D1759206

The Public Management and Leadership series

Public management and, more recently, public leadership have over several decades emerged as increasingly central elements in the study and practice of governance, public administration and public policy.

Around them have developed important new strands of research, debate, education and professional formation. And these in turn have informed a wide range of initiatives in many parts of the world to 'modernize', 'reform', 'innovate', 'de-bureaucratize' and 'professionalize' existing institutions and practices.

The *Public Management and Leadership* series aims to provide a set of key texts to meet the changing needs of the growing range of graduate and post-experience courses in this area as well as concise and accessible reading for busy practitioners.

Genuinely international in scope and conception, accessible in style and presentation, and drawing on empirical information and illustrations from a wide variety of jurisdictions and policy sectors, each title will offer an authoritative review of the state of theory and practice in its respective field, and identify the key challenges and the most promising conceptual and practical tools to tackle them.

The Public Management and Leadership series

Series Editor: Paul 't Hart, Utrecht University & Netherlands School of Public Administration

Published:

John Alford and Janine O'Flynn
Rethinking Public Service Delivery: Managing with External Providers

Martin Lodge and Kai Wegrich
Managing Regulation: Regulatory Analysis, Politics and Policy

Sean Lusk and Nick Birks
Rethinking Public Strategy

Richard Mulgan
Making Open Government Work

Paul 't Hart
Understanding Public Leadership

Forthcoming:

Mirko Noordegraaf
Perspectives on Public Management

John Uhr
Ethical Public Leadership

In preparation:

Strategic Public Management
Political/Administrative Relations
Public Management and Public Finance
Public Management and Collaboration
Public Management and the Media
Public Management in an Information Age
The 21st Century Public Manager

The Public Management and Leadership Series

Series Standing Order ISBN 978–0–230–23657–8 hardback
Series Standing Order ISBN 978–0–230–23658–5 paperback

(outside North America only)

You can receive future titles in this series as they are published by placing a standing order. Please contact your bookseller or, in case of difficulty, write to us at the address below with your name and address, the title of the series and an ISBN quoted above.

Customer Services Department, Macmillan Distribution Ltd
Houndmills, Basingstoke, Hampshire RG21 6XS, England, UK

Understanding Public Leadership

Paul 't Hart

 palgrave

First published 2014 by
PALGRAVE

Palgrave in the UK is an imprint of Macmillan Publishers Limited, registered in England, company number 785998, of 4 Crinan Street, London N1 9XW

Palgrave Macmillan in the US is a division of St Martin's Press LLC, 175 Fifth Avenue, New York, NY 10010.

Palgrave is the global imprint of the above companies and is represented throughout the world.

Palgrave® and Macmillan® are registered trademarks in the United States, the United Kingdom, Europe and other countries.

ISBN 978–0–230–20552–9   hardback
ISBN 978–0–230–20553–6   paperback

This book is printed on paper suitable for recycling and made from fully managed and sustained forest sources. Logging, pulping and manufacturing processes are expected to conform to the environmental regulations of the country of origin.

A catalogue record for this book is available from the British Library.

A catalog record for this book is available from the Library of Congress.

Printed in China

In memory of

Willem 't Hart (1921–2005), musician, romantic, father

and

Alexander George (1920–2006), scholar, gentleman, role model

Contents

List of Illustrative Material

Boxes

Figures

Tables

Preface

Yes, this is another book about leadership. I apologize. And to tell you the truth it has been extremely hard to convince myself that the world really needed one, and that I had something useful, original and teachable to say about the subject. That is probably why this has been by far the most difficult book to write in well over twenty-five years of academic writing. But now, I have convinced myself that it has all been worth it, so now it is time for me to convince you that this book is worth your time too.

Many would argue this is a mission impossible as the subject of leadership has been over-studied by academics and over-sold by consultants and gurus. It has certainly become a ubiquitous and inevitable subject in late modern Western societies. Strong critiques of existing institutions abounded, and the creative–destructive power of extraordinary individuals in changing these institutions was amply illustrated throughout the early decades of the twentieth century, in both politics and business. The power of leadership has been loathed, feared and admired, but can hardly be denied. And therefore it has been reported on, studied and propagated.

Leadership has become both a field and a fad. It has espoused a bewildering array of concepts, frameworks, propositions, stories, assessments, prescriptions and clichés about leadership across a range of academic disciplines and professional domains. Inspirational books by leadership 'gurus' and biographies of celebrity chief executive officers (CEOs) have been stacked side by side with the latest offerings by John le Carré and Jamie Oliver in bookstores around the world. An entire industry of leadership training and consulting has sprung up in its wake, starting in the corporate sector but spilling over into the government and third sectors since the late 1990s.

Years of reading leadership studies have left me both inspired and bewildered. I have been inspired by the skill and wisdom of the authors of those studies that to me seemed to contain nuggets of insight in what too often felt like a desert of trivial industriousness and fact-free speculation. But I was bewildered by the lack of coherence between the claims of the many studies I digested. Surely the work of public leadership is not so opaque and ambiguous as to defy any kind of integrative understanding?

Years of observing and interviewing mainly senior public servants and politicians in different places on the planet certainly seemed to me to suggest otherwise. Different institutional traditions and contextual imperatives notwithstanding, many of them seemed to live largely similar professional lives, appeared to face similar types of challenges and were subject to remarkably similar incentives and constraints. They maintained similar sorts of relationships with associates and stakeholders and put on highly similar public performances. This book attempts to capture these common denominators of the practice of public leadership.

Years of classroom interaction with regular and mature students has left me wondering how best to teach leadership; is it in fact something that can be taught at all? If so, is a lifelong academic like me a credible source of leadership teaching? I know many government practitioners who argue that one needs to have been in the hot seat oneself in order truly to understand what life a the top is really like – both the promises and the pitfalls of leading. I don't believe that, and I hope this book disproves them, or at least convinces them that academic observers of public leadership also have something useful to contribute.

A key caveat is in order. This book is about public leadership – the work performed by politicians and political activists, senior as well as less senior public servants, and people active in civil society and non-profit organizations – in democratic polities. The concepts, conjectures, observations and lessons developed in this book stem from research into (and are focused on) political systems where there is a rule of law, freedom of speech, free and fair elections, a professional public service, and an open civil society. I have no way of telling how much of this has relevance for public leadership in non-democratic polities, but would be interested to learn from readers with more experience and expertise in those settings.

The fact that there is a book at all today is due in no small part to my publisher, the formidable Steven Kennedy, who will not let up when he senses a book he thinks should be written. I am grateful to him for that. But the main reason I have returned to what in effect had become an aborted project, have been the public sector professionals and university students I have the continuous privilege of lecturing about leadership. Throughout the period during which this book was written, I have taught public or political leadership classes to fresh-faced bachelor students, keen and hard-working mid-career public managers pursuing postgraduate degrees, in-company management teams and groups of professionals, and weary and wise senior executives at the very apex of government and non-profit organizations in the Netherlands and Australia. I have relished the challenges involved in tailoring both the content and format of 'teaching leadership' for these radically different settings. And I have benefited enormously from their by now countless presentations, debates and papers, but most of all from the incisive questions they asked. This book is, first and foremost, an attempt to give a new generation of students of public policy, public management, public organizations and political science a bit of a roadmap of the awe-inspiring but treacherous terrain.

I have incurred many debts along the way. First, I would like to thank the former dean of the Australia New Zealand School of Government (ANZSOG), Allan Fels, for taking a risk back in 2007 in letting an unknown foreigner loose on the future public service leaders of both nations, and then for encouraging me to develop and teach my own particular brand of leadership development programme over the years. And I thank his successor, Gary Banks, for continuing to tolerate me within the ANZSOG family despite the considerable logistical costs of doing so since I moved back to the Netherlands from Australia in 2011. Within ANZSOG I owe a depth of gratitude to welcoming and generous colleagues such as John Alford, Peter Allen, Pauline Clancy, Peter Debus and Glen Sheldon, and most especially to simply the best academic support staff in the entire world, who have indulged my every whim and yet kept me on track in managing the large-scale programmes around the capital cities of Australia and New Zealand: Libby Buckle, Rosetta Colosimo, Jane Durlacher, Tracey Fischer, Samantha Hicks, Linda Losanno, Tim Wigg and last, but most certainly not least, Sophie Yates. Thanks also to Janet Tyson for stewarding ANZSOG's inspiring case programme to which I have also been given the opportunity to contribute. Finally, special mention should go to Amanda Sinclair of Melbourne Business School, and subsequently Robbie MacPherson of AdaptAble Leadership, who have been my companions in creating and facilitating the Towards Strategic Leadership (TSL) programme. Working with them has been for me the single most challenging and gratifying professional experience of the past five years. Robbie has become a close personal friend in the process, and I cherish the thought of, I hope, many more years of co-teaching TSL with him.

In the Netherlands, I am indebted to co-deans Paul Frissen and Mark van Twist of the Netherlands School of Public Administration (NSOB) – themselves excellent examples of highly effective shared leadership (see Chapter 5) – for taking me back in when I returned from more than five years 'down under', and for not thinking twice about unleashing someone who had in effect become a foreigner (I am now a proud Australian citizen) on the *crème de la crème* of the Dutch public service. At NSOB, I have received exemplary collegial encouragement, and managerial and staff support from Hera Tseng, Martijn van der Steen, Mohammed Ayyadi, Nancy Chin-A-Fat, Hetty Fischer, Linda Frauenfelder, Irmi Dekker, Michelle van den Oever, Rik Peeters, Sandra Poldermans, Jorren Scherpenisse, Jaap van der Spek, Saskia

Wiersma, Wanda van der Werf, Stavros Zouridis and Arthur Docters van Leeuwen. Within NSOB, it is furthermore a privilege to be able to co-facilitate a learning network for Dutch public sector CEOs with one of the Netherland's truly outstanding civil servants, Wim Kuijken. Wim gave me the chance towards the end of the 1990s of penetrating the inner sanctums of the Dutch bureaucracy and I have continued to learn from him ever since.

I have received some useful and encouraging feedback from the doyen of leadership studies in European political science, Professor Jean Blondel. His 1987 book on the subject was a great inspiration to this young scholar at the time, and it is a great pleasure that we have been able to be involved in various collaborations in recent years. Thanks also to my Spanish–English–Dutch friend, Professor Luis Garicano, for helpful comments on parts of the manuscript.

My initial academic home when this project began was the Political Science Program at the Research School of Social Sciences of the Australian National University. I thank Bob Goodin for nudging me towards it, Rod Rhodes for letting me in and allowing me to draw him into the world of leadership studies in a number of collaborations. I thank John Uhr for a whole series of highly enjoyable collaborations, and John Wanna and John Dryzek for their companionship. During my years in Australia and since then, I have learned a lot more about 'understanding public leadership' from my ongoing collaborative projects with James Walter and Paul Strangio of Monash University, Melbourne. They continue to teach me how political leadership in Australia works.

My previous and current academic home in the Netherlands is at the Utrecht School of Governance (USG) of Utrecht University. This place is not just intellectually engaging and a model of best-practice teaching, it is truly a 'home' that bears no resemblance to the average academic department where aloofness, social awkwardness and competitiveness all too often shape the social climate. At USG we work hard, we play hard, and we look after each other. That this is so because of the exceptional academic leadership of my old friend and collaborator Mark Bovens and his co-leader Paul Verweel. Their successors, Maarten van Bottenburg and Mirko Noordegraaf, are carrying the torch with enthusiasm, and I thank them for taking on the daunting challenge. Returning to Utrecht also meant reuniting with my long-standing partner in the area of crisis leadership studies, Arjen Boin, with whom I have been working happily for a good twenty years. As part of my Utrecht work, I have taken on the job of being academic dean of a university-wide interdisciplinary honours programme for master students called the Young Leaders League (YLL). Building and managing the YLL as an entirely 'outside the box' academic programme, along with my co-conspirator Fried Keesen and a dedicated team of teachers and coaches has been a joy, and I hope this book reflects some of what I have learnt along the way.

Jean Hartley of the Open University deserves special mention. I have long valued her work on leadership and when I got stuck on this manuscript, I invited her to join me in revising and finishing it, only to lose heart yet again and I shelved the project entirely for several years. Throughout all this time she has been unfailingly supportive and gracious. That I eventually felt that I had to finish this book on my own, and did so in a spurt of creative energy while being unexpectedly bedridden for several weeks, is something neither she nor I could have foreseen. It certainly had nothing to do with my professional and personal respect for her. I am also grateful to her for asking me to write the article that forms the basis of Chapter 7 for a special issue she was editing of *Public Money and Management,* and am glad that we are now working together on another joint project.

Finally, and most importantly as always: Marieke, Sarah and Naomi. They have had to share me with this 'wretched book' and various other manifestations of my inexplicable passion for academic pursuits. They have done so with utter grace, and have filled our house with love. Sarah and Naomi even helped to compile the bibliography. I owe it to them all never again to take on a project quite as tortuous as this one has turned out to be.

This book was conceived and written as an integrated project but its long gestation has meant that parts of it have been tried out in lectures, courses and articles along the way. In addition, when it looked as though I would never complete it, I published versions of sections of it in contributions to a number of books and journals, some sole-authored, others with co-authors. I would like to thank my various students, course participants and collaborators for their help in sharpening my ideas and the various publishers concerned, most particularly Oxford University Press and ANU Press (formerly ANU E Press), for their help in unscrambling copyright and permission issues. Some sections of a draft of Chapter 1 found their way into 'Puzzles of political leadership' in Rhodes and 't Hart (2014). Some small sections of a draft of Chapter 2 were incorporated into 'Understanding public leadership: perspectives and practices' in 't Hart and Uhr (2008). Chapter 3's presentation of a Leadership Capital Index rests on ideas first aired in a conference paper (Bennister *et al.*, 2014). Some sections of a draft of Chapter 5 found their way into 'Contextual analysis' in Rhodes and 't Hart (2014), and others into 't Hart (2011a). Chapter 7 draws on and extends 't Hart (2011b), with kind permission of the publisher. Chapter 8 was adapted from 't Hart, 'Epilogue: Rules for reformers', in Lindquist *et al.* (2011). Parts of Chapter 9 were gleaned from 'Public sector leadership: moving beyond mythology' (Paul 't Hart, 2009). Figure 4.1 was taken from Chris Ansell and Alison Gash, 'Collaborative Governance in Theory and Practice', *Journal of Public Administration Research and Theory* (2008) 18 (4): 543–71, and is reproduced here by kind permission from Oxford University Press and the authors.

Driebergen, The Netherlands   PAUL 'T HART

Chapter 1

Unlocking Public Leadership

Why bother?

Every group or society needs to be governed if it is to survive and its members are to thrive. And every system of governance requires what we have come to think of as 'leadership', at least from time to time: protection, direction, order, inspiration, challenge, transformation. Institutional rules, procedures and routines alone are never enough to tackle the conflicts, changes, surprises, opportunities and challenges that groups and communities encounter. Judging when and how to design, protect, supplement or change governance institutions and creating momentum to act upon those judgements are key functions of public leadership. In most governance systems there are designated roles – high offices in politics, government agencies and professional spheres – that come with a warrant for their bearers to exercise such leadership. But these offices also come with constraints – institutional, professional, ethical – on the ways in which leadership can be exercised. We realize we need the creative force that is leadership, but we are also acutely aware of the risks of channelling too much power, authority and public adulation towards only a few people. These public office-holders moreover do not have a monopoly on the exercise of public leadership: people and groups outside the formal leadership stratum can espouse ideas for tackling governance challenges, gather support for them, and so challenge or complement the leadership of public office-holders. Public leadership is thus part of the job for some, but a calling, a duty, an opportunity or a coincidence for many others. Its exercise is necessary, but also dangerous. It can elevate and motivate us, but it can also drag us down.

The main challenge is how the pivotal but fickle function that is leadership can be harnessed yet also constrained within the overall framework of democratic governance. The sheer number and variety of offices and platforms for exercising public leadership in liberal democracies have produced governance systems that are both complex and opaque. How do the various spheres of public leadership – political, administrative, and civic – intersect, reinforce and/or conflict with one another? How can the 'creative tension' between them best be governed and utilized? One thing is certain: we gain little from limiting our understanding of public leadership to the traits, skills and deeds of the

1

limited number of individual office-holders at the heart of executive government who tend to get all the media attention. Holding office and being in the spotlights do not in and of themselves amount to exercising leadership. In open societies, public leadership work can be, and needs to be, performed by many actors, both inside and outside government.

A big question for custodians of democracy and governance is: how much space do we accord to different leadership roles and vehicles, and how do we prefer that they interrelate? In effective governance systems, multiple leadership offices and roles tend to exist in parallel – leadership opportunities are thus more often than not *distributed* (Kane *et al.* 2009). In interactive, democratic governance settings, leadership agents have inducements to act in concert and thus exercise what has come to be called 'shared', 'collaborative', 'team' or 'tandem' leadership (Pearce and Conger 2003; Hartley and Manzie 2014; Strangio *et al.* 2014). But there can also be significant incentives to 'go into bat' against one another, with leadership becoming a more dialectic if not outright competitive process. Think of the organized competition between government and opposition, and the roles of their respective leaders as symbols of this struggle for authority, support and power – and ironically as implicit co-creators of one another's leadership impact (McCaffrie 2012). Or think of the credibility contests between corporate CEOs and the leaders of the NGOs that scrutinize and publicly criticize those corporations' behaviours.

Distributed leadership may look messy to those who prefer the clarity of hierarchy and leadership as command and control. But the evidence is clear: like any resilient socio-cultural or socio-technical system, systems of governing thrive on variety, overlap and competition among loci of initiative, voice, authority and accountability. Certainly, these systems have their transaction costs. Aligning enough people and organizations behind any particular set of ideas or policy proposals can be a time-consuming and convoluted process. But, as Lindblom (1965) and others (Landau 1969; Bendor 1985; Thompson *et al.* 1990; March and Olsen 1995; Torfing *et al.* 2012) argue, such institutional pluralism in the end produces smarter, more robust public policies as well as keeping the ever-looming arrogance of power at bay.

In contrast, governance systems built around top-down, 'great man' and charismatic leadership are not only inherently unstable and normatively unpalatable but also lack institutional capacity for effective social problem solving. They are only governed reasonably well when the supreme leader and his or her clique are smart, wise and honest. But they are quick to slide into the abyss of tyranny, stupidity and corruption when the ruling elite becomes addicted to its own power, or is replaced by less capable and morally upright characters. Examples of this abound in both politics (ancient Rome, absolute monarchies, the communist experience, the Roman Catholic Church, post-colonial and post-communist dictatorships) and business (the Enron scandal; Firestone's use of child labour; and, most of all, the hubris of upper echelons within the banking and financial services sector as exposed by the global financial crisis that exploded in 2008).

But before we can get around to (re-)designing the institutions that empower leaders and hold them accountable, we must first understand the nature of the beast. How do we know 'public leadership' when we see it? How do we describe, explain, evaluate and improve it? Because leadership studies is such a complex and disjointed interdisciplinary enterprise, it is important to locate this book within it. So, in the remainder of this chapter I shall outline the book's key assumptions.

Understanding leadership: art, science, industry

Leadership can be taught – but can it be learnt? From the time of the ancient Greeks to the present day, many observers of public leadership have chosen to portray it as an art. Leadership, this view holds, cannot be captured in scientific generalizations based on cool, detached observation (Wren 2006). And, by inference, it cannot be taught in the cerebral environment of an academic classroom or executive seminar. As always, Max Weber (1970: 115) was right on the mark when he suggested that the challenge of leadership is to forge warm passion and cool judgement together in one and the same soul – and that in practice this condemns those aspiring to political leadership to a life of tough judgement calls between the passion that fires them up, the feeling of personal responsibility that drives them on, and a sense of proportion that is necessary to exercise good judgement.

Leadership as conceived by some its most authoritative scholars involves a large component of practical wisdom: insight that can only be obtained effectively through direct personal experience and sustained reflection. The vital intangibles of leadership – empathy, intuition, creativity, courage, morality and judgement – are largely beyond the grasp of systematic inquiry, let alone comprehensive explanation and evidence-based prescription. Understanding leadership comes from living it: being led, living with and advising leaders, doing one's own leading. Some understanding of leadership may be gained from vicarious learning: from digesting the experiences of other leaders. Hence the old-established and steady appetite for (auto-)biographies of CEOs and politicians, and the more contemporary market for 'live encounters' with high-profile leaders during seminars and conferences. And if we cannot gain access to 'the real thing', we are still willing to pay buckets of money for the next best thing: books and seminars by the exclusive circle of leadership 'gurus' who do manage to observe and interrogate up close the great and the good.

Defying this entrenched view, a 'science of leadership' sprang up from the latter half of the twentieth century. Thousands of academics now make a living treating leadership as they would any other subject in the realm of human affairs – as an object of study, which can be picked apart and reassembled via systematic inquiry (whether of the classical 'scientific' or more interpretive kind), filling journals, handbooks, conference programmes and lecture halls. Many among them make inroads into the real world of public leadership as consultants and advisers, often very well paid. Surely all this would not persist if the kind of knowledge they offered was useless in solving at least some of the puzzles that leaders face and leadership poses?

It is this kind of leadership that we now see echoed in widespread attempts to erect a leadership profession. The language of leadership has pervaded the job descriptions, training and performance management systems of public servants, even at junior management levels. Many public service commissions or equivalent bodies have embarked on developing integrated leadership frameworks in which set bundles of leadership skills are linked to the successful performance of different leadership roles (usually indicated simply by general hierarchical rank rather than specific job characteristics).

People wanting to move up the hierarchy must jump through the hoops thus constructed: they must attend set courses, adhere to a set of shared values, write structured job applications, and be subjected to standardized tests. When they manage to get all the boxes ticked, they are ushered into a fraternity rather like a Masonic Lodge. Uniformity is nurtured and celebrated through lucrative rewards packages. Leadership education is ubiquitous. Everyone attends meetings where leadership gurus perform. The aim is not to impart knowledge, but rather to solidify a shared notion of professionalism. The means for such sharing are the latest nostrums, models and metaphors. The audience is captive, and willingly so, though one might – like leadership 'guru' Barbara Kellerman (2012) – wonder for how much longer.

Clearly, when taken to extremes, each set of assumptions about 'understanding leadership' leads to preposterous results: the mystification of idiosyncratic 'charisma' in a nearly evidence-free environment versus the imposition of a quasi-scientific 'one size fits all' of the kind to which many public servants are currently subjected around the world. Both privilege one form of knowledge over all others. Both generate their own quacks and true believers, who both do very well out of the transaction – but with dubious results as far as quality and particularly diversity in leadership are concerned.

This book shies away from these extremes. By its very nature as a text designed to convey 'what we know about leadership' to a range of students and public sector professionals it embodies the second approach more than it does the first. But I recognize that there is only so much 'understanding' of the subtle, complex and often paradoxical process of public leadership that academics and other observers can distil and transmit. Where and when I can, for illustrative and reflective purposes I shall take a closer look at the world of public leaders, but beyond that, reader, you are on your own.

Public leadership as cause and consequence

Let us begin at the beginning. There are two fundamentally different points of departure in understanding leadership. One is to see it as a force within public life, and explore how, when and why it works, and to what effect. It is a force that energizes otherwise inanimate objects. Likewise, leadership is commonly portrayed as a dynamic factor in the polity, breathing life into public institutions and political processes as they struggle to come to terms with major environmental changes. In this view, leadership is about injecting ideas and ambitions into the public arena; and is about grasping existing realities and recognizing their transformative potential. Leadership produces collective meaning and harnesses collective energy in the service of a common cause. Great leaders are often conceived of as 'event-makers': people who were able to gather so much momentum for the hopes and ambitions they held out to their followers that the course of history was affected conspicuously by their presence. Call them pied pipers, call them visionaries, call them entrepreneurs, call them reformers: leaders are seen to be both reading and moving their followers' minds, and inducing them collectively to go on journeys they would otherwise never have contemplated, let alone taken.

Likewise, many accounts of leadership focus on leaders as the ultimate decision-makers. When all is said and done and the organization or nation faces high-stakes choices that no one else is able or willing to make, somebody has to cast the die and take responsibility. A sign on Harry Truman's Oval Office desk read 'The buck stops here', and he practised what he preached, committing the USA to the use of two nuclear bombs within a week and proudly claimed that he never lost any sleep over doing so. Some leaders revel in being in that position, and do what they can to make sure that every big decision crosses their desk. They feel confident in analysing complex problems, working through the risks and uncertainties and probing the vested interests and unstated assumptions of the experts, advisers and colleagues attempting to push them into (or away from) particular courses of action.

Others leaders may loathe making decisions, particularly risky ones they cannot avoid. Some may feel overwhelmed by the very complexity of the issues and of the policy-making process itself. George (1974: 187) quoted US president Warren Harding as he confided to a friend how stressful he found his role:

> John, I can't make a thing out of this tax problem. I listen to one side and they seem right, and then God! I talk to the other side and they seem just as right, and there I am where I started ... I know somewhere there is an economist who knows the truth, but hell, I don't know where to find him and haven't got the sense to know him and trust him when I find him. God, what a job.

The point is, whether they enjoy it or not and whether they display sound judgement or not, the very notion of leaders as strategic decision-makers portrays them as being at the helm, in control and reshaping the world around them.

Trying to understand leadership as a cause is important. Though much of social life is governed by shared traditions, rules and practices, there are always public problems that defy routine solutions. Sensing that, diagnosing it, and making a persuasive case for adapting routines or abandoning them completely is a leadership task. Study the history behind every great reform and you will find leadership at work, though usually in a form of collective or distributed leadership rather than the single 'heroic' activist that might get all the public credit for it. Understanding leadership as a cause implies raising many important analytical and practical questions about the impact of different leadership configurations, styles and discourses in different types of contexts, communities and situations. What 'works' when? Can it be emulated and transplanted? How do particular people or groups matter? What kinds of characteristics and skills make them matter?

The other main point of departure for understanding public leadership is finding out how it comes about, consolidates and erodes – leadership not as a cause but as a *consequence*. In academic jargon: taking leadership itself as the dependent variable, which is to be explained by looking at a range of other variables that impact upon it. For example, if we agree that people in the highest public offices of the land are at least potentially pivotal public leaders, we might want to know what sorts of people come to hold these offices (and, by implication, what sorts of people do not). How do people make it to the top in political parties, social movements and public bureaucracies? What leader selection mechanisms apply in these spheres? What happens to leadership aspirants on their path to the top – how are they socialized, what debts do they incur – and how does all this affect their scope for exercising leadership? What if access to senior leadership positions is biased in favour of people from certain social or professional backgrounds? We may also want to know about the offices themselves: what are the responsibilities, expectations and resources attached to them? What likely implications do they have for the scope of their occupant's authority and support among those they lead? And how have these evolved over time?

Obtaining knowledge about who get to lead can teach us much, not only about the leaders themselves but also about the nature of the societies in which they operate. Nicolas Sarkozy's and Barack Obama's elevation to the presidency of their respective countries would not have been possible just a few decades ago. That they made it all the way to the top is evidence of changes within both French and American society – for example, of possibilities for upward social mobility and political influence of immigrants and minorities, which in turn influences the leadership agendas and incentives of whoever holds these presidencies into the future.

Public leadership and public management

Thirty-odd years ago, people in senior positions within the public sector in the Anglo-Saxon world in particular were being reconstructed as public 'managers' (rather than public servants, officials or administrators). The professional reading and courses they were fed were all about adopting management frameworks and techniques developed in the business sector. Yet, as this was happening, people in senior positions in business were expected to be *more* than mere managers; they were to become 'leaders', and preferably 'transformational' leaders. Managers were now conceived of as people competently minding existing stores, while leaders were people who were founding and modernizing these stores (Bennis 1989). Management was about professional craft of planning, organizing, staffing, motivating, deciding and reorganizing in a 'business as usual' fashion; leadership was about the personal art of visioning, inspiring, innovating, revaluing and reframing in times of uncertainty and turbulence (Zaleznik 1977/2004).

Though initially posited as a descriptive, value-neutral distinction between various philosophies and skill sets in governing organisations, a normative hierarchy crept in quite quickly. Management remained a necessary but distinctly unheroic and slightly dull occupation; the real difference between 'good' and 'great' corporations was being made by the leaders. Managers solve existing problems and are naturally inclined to contain crises in order to preserve existing structures, while leaders define new challenges and exploit crises in order to forge structural change. Management became a respectable norm for middle-level executives, but anyone aspiring to top-level jobs was expected to echo the mantra of leadership. A decade or so later, these distinctions reached the public sector, and they persist today. And so we can routinely overhear senior public servants describing one of their colleagues as 'a good manager, but not a leader'. This is not even faint praise; it means that this colleague's chances of promotion are dead.

I am comfortable with making an analytical distinction between leadership and management, but not with extolling leadership above management. Both are vital functions in running organizations, and one cannot properly function without the other also being performed. Business scholar John Kotter's (1996: 114–15) assessment is sensible, and can be applied with some modification to the world of public policy:

> Leadership and management are two distinctive and complementary systems of action. Each has its own function and characteristic activities. Both are necessary for success in an increasingly complex and volatile ... environment. Each system of action involves deciding what needs to be done, creating networks of people and relationships that can accomplish an agenda, and then trying to ensure that those people actually do the job.

The key difference between the two lies in their main ambit and focus, Kotter argues. Management is about coping with complexity, and it aims to bring 'a degree of order and consistency' to key dimensions of governance such as the quality and efficiency of (public) programmes and services. Leadership, then, is about coping with change – that is, abrupt or creeping technological, demographic, economic, strategic-military, regulatory and socio-cultural changes that put pressure on existing public policies and institutions. That is not the same as saying that every leader is, or should be, an agent of change. In this book, the chief focus of leadership is taken to be *to induce groups to reconsider their underlying values and purposes in light of changes in the group's context, and to make strategic choices about whether to conserve, defend and adjust or repudiate and transform key features of the group's rationale, make up and ways of working.* Or, as Bennis (1989: 145) puts it, 'learning to lead is ... learning to manage change'.

This book focuses on understanding how public leadership is exercised, not on a priori sanctification of it above all other sets of roles and skills in conducting the public's business. The series of which this book forms a part is therefore called Public Management *and* Leadership, and within it this general introduction to public leadership co-exists with a general introduction to public management (Noordegraaf 2014). In Chapter 2 we outline the distinctive features and forms of the work of public leadership in which politicians, public servants and civic leaders engage.

People and process: leaders, followers and relations

We also need to decide who or what it is we want to understand: the people we commonly call leaders, or the process we call leadership? For many scholars and practitioners, understanding public leaders comes down to studying the characteristics, beliefs and deeds of people said to be playing pivotal roles in public life. These are, first and foremost, senior politicians: heads of government, cabinet ministers, senior legislators and key party officials. In this category we should also include key advisers to these senior politicians, who generally remain behind the scenes but are often said to be highly influential.

Less evident to outside observers, but all too obvious to those who know how government really works, are senior public officials. This category includes top executives within the departments that advise ministers and prepare and administer policies and programmes, as well as the heads and senior ranks of administrative organizations whose job it is to implement policy and deliver public services on the ground. While their institutional role and professional ethos is to be public *servants* and *managers*, there is little dispute that the upper echelons of the bureaucracy are often vitally important in shaping what governments do, and when and how they do it, in view of the ever-changing public agendas and dynamic social, economic and technological contexts. Likewise, but clearly distinct from public administrators, senior members of the judiciary are sometimes thought of as public leaders. Their statutory independence and pivotal role in interpreting the law and adjudicating conflict provides them with a platform for shaping public policies, norms and debates.

Finally, many public leaders do not hold any formal public office at all. The world of non-government organizations is vast, varied and vital in its own right. Certainly, democracies nurture a large and active civil society, and value its contributions to the political process, however critical of the government of the day some civic organizations and their leaders might be. Standout individuals at the helm of trade unions, churches, social movements, mass media, community organizations and even business corporations are widely thought of as important public leaders. They do not have the power of office but may well have the power of numbers (supporters, viewers, money), ideas, access, moral authority or popular support to shape public problem-solving in pivotal ways.

Understanding public leadership through the lens of public leaders takes one to the province of biography and personality psychology. It rests on the idea that 'who leads matters' (Hermann 2014). It entails an agent-centred view of politics and government: public debates and decisions are shaped by the views, drives, skills and styles of individuals who happen to be in the right place at the right time to make a difference. This form of leadership analysis has long been dominant in the field of history and has underpinned almost all of the countless books and papers on business leadership.

The leader-centred form of leadership analysis has proved to be immensely popular. So much so, however, that it has crowded out the more functional, process-centred view of leadership as the distinct and crucial work of getting groups to engage with change. In his monumental study *Leadership*, Burns (1978: 1–2) was scathing: 'if we know all too much about our leaders, we know far too little about leadership. We fail to grasp the essence of leadership that is relevant to the modern age and hence we cannot even agree on the standards by which to measure, recruit, and reject it'. In the decades since Burns made these comments, the balance has been somewhat redressed. There is now a firm body of thought and research that chooses to understand public leadership as an interactive process between those we call leaders, the people that choose (or feel forced) to be led by them, and the environment in which their interaction takes place. This take on leadership analysis set up a different agenda. In addition to Kotter's assertion that leadership is about coping with environmental change, it also includes the idea that 'who are being led matters'. With this in mind, the first thing to know about leadership is its *relational* quality.

In democracies, individual leaders are never free agents. The warrant to lead is conditional, and leadership roles and resources are dispersed. Even in the intimate setting of the cabinet, few if any prime ministers get their way all of the time. They know that, if pushed too far for too long, their cabinet and parliamentary colleagues have ways of undermining their leadership (Weller 2007; Strangio *et al*. 2013). Public leadership analysis can thus never be confined only to the attributes of leaders. To understand leadership is to grasp when, how and why particular groups of people come to view and accept some individuals or small groups of people to perform leadership work. This put the focus on at least two things other than the personal properties of leaders. First, the states of mind, needs, emotions and identities of the non-leaders – in other words the 'followers', 'constituents', indeed the 'group(s)' who are being led. Who are the 'we' that leaders appeal to, implicitly and explicitly? What is it that is sought in leaders? What services are leaders performing for the groups they aspire to lead? Second, the focus moves towards the nature, sources and limits of leaders' authority claims in relation to their constituencies. What psychological contract exists between leaders and followers, and what licence to operate can leaders derive from it? How can leaders persuade groups to pay attention to their voices and abide by their decisions? What, in fact, are different kinds of groups willing to tolerate from leaders? And how do groups elect, authorize and remove leaders? Leadership is a two-way street.

In its most radical form, the focus on leadership rather than leaders entails a follower-centric perspective, in which leaders are primarily a product of the identities, needs, desires and fears of the groups that put, and keep, them in place. But it is more productive to think of leadership as a genuinely interactive process, which also includes scope for the ambitions, skills and resources of leaders in appealing to or modifying the social identities of their followers when gaining or using their positions. Likewise, James M. Burns' famous distinction between transactional (based around leader-initiated exchange relationships between leaders and followers) and transformational (a mutual engagement between leader and followers in which a fusing of their purposes leads to higher levels of motivation and morality) types of leadership epitomizes a similarly interactive approach to conceptualizing leadership processes (Burns, 1978: 19–20).

In Chapters 3 and 4 we develop a relational and process-based perspective on public leadership. We explore the nature of leader–follower relations, as well as the specific features of the type of leadership that exists when authority is dispersed and there is no formal or clear hierarchy (as in networks and partnerships, for example). Leadership becomes possible because non-leaders select people they identify with and trust, or whose authority claims they respect. But each of these levers for leadership is conditional and temporary in all but the most spellbinding cases of charismatic leadership (and 'blind' followership). Leaders have to build and maintain their leadership capital carefully, but the very process of leading – rather than just office-holding – also entails spending much of that capital. Leaders cannot please all of the people all of the time; they have to introduce unpleasant realities, make trade-off choices, and embrace some values while repudiating others. Moreover, leaders hardly ever succeed in accomplishing all they promise, so they rarely meet all their followers' hopes.

Who leads matters, sometimes: people, contexts and situations

Of course it matters who leads. Comparisons of different leaders in highly similar circumstances show how their personal beliefs and styles impact on the lives of citizens. During the late 1990s, Nelson Mandela and Robert Mugabe headed governments in the neighbouring countries of South Africa and Zimbabwe, but took these countries in very different directions. Mandela embodied reconciliation, and sought to weave broad political coalitions, but Mugabe whipped up and exploited racial tensions. Mandela sought to institutionalize democratic norms and practices; Mugabe purposefully eroded them. Mandela stepped down voluntarily, and made way for a democratically elected successor, while Mugabe sought to extend his rule indefinitely and waged war on the democratic opposition, before reluctantly accepting a power-sharing deal, which he subsequently sought to manipulate to consolidate his power.

Looking at the convictions and choices of individuals and their successors in the same senior public office suggests that leaders can make and break the momentum of an organization. After the Berlin Wall came down and the Cold War ended, security and intelligence agencies around the world were suddenly robbed of a pivotal part of their *raison d'être*. All were scrambling to find new roles and new justifications for their continued existence. The Dutch intelligence service (BVD) was a case in point. In mid-1989, just before the Wall collapsed, a new person was appointed to lead this hitherto largely unseen and widely taken-for-granted agency. At the time of his appointment, Arthur Docters van Leeuwen, a former Home Office heavyweight, was given to the task of modernizing the organization, but just few months later he found himself caught in a struggle for its very existence. He embarked on a path of radical innovation, sensing that the organization would either reinvent itself quickly, or else would be killed off. He identified new threats, new forms of uncertainty and new clients inside and outside government for his organization's intelligence products. Those products themselves, and the ways in which they were to be manufactured and communicated, would also have to change drastically. To this end, he embraced nothing short of a paradigm shift in the agency's mission and methodologies, followed by radical changes in organizational structure, technology and human resource management (HRM) policies. All this happened in the space of a few years – a veritable whirlwind of change. His tenure ended in 1994. When he announced his departure, many in the organization held their breath: who would succeed him? When his successor was announced, a former admiral who made it clear that his philosophy was one of 'back to basics', the proponents of change within the BVD despaired, while its opponents rejoiced. Both sides knew that the new leader would have both the ability and the desire to temporize or even reverse van Leeuwen's innovations ('t Hart 2007).

Counterfactual questions about the roles of leaders at critical historical junctures make one ponder the point. What if not Margaret Thatcher but James Callaghan had still been the British prime minister at the time of the Argentinian junta's move to physically reclaim the Falklands Islands? What would have happened to the course of the Vietnam war or to American-Chinese relations if Robert Kennedy rather than Richard Nixon had won the 1968 US presidential election? And would America have waged war in both Afghanistan and Iraq following the 11 September attacks on its soil if Al Gore had won the Florida recount during the 2000 presidential election?

BOX 1.1   Understanding leadership styles

A good working knowledge of leaders' personal styles is useful in gauging their key strengths and weaknesses in the jobs they hold. US presidential scholar Fred Greenstein (2000), for example, suggests six key skill areas of leadership style that one can use to explain and evaluate the perform-ance of the holders of that office, and which can usefully be applied also to gauging the styles and performance of other democratic heads of government. These are:

- *public communication proficiency*: how do presidents 'get the message across' to ordinary citizens as well as other key audiences that they typically cannot engage with on a face-to-face basis?
- *organizational capacity*: how do presidents harness the vast and complex machinery of government to serve their aims?
- *political skill*: how do they consolidate their authority and 'get their way' in a system of democratic, divided government, where power, responsibility and resources are purposefully dispersed across a range of institutions and actors?
- *policy vision*: what beliefs and ideals do they hold, and how are these articulated in a recognizable, coherent agenda they seek to accomplish while in office?
- *cognitive style*: how do presidents form their beliefs, and how do they process information and advice?
- *emotional intelligence*: to what extent and how do they engage with other people – for example, with their needs, drives and moods?

Greenstein is part of a small army of analysts across the social sciences who have tried to capture key dimensions of leadership style and develop them into tools such as analytical typologies and performance assessment instruments. Looking at leader behaviour through these lenses is not just an academic exercise. Doing so also affords others who engage with those leaders an opportunity to 'deal' with them effectively – to inform, advise, lobby, outmanoeuvre and upset them. This is precisely why intelli-gence agencies such as the CIA have long invested heavily in profiling techniques allowing them to monitor and interpret the psychological make up and leadership styles of key political figures around the world (in its Center for the Analysis of Personality and Political Behavior; see Post 2004, 2005).

The behaviour of people holding high public office has been, and will be, observed incessantly by leadership scholars. 'Reading' leaders' behaviour is seen as the key to understanding what motivates them, and a predictor of what impacts they might have. Peers, advisers, subordinates, opponents and other stakeholders all watch how they allocate their attention, make decisions, relate to people, deal with pressure, conflict and criticism, and perform in public situations. They do so for good reasons. Like all of us, leaders are creatures of habit. In the course of their personal and professional lives they develop distinctive styles of thought and action. This allows others to make educated guesses about what they may be feeling and how they will act when a new situation comes along (see Box 1.1). The more intimate one's knowledge about a leader's personal style, the more accurate those educated guesses are likely to be.

Why do individuals holding identical or similar leadership roles display such widely different styles? The answer almost *has* to be: because of the people they are. But what is it about certain people that makes them end up on top? Are leaders smarter than ordinary people, and are successful leaders even smarter than those that are not? Are they fitter? Do they have greater self-confidence? Are they morally superior? In contemporary democratic societies few will answer these questions instinctively in the affirmative – if only because the evidence to the contrary seems to abound wherever we cast our glance. Quite a few American presidents suffered from low self-esteem rather than the reverse (Greenstein 2002: 8); some, like Calvin Coolidge, were clinically depressed (McDermott 2008: 34).

As far as 'smartness' goes, Ronald Reagan is an interesting case. He had no great desire to know things before he acted and was dismissed as a second-rate mind by many, and in his second term the effects of his advanced age and the onset of Alzheimer's disease became more evident (McDermott 2008: 28, 31). He nevertheless eventually became one of the twentieth century's most highly rated US presidents, mainly because his communicative capacity and his high EQ (emotional intelligence quotient) compensated for what may have been a modest IQ (intelligence quotient). In contrast, intellectually gifted but emotionally impaired individuals such as Richard Nixon and Bill Clinton consistently rank much lower than Reagan, mainly because they failed to control their darker impulses while in office. James Buchanan, Jimmy Carter and Gerald Ford were widely seen as both bright and morally upright, but all three ended up in the dustbin of presidential history. Two of the USA's most revered presidents – Franklin D. Roosevelt (FDR) and John F. Kennedy (JFK) – were effectively cripples, and the latter, holding office in the television rather than the radio age, took irresponsibly high doses of heavy medication to hide that fact from the public (McDermott 2008; Owen 2008). In short, even if we assume that in the balance between actors and contexts it is the former who matter most, there is plenty of space for debate about what precisely it is about those particular actors that matters for their leadership. One of many such personal factors that has been paid a lot of attention by leadership researchers is motivation. The assertion is that the reasons why people seek leadership positions and roles matter

BOX 1.2   What makes leaders tick?

Why do people aspire to hold high public office? What keeps them going in the face of unmanageable workloads, relentless public criticism and an often toxic stakeholder environment? Why do some leaders take huge gambles with history? Why do they act in a sometimes blatantly self-defeating manner, as did US president Woodrow Wilson, who undermined his own burning desire to create a League of Nations in the wake of World War I by treating anyone expressing reservations about American accession to the new body with such hostility and contempt that he virtually organized his own opposition, and eventual Congressional defeat (George and George 1956)? Why do some otherwise highly successful and long-serving heads of government, such as Konrad Adenauer (West German chancellor, 1949–65) or Tony Blair (British prime minister, 1997–2007) cling to office long beyond their political sell-by date, dragging down their party, their government, their successor and their reputation in the process? Why do some corporate giants not previously known for their commitment to public values restyle themselves as mega-benefactors (for example, Bill Gates, George Soros and Warren Buffett)? To answer such questions, leadership scholars have delved into the personalities of leaders, and particularly into their underlying motives: the ends or purposes for which their personal skills and resources are being mobilized and directed. Two traditions of motivational analysis can be juxtaposed: the psychoanalytical and the behavioral. The former is inspired by the intellectual legacy of people such as Sigmund Freud and Erik Erikson. It assumes that the roots of people's motivation and character lie in their childhood and early life experiences, which shape both their conscious and unconscious selves (Post 2013). Zaleznik (1977/2004) makes an interesting distinction between once-born and twice-born leaders. The former's transition from the home and family of their childhood to independence as an adult is relatively easy. Their leadership later in life is therefore a product of their early circumstances. The latter suffer as they grow up, feel different and isolated from their family and peers, and develop an elaborate inner life as a coping device. As they grow older, this allows them to become truly independent and self-reliant, inner-directed and self-assured. Their leadership is the product of self-invention.

The behavioural tradition is best exemplified by the work of David Winter and his many associates (see an overview in Winter 2002). Their work is informed by a different tradition of social science research: the systematic measurement of specific aspects of the behaviour of large numbers of individuals. Winter *et al.* studied the speech acts (speeches, interviews, letters, writings etc.) of a great number of US presidents and other political leaders. They coded the contents in terms of the indications they contained for the presence of three types of fundamental human motives they had drawn from their reading of the literature: the drives for power, achievement and affiliation. They then illustrated how the presence/absence of these motivational drives related to particular leadership actions and outcomes. Table 1.1 clarifies what the three motivational types entail, and to what sorts of leadership behaviour they are likely to give rise.

in relation to how (and how well) they lead (see further Box 1.2 and Table 1.1).

Clearly, who leads does indeed matter. But *where, when* and *on what* leadership is called for matters just as much. When studying governance in terms of leadership we should not fall into the trap of assuming that particular individuals comprehensively dominate governments, parties and public or non-profit organizations. In a world of distributed leadership, policy decisions and public institutions tend to have a host of fingerprints on them. Paradoxically, some public choices and organizational policies issues have 'no' fingerprints on them at all, in that their course and outcomes arguably are in fact shaped not by particular actors but are largely predetermined by impersonal, external forces (for example, the economic climate, legal obligations, international pressures).

This leads us into another important set of assumptions, about matters of agency. Do we take leaders to be relatively autonomous actors who are able to make their own luck, and whose main sources of influence derive from their personal make-up and behaviour? If we do, studying their personalities and actions in depth makes all the sense in the world. Or do we see them as frail humans afloat on a sea of forces greater than themselves that set the stage for their emergence, performance and demise? In this case, it makes at least as much sense to study the properties of the context in which leaders have to operate.

In facing this question, the study of leadership is no different from that of any other social phenomenon. The so-called agency–structure duality lies at the very heart of the social sciences, as does the closely related duality between ideas and reality: is human behaviour shaped by objective physical and social realities, or by socially constructed, and therefore contingent and contestable, interpretations of these realities? Academics have long debated this, and the most sensible position on it lies somewhere in the middle ground. Who governs does not matter always and all of the time. Economic and political conditions may highly constrain the range of policies leaders may pursue – but they never fully determine them.

The sensible position, therefore, is to assume that 'it depends', and not get caught in exclusively agent-centred, ideational or structure-centred, material accounts of leadership. As Joseph Nye (2008) argued, good leadership is also about being 'smart': seeking and exploiting a thorough understanding of the context in which the group finds itself. If we want to understand leadership, we must also grasp how and why (mis)alignments between leader and context occur.

So what 'understanding public leadership' entails in both analytical and practical terms can vary greatly. Greenstein (1969) long ago summed up when it makes sense to take an actor-centred approach to explaining public policies or decisions. This is when, in the given situa-

TABLE 1.1   *Leader motives: achievement, affiliation and power*

Motivational drive	Achievement	Affiliation	Power
Leader is likely to be prioritizing:	Achieving excellence, setting standards for quality of performance, prevailing in competitive situations, or delivering unique and unprecedented accomplishments	'Keeping things together': establishing, maintaining or restoring friendly relations among individuals, groups, constituencies	Having control over or being able to influence, persuade or help others by strong, forceful actions, controlling or regulating others, and to gain prestige in the process of doing so
Likely to engage in:	Moderate risk-taking Using information to modify performance Achieving entrepreneurial success	Co-operative, friendly, approval-seeking behaviour when feeling confident and safe Defensive, cold and even hostile behaviour when feeling vulnerable or criticized	Ranging from proactive, nurturing, inspirational behaviour to profligate, impulsive, excessive, narcissistic behaviour
Basic strategic posture:	Co-operative and 'rational'	Co-operative when safe; defensive and hostile when under threat	Exploitative, aggressive
Values advice from:	Technical experts	Friends and other liked sources	People who know the political game

Source: Adapted from Winter (2002)p.27.

tion: (i) there was a non-trivial degree of freedom for actors – including actor A to chose various alternative courses of action with respect to X or Y; (ii) A had the formal and/or the informal power resources *vis-à-vis* all other potentially relevant actors (B–n) to make a pivotal, potentially decisive contribution to the handling of X or the course of Y; (iii) A had the intention of doing so; (iv) A had the personal strength and skills to use his/her power resources effectively with regard to X or within Y (Greenstein 1969).

The extent to which these conditions are met varies greatly from issue to issue, and context to context. In many cases, it will simply not make sense to pay much attention to the personal characteristics of a particular leader, because the evidence overwhelmingly suggests that the leader was either not motivated or not powerful enough to make a difference. So this leads to the general proposition that leader-centred explanations of public policy choices and the behaviour of public organizations are most likely to hold sway in the case of: (a) leaders with a reputation for having and wielding a great deal of power and influence; (b) issues of strong personal interest or strategic importance to leaders; and (c) issues that cannot easily be handled by institutional routines of policy preparation and collective decision-making (for example, unprecedented, acute, highly risky and/or contentious issues such as 'crises').

The extent to which such general propositions and contingency rules can capture the complex public leadership equation should not be overestimated. We need a more finely grained analysis. Therefore, in Chapters 5 and 6 we shall explore the importance of particular types of contexts and situations in producing particular leadership opportunities and challenges.

When is leadership 'good'?

Is public leadership inherently desirable? Should we distinguish, as Burns (1978) does, between 'leaders' who rely primarily on bargaining, persuasion and genuine engagement with followers, and who accept the constraints of democracy and the rule of law, and Machiavellian 'power-wielders' who do not shy away from manipulation and coercion to prevail upon the led? If we adopt this explicitly normative, even moral, distinction, people like Napoleon, Hitler, Stalin and Mao disappear off the leadership map. Each of these authorized the use of brutal force against millions whom they deemed unworthy or dangerous. Still, to brand them mere power-wielders would overlook the fact that, whether we like it or not, each of them was able at least for some period of time to articulate a vision and persuade millions of others to share it. Moreover, all of them were in the business of both coping with and engendering major social change. The fact that their values and purposes are morally repugnant to our contemporary democratic sensibilities should not blind us to the fact that leadership was exercised. Conversely, democratically elected leaders such as George W. Bush and Tony Blair have been criticized widely for using deception in launching the war in Iraq and condoning torture in running it. Does that disqualify them from leadership analysis, or is it perhaps more productive to see these episodes as forms of 'bad' leadership (Kellerman, 2004)?

Public leaders, particularly those holding executive or legislative office within democratic societies, live in a complex moral universe.

Democracy requires good leadership if it is to function effectively. Yet the very idea of leadership seems to conflict with democracy's egalitarian ethos. The more that democratic leaders lead from the front, the less democratic they appear; and the more they act like good democrats, the less they seem like true leaders. Confronted with this dilemma, the general tendency among scholars has been to accept the need for leadership in practice while overlooking it in theory, and consequently failing to offer a yardstick for assessing leadership within democracy. Leadership cannot be eliminated, at least not without jeopardizing the conduct of public affairs. In practice, democracy's tendency is not to eliminate leadership but to multiply leadership offices and opportunities, and keep office-holding leaders in check with a web of accountabilities (Geer 1996; Ruscio 2004; Wren 2007; Kane *et al.* 2009).

Yet, at times, democratically embedded leaders also have to make tricky trade-offs: using debatable means to achieve inherently respectable (if perhaps politically contested) ends (Uhr, 2005). In the process, some succumb to the fallacy of thinking that the power of their office alone provides them with the moral authority to lead: 'If the President orders it, it cannot be illegal,' exclaimed US president Richard Nixon, justifying to interviewer David Frost his authorization of the Watergate break-in and subsequent cover-up activities. Going too far is a grave error for which many – including sooner or later the leaders that do so – may pay a serious price. But the story does not end there. The same Richard Nixon is credited with a number of bold, historic policy initiatives that have met with broad and lasting acclaim. To avoid the full complexity of this man and his period in office by removing him from consideration as a public leader is not helpful. Likewise, heads of government who have gained power by non-democratic means and occasionally govern by fear, intimidation and blackmail may at the same time pursue a range of widely shared and morally acceptable goals. They may even pursue those goals with inherently respectable means, to the contentment of an overwhelming proportion of the population. Are they not exercising leadership? Understanding public leadership is to take it in all its shades of grey: leading and following, heroes and villains, the capable and the incompetent, winners and losers.

This is precisely why the job of evaluating public leadership – which, after all, is one crucial form of understanding it – is so difficult. In Chapter 7 we shall explore these complexities and offer a normative framework for public leadership assessment in which the inherent dilemmas of exercising leadership are built into rather than organized out of the equation.

The art and profession of leading

If they have a viable coalition behind them, leaders may choose to disrupt the status quo, take a gamble on history, and really drive major innovations and reforms. Many leaders who do so are written off as quixotic and face punishment in one way or another. But some of them succeed: Martin Luther King on US race relations in the 1960s, Ronald Reagan on macro-economic management in the early 1980s, and Hugo Chavez on undermining the US's authority claims in its self-proclaimed Latin-American backyard in the 1990s.

It pays, therefore, to ask why some leaders are able to swim against the tide of existing structures, traditions and conventional wisdoms, and to achieve policy reforms and social changes against the odds. The temptation is always there to attribute this to some special qualities they possess – the 'great man' theory of leadership. But on closer inspection that account is almost always unpersuasive: no public leader I know managed to achieve all his or her objectives all of the time, yet the individual presumably possessed roughly the same set of personal qualities throughout. Even people like Abraham Lincoln, Mahatma Gandhi and Winston Churchill suffered many defeats and made many discernible errors of judgement before they achieved historical greatness.

Nor did they ever work completely alone. Behind every 'great' leader are some indispensable collaborators, advisers and mentors, without whom the leader's achievements would not have materialized. In Chapter 8, in a deliberate perspectivist break with the rest of the book, we take on the mantle of such an associate of a leader with major reform aspirations. Building in part on the fast-growing knowledge from both political science and management studies about the dynamics of 'leading change' in sticky systems with lots of 'veto players', and in part following in the footsteps of Machiavelli and other hands-on advisers to leaders whose maxims were more steeped in first-hand observation of leaders at work then in systematic theory development, we move from diagnostic into prescriptive mode. We articulate a number of key 'dos and don'ts' for public leaders trying to perform the archetypal work of change agent. In Chapter 9 we conclude the book. Retaining the practical hands-on perspective of Chapter 8, we move back into diagnostic mode and reflect on the future challenges and shape of public leadership in a fast changing world.

Chapter 2

The Work of Public Leadership

The 'public' in public leadership

This is a book about *public* leadership. That fact alone sets it apart from the bulk of the leadership literature, which is focused on corporate or organizational leadership. These insights cannot simply be transplanted into the public sector context. The pressures of expectations and responsibilities that both types of leaders face are not perhaps wholly dissimilar. The spheres in which they operate are distinct but inevitably intertwined in important ways, yet their craft and the conditions under which they practice it are fundamentally different in important respects. I shall not repeat all the familiar arguments made in support of this contention. They boil down to the one key point: public and private leadership perform fundamentally different functions in society, and because this is so, public and private leaders are subject to fundamentally different incentive structures and accountability regimes.

Public leadership is what breathes life into the institutions that inhabit and constitute the world of politics and government: parliament, cabinet, the presidency, the courts, government departments and agencies from the very top down to the 'street-level bureaucrats', as well as the arm's-length agencies such as central banks and national regulators, non-governmental organizations, international organizations, and – formally on the outside but de facto highly influential – the mass media. It is these public institutions and their interplay that determine how our societies, and indeed our personal lives, are governed. Leadership is involved in building, managing, legitimizing, controlling, changing and abolishing the public institutions. Taxpayers' money is involved in running them, political mechanisms are involved in steering them, and they are kept in check by a range of very public accountability arrangements.

Opportunities to exercise public leadership are vested particularly (but not exclusively) in the holders of senior offices within these institutions. Inside government, the key offices and their holders are readily discernible: they include the head of state, head of government, leaders of parliamentary political parties, heads of the judiciary, and the top layers of the civil service. Outside government, the term 'office-holder' is less reliable as an expression, but it is clear that public leadership can also be exercised by chief executives of non-government organizations, major corporations, social movements, organized interest groups, churches and trade unions. These are all leaders within civil society who may, for whatever reason, become involved in public affairs. Their position or informal stature enables them to wield influence and in some cases gives them considerable public authority to speak and act on behalf of significant groups, values or interests within society. Note that this broad view of civil society leaders also includes actors who legally or technically are commonly defined as belonging to the 'private sector', such as executives of firms, artists or journalists.

However big the differences in their respective roles, resources and regimes of accountability, all three forms of public leadership discussed here – political, administrative and civic – are performed in the public sphere, and aim in some way to address social issues and problems of collective action. This is what, as a cluster, sets them apart from corporate leadership. What, then, is it that public leaders 'do' in society that is not already done by anybody or anything else? The answer to the classic question of 'Who governs?' cannot be 'Nobody' – and not just for logical reasons. The many public institutions, rules and routines notwithstanding, at the end of the day it is down to individuals and groups taking up the strategic challenges and dilemmas of 'managing the public's business' (Lynn 1981) to give direction to the governance of societies. There is a range of things that citizens tend to look for in public leaders that they would not dream of expecting from business leaders. Public leadership as covered in this book encompasses three key spheres: politics, administration and society. Each sphere entails its own cluster of public leadership work (see Table 2.1). This chapter provides an introductory overview of what these eight areas of leadership work entail.

And once we have gained a sense of *what* the work of public leadership entails, we can start to wonder *how* it is being performed. What does 'doing' leadership actually involve? More specifically, what 'tools' are – or should be – in the kit that public leaders take to work every day? The latter part of the chapter will provide a glimpse into that toolkit. But first let us turn to the three spheres of public leadership work: political, administrative and civic.

Political leadership

In the day-to-day world of politics, much of the public attention revolves around the aspirations, acts and achievements of leaders of parties and governments. This is echoed in a growing awareness

TABLE 2.1   *The work of public leadership*

Political leadership

1. Constructing identities
2. Forging and selecting public policies

Administrative leadership

3. Balancing responsiveness and professionalism
4. Directing and adapting public organizations
5. Making government work on the front line

Civic leadership

6. Challenging and exhorting political and administrative actors
7. Holding governments accountable
8. Providing meaningful community services

among political scientists that leadership is not a subject that can be ignored, as it has long been, in the study of politics and government. In a world of declining voter loyalty to parties, far-reaching transformations of governance structures, omnipresent media coverage of political life and constant 'crises' of one sort or another, individual leaders have gained both visibility and relevance as moulders of political agendas and shapers of political outcomes (Blondel 1987; Aarts *et al.* 2011; Mair 2013). What, then, are the key roles of political leadership? The simple answer would be: to get elected, and elected, and elected once again. But that would confuse political office-seeking and office-holding with exercising political leadership. Instead, we have to wonder what it is that political actors can contribute to the governance of societies that no other players can. Without assuming that is all there is to it, two key roles should be highlighted.

Identity entrepreneurship

'Leadership', British leadership scholar Keith Grint argues, is 'essentially a social phenomenon: without followers there are no leaders. What leaders must do, therefore, is construct an imaginary community that followers can feel part of' (Grint 2000: 6). Including and excluding particular social groups and categories from the community is an often implicit, but in effect an essential task of political leadership, in which leaders both respond to and shape followers' perceptions (of themselves and others) and emotions – solidarity, but also fear and enmity (see Turner *et al.* 2008). In order to become accepted as leaders, politicians engage in 'identity entrepreneurship': they attempt to weave believable narratives about who and what it is they embody and claim to represent. The personas they project – their public self, and the beliefs and values they embody – need to take into account their intended constituencies' social identities – for example, their perceptions of 'we-ness' (and, by implication, their reasons for including and excluding others from their imagined community) (Haslam and Reicher 2007; Reicher *et al.* 2014).

Political leaders are sometimes faced with stark choices as to how to represent themselves and the group(s) whose leadership they seek. Do they aim for a profile as a factional warrior or as a unifying figure within their parties? Do they claim to rule first and foremost for their own ideological, religious or ethnic tribe? Such a strategy may earn them a cohesive and committed following, but may push their grouping towards the fringe of the political spectrum, or indeed perpetuate (and even escalate) simmering intergroup tensions within the community. When Marshal Josip Tito died in 1980, the members of the collective leadership that succeeded him as rulers of Yugoslavia each faced such a choice: would they to continue his project of forging a superordinate Yugoslavian identity on a patchwork of ethnically and religiously diverse and historically bitterly divided communities? Or would they seek to project themselves as flag bearers for their respective ethnic-religious groups? We all know what choices they made, and the tragedies resulting from them. When apartheid ended in South Africa, long-suppressed tribal divisions within the black community surfaced, and some militant ethnic identity entrepreneurs whipped up Zulu nationalism, plunging the country into violent conflict. It took the compensating force and authority of the highly inclusive 'rainbow nation' identity frame espoused by South African president Nelson Mandela, combined with persistent conciliatory gestures towards ethnic radicals, to stave off civil war.

Conversely, when long-divided societies are exhausted by conflict and possibilities for peace-building occur, as in Northern Ireland during the 1990s, political leaders supporting such initiatives face the challenge of taking their communities along on a path of abandoning some of the beliefs and stereotypes that sustain division in favour of a commitment to a more inclusive way of thinking about themselves and the community in which they live. The same applies to the leaders of political parties seeking to repair traumatic, long-running internal splits, or to public service leaders overseeing a politically imposed merger of two hitherto distinct departments or agencies.

In contemporary 'liquid societies' (Bauman 2007), where many parts of people's lifestyles and perceptions are more ephemeral, fluid and partly 'globalized', identity work has become a particularly daunting leadership challenge for politicians. How to respond to secularization when you're running a Christian-democratic party? What stance to take on largely uncontrolled mass migration into one's country? How does the archetypal leader of a staunchly WASP (White Anglo-Saxon

Protestant) community in the South-western United States position himself and his community in relation to the growing size and political power of Hispanic Americans? How to turn the traditionally wary British, Danes or the recently acceded Bulgarians and Romanians into committed 'Europeans?' (Shore 2000). In other words, how to mobilize public internalization of transnational 'nation-building' projects such as the European Union, which propose to transcend centuries-worth of national and regional sentiments, hardened by economic competition and wars? What stance to take on Islamist extremism in a traditionally Christian/secular community with considerable and fast-growing Muslim populations?

When the boundaries of hitherto cohesive and fixed social identities are tested, leaders are faced with dilemmas. The mayor of Amsterdam, Job Cohen, earned praise from one half of the population and scorn from the rest when he reiterated his well-publicized commitment to inclusiveness and conciliation in the face of peak ethnic tensions following the political assassination by a Moroccan-born young Muslim of a controversial film director and columnist known for his highly critical stance towards Islam. An inclusive stance in the face of active mobilization of bias, growing cleavages and emotive incidents can easily be cast as a form of weakness or naivety in leaders. It can destroy their authority and pave the way for partisan identity entrepreneurs on either side of the divide (Hajer and Uitermark 2008). One way or another, all political leaders will have to come to terms with the fact that 'social identities exist and are acquired, claimed and allocated within power relations. Identity is something over which struggles take place and with which strategies are advanced: it is means and end in politics' (Jenkins 2013: 23).

Policy entrepreneurship

These are the moments where there is the potential to rally forces around a push for major – rather than incremental – change. Such critical junctures are therefore often referred to as 'windows of opportunity' for reform (Keeler 1993). Think of Helmut Kohl's strategic choice when the Berlin Wall came down: pursue the policy of coexistence with the German Democratic Republic, or push for German reunification now that Soviet dominance of Eastern Europe was clearly on the wane, and all the established beliefs about the architecture of Europe seemed to be ready to be taken? Kohl chose the latter, seized the moment, and forged what had been unthinkable just months before into existence within the space of a year (Zelikow (with Rice) 1995; Maier 1997). Inspirational public rhetoric by leaders can play an important part in this, but so can their ability for backstage wheeling and dealing. Kohl, of modest rhetorical ability, was highly astute in massaging the egos and allaying the fears of the four veto players in the reunification game: the leaders of the allied powers. He worked on them one by one, carefully picking the sequence, starting with the most powerful among them (who was also the most positively predisposed towards unification) – George H.W. Bush. Tackling Mikhail Gorbachev required not just hard bargaining – a big line of credit flowed from Germany to the Soviet Union – but more important, levelling with him on a deeper emotional level, as leaders of countries that were both scarred immeasurably by the devastation of the Second World War. Kohl understood this instinctively, and rose to the occasion.

The idea of leadership as a combination of exploitation and mobilization lies at the heart of John Kingdon's (1984) notion of 'policy entrepreneurs'. These are individuals who are adept at playing the political game of policy change. They aim to join hitherto disparate streams of problem definitions, political priorities and coalitions of actors in the policy arenas to destroy support for existing arrangements and wield support for particular reform ideas and designs (Bryson *et al.* 1992). Policy entrepreneurship is about the embracing of novel policy ideas, selling them to diverse constituencies, building powerful coalitions around them, and seizing the moment when opportunities to do so present themselves. It is about practising the political art of the possible in proactive and creative ways (Ignatieff 2013: 34).

Administrative leadership

Senior officials feed political executives with sound and usable ideas, information and advice. The privileged access they enjoy to political decision-makers offers senior officials the opportunity to 'manage up' and 'lead from below'. They can frame, time and distribute their strategic advice selectively. They can thus serve as important gatekeepers in the policy-making processes. Administrative leaders also face the daunting task of making the massive machinery of government implement political choices and deliver public services. Keeping this going in today's complex and fast-moving environments requires much more than the technically competent 'administration' as envisaged by Woodrow Wilson; it presupposes both transactional and at times transformational leadership, stewardship, reform, networking and alliance formation (Selznick 1957; Lewis 1980; Terry 1995; Moore 1995 and 2013; Boin 2001).

In the American tradition in particular, the leadership expectations attached to senior administrative positions are emphasized strongly, and in part embedded in the Constitution. In other places – such as France and to some extent Germany – a remarkable degree of officially sanctioned 'hybridity' exists between political and administrative leadership roles and cadres. In Westminster (UK) systems, official doctrine almost exclusively, and sometimes quite narrowly, emphasizes the 'servant' aspect of administrative roles ('the government of the day'), but the realities of modern governance are such that senior departmental and agency officials must also be exercising leadership – leaving them more vulnerable than their US counterparts to charges of being 'unresponsive' (see Rhodes and Wanna 2008). We can discern three distinctive challenges of administrative leadership: serving the democratic process while at the same time remaining a credible leader of a cadre of professionals; making policy work at the front line of implementation; and building and nurturing the organizational capacity to accomplish this.

Serving democracy while leading professionals

In the traditional understanding of the relationship between bureaucrats and politicians there is a clear distinction and hierarchy of labour between them. The politician functions as a sovereign representative of political values and interests, while the bureaucrat is the subordinate 'expert adviser and policy executor', whose major concern is efficiency. In this conception, leadership (charting and adjusting the course of public policy) is by definition exercised by politicians, with bureaucrats specializing in management (creating order and proposing workable alternatives in the face of complex social problems).

Several studies have suggested that in reality the respective role conceptions and interaction patterns between politicians and administrators are more differentiated (Putnam 1975; Aberbach *et al.* 1981) pointed to a growing hybridity in the role conceptions of politicians and senior public servants. Peters (1987) deduced five ideal-typical modes of interaction on a continuum between, on the one hand, formal Weberian separation and a hierarchy that sees politicians lead and bureaucrats follow, and on the other hand, 'bureaucratic government', in which bureaucratic expertise and activism dominate the policy process and the role of political officeholders is marginal. In this model, bureaucratic leadership eclipses political leadership – an unwanted prospect for democrats. In between both ends of the continuum there are the intermediate categories of 'village life' and 'functional village life', in which the roles are more diffuse and the interaction between bureaucrats and politicians more collegial. The final type is 'adversarial politics', referring to a strongly politicized relationship in which politicians and bureaucrats compete for control over public policy. These classical studies suggest that, in order to 'serve' properly, senior bureaucrats ultimately do a good deal of 'leading' during the process: conducting and continuously recalibrating a delicate form of institutional role play with an ever-changing cast of political masters.

Peters and Pierre (2001) argue that ongoing waves of public sector reform and administrative reorganization since the 1980s have had a profound effect on the relationship between politicians and administrators. Agencification and the changing recruitment and career patterns of officials tend to undermine both the classical dichotomy and the more co-operative 'village life' in which jointly socialized politicians and top officials blend smoothly. Politicians seem to want to play it safe and opt for civil service reforms that appear designed to curtail the autonomy of senior public servants: temporary appointments, targets and performance management. Moreover, in some countries, ministers and heads of government now have significant numbers of advisers whose prime loyalty is to them and whose orientation is on 'good politics' rather than 'good policy'. The growing number and clout of these advisers has been a two-edged sword for the senior public service. Ministerial staffs potentially present opportunities to get the public service's message into ministers' ears; but equally they can become a difficult to manage third partner in the interface between politics and administration – one that potentially has much power but very little accountability (Tiernan 2007; Eichbaum and Shaw 2014). At worst, the public service leader is thus (re-)cast as a public *servant* in a narrow sense, not the servant of the public interest but an 'agent' of the 'principal' that is the democratically elected or mandated political office-holder (Hood and Lodge 2004).

And it is true: serving the government of the day and serving the public interest more broadly do not always amount to the same thing. In a climate of popular mistrust of politics and popular scepticism about the quality of public service delivery, criticism of current or intended policies and programmes may give rise to awkward 'blame games' within government. Senior bureaucrats have at times felt unjustly victimized by ministerial blame deflection exercises that have left them to 'take the heat' when the going got tough. To them, this amounts to 'breaking the bargain' (Savoie 2003) between politics and administration, which is centred on the idea that with the politician's right to direct the bureaucracy must also come their acceptance of public accountability for its performance. Hence a significant leadership challenge has arisen for senior public officials: how to reinvent a tolerable compact between themselves and their political masters in an era when old assumptions have lost their relevance and the pressures on the relationship have both multiplied and intensified?

Most crucially, while they are supposed to be responsive to their political masters, administrative leaders are not merely required to serve the government of the day, but also to protect the professional and ethical integrity of the administrative process – even, or more aptly, particularly when members of the government want to cut administrative corners to achieve their political ends. Balancing these three imperatives at any given time, but in particular when they are directly at odds with one another, is perhaps the supreme test of administrative leadership. At the same time, the growing currency of the notion of distributed leadership has also given some traction to the idea that it is not the distinction and separation between political and administrative leadership that should be emphasized, but rather their complementarity: political office-holders (and their staffs) and senior public servants as 'tandems' that work most effectively when they collaborate and thus engage in shared leadership of ministerial portfolios and priorities (Svara 2002; Hartley and Manzie 2014).

Implementing: making government work at the front line

Harvard scholar Mark Moore (1995, 2013) is credited with the phrase 'public value creation' as a descriptor of the type of leadership exercised by senior public administrators. The emphasis in Moore's account is on the creative element, which can be seen as the contemporary restatement of the delegated discretionary power so valued by Wilson a century earlier. What is new in Moore's account is the explicit recognition that those who 'implement' the law have a legitimate role in shaping and forming the policy that supposedly informs the law. Even where officials have had very limited input into the formal policy being authorized and implemented, they have substantial control over *how* the policy will be implemented, and that discretionary capacity over the mechanisms of implementation marks out the legitimate expectation of officials that they will 'create public value' from the often incomprehensible and sometimes incoherent public law that is handed to them.

Of special importance in Moore's framework is stakeholder negotiation: the many ways that public servants can lead the implementation process through their management of who is heard when policy is translated into administrative practice. Carefully aligning the 'managing up' to authorizers, 'managing out' to partners and stakeholders in the public service delivery process, and 'managing down' to optimize their own organization's operational capacity is the name of this leadership game. Moore (2013) has his gallery of exemplary public managers who can bring public legitimacy to policy implementation by exercising the sort of leadership that can be wielded through astute political management designed to create and maintain mandates, tolerable levels of resources and ample discretion for the organization. Police chiefs at their best illustrate these processes.

There is robust debate on how applicable this interpretation of assertive public service leadership is outside the American administrative system, particularly in the Westminster context. In the parliamentary Anglo democracies, the formal autonomy positions of agency

30

BOX 2.1 Helping government deliver

Contemporary public service leadership is as much about strategic management of policy implementation as it is about producing strategic policy advice. In the words of Peter Shergold, the head of the Australian Public Service (2003–08):

> Public servants bear a particular responsibility, directly and indirectly, for the delivery of government policy. Every government knows that its future depends not only on how wisely it makes decisions but on how effectively its public service delivers them. In my interpretation of the Westminster tradition governments should continue or fall on how the electorate perceives the quality of their policies not on the competence of public officials to execute them. Indeed I think that public servants should exhibit bias ... but the bias they display should be for delivering public policy with vigour.
>
> Implementation is necessarily a learning process. The changing circumstances and the experience of executing a policy decision have to be taken into account. Indeed they may require the policy decision to be revisited. Getting things done well in government requires more than a series of commandments (regulations, rules and guidelines) handed down to those below or transmitted from the national office to regional offices. Communication and learning have to work both ways. Policy prepared without the experience of those who deliver it across counters or from call-centres is almost certainly policy that will be poorly designed and difficult to implement.
>
> Successful implementation of policy is not about the adoption of any particular project management methodology, although it is essential that an appropriate methodology be employed. Increasingly it has become apparent that the pathway to better implementation is that it be consciously driven from the top down with continuing executive oversight.
>
> Senior public sector managers, who find themselves charged with the oversight of major programs [sic] and projects must know what the right questions are, who might be able to answer them and how to assess the validity of the answers.
>
> Senior management has to play an increasingly important role in linking individual projects to wider organisational strategies and goals, and shaping those goals on the basis of what has been learned from individual projects. They need to understand that policy development and service delivery are not in a linear chronological relationship. The making and executing of government policy is an iterative process. We can only avoid policy blunders by ensuring that policy-making is routinely and constructively informed by service delivery, in a way that transcends traditional boundaries and structures.

Source: Excerpts from: Peter Shergold, 'Driving change to bring about better implementation and delivery', in Wanna (2007), pp. 11–21, reproduced by permission of ANU Press.

heads tend to be smaller, less emphasis is placed on their roles as 'stewards' of programme and agency continuity, and the ethos of 'serving the government of the day' is more dominant. Whether this obviates the whole idea of proactive public value creation by public servants, particularly by leaders of arm's-length agencies, or of major public projects and programmes is another matter (see Alford 2008 versus Rhodes and Wanna 2007).

Building and preserving organizational capacity

First and foremost, administrative leaders need organizations that enable them to create such public value. Public organizations are, however, not simply tools at the disposal of leaders. They are complex entities whose structures and set ways may help but equally may hinder the creation of public value as envisaged by their leaders. Moreover, they exist in similar complex and often unforgiving social and political environments. Organizational leadership is about building, consolidating, safeguarding and transforming public organizations in the face of ever-changing environments and potentially volatile political sentiments and preferences. Ideally, such leadership is instrumental in 'institutionalizing' public organizations into well-oiled machines whose missions and methods are fully aligned and at the same time have become near-unassailable 'strong brands' that are widely 'taken for granted' by both internal (employees, political masters, other public organizations), and external (clients, mass media, legislators) stakeholders (Selznick 1957; Terry 1995; Boin 2001).

Institutions combine reliable performance with high levels of public legitimacy. They are special because they have developed and incorporated an effective way of dealing with complex and elusive goals. This way of working helps employees to do their jobs. It tells them what works and what does not. It also helps them to make sense of the world around them. As this 'adaptive belief system' proves its worth, institutional members come to value it and voluntarily reproduce it. Externally, their way of working has become their trademark. Public institutions are valued not only for what they *do* but also for what they *are*. A generalized perception or assumption exists outside the organization that the organization is 'desirable, proper, or appropriate' within the socially constructed system of norms, values, beliefs and definitions.

Some public organizations seem to have no clear sense of purpose, no shared culture of any kind, no consistent way of working and no solid support base. Some public organizations are highly institutionalized (many fire brigades, successful schools, and military services, for example). Some – such as NASA or the FBI – used to be but have since 'deinstitutionalized' under the pressure of botched performance, public scandal or politically imposed reorganization. To enable organizations to reach that Nirvana-like state of becoming 'institutions' and to keep them there requires astute leadership (Boin and Christensen 2008). This is particularly so for public organizations, whose chief mission may not automatically endear them to their principal clienteles or the general public, and whose occasional errors can make for great and highly emotive negative publicity (for example, mistakes by tax offices, prisons, environmental regulators, competition regulators, child protection agencies and so on).

Leading the latter category of organizations has sometimes been likened to an 'impossible job' (Hargrove and Glidewell 1990). And indeed, how *does* one keep organizations afloat that are characterized by several of the following conditions:

- a fuzzy mission full of internal contradictions (for example, in prison systems: the need to keep people locked up reliably, yet humanely, while at the same time working towards their rehabilitation and reintegration into society);
- an ill-defined and/or ill-respected contested professional technology for achieving their goals (for example, social work, child protection);
- low-legitimacy clienteles, such as single mothers, ethnic minorities or parolees, which impede the agency's ability to attract funding and political support; or
- intense conflict among its various constituencies (for example, farmers, environmentalists, grocery chains and consumer organizations) in a department of primary industries, food and consumer affairs).

The terminology of 'impossibility' is inappropriate: in the public sector, thousands of such organizations exist and persevere without their clients rising in revolt or their political masters pulling the plug on the clients. Some may cynically call them 'permanently failing' organizations (Meyer and Zucker 1989), which survive because of the lack of competitors and society's need for some agencies to do its dirty work, however ineptly. That, however, does not explain why some prison systems or child protection agencies manage to beat the odds, avoid the front pages much of the time, and achieve fairly high levels of institutionalization, whereas others are perennially bogged down in controversy, suffer entrenched low staff morale, and produce little discernible public value. The difference, I would argue, is not in their contexts, but in the way they are being led (see also Goodsell 2011).

In practice, public organizations (or parts within them) move between the extremes of full institutionalization and complete de-institutionalization. The administrative leadership challenge is about finding achievable equilibriums given the nature of the context and the organization's key parameters at particular points in time (see further, Chapter 5). Figure 2.1 sums up the balancing act of leading public organizations.

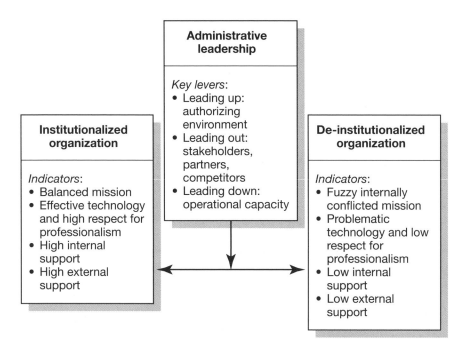

FIGURE 2.1　*The balancing act of leading public organizations*

Civic leadership

The third sphere of public leadership focuses on actors/roles outside the governmental system. Most studies of public leadership ignore this sphere completely, which is a gross omission, since civic leadership quite often is what animates innovation, controversy and change in polities – all leadership functions *par excellence*. Vibrant civil societies provide democracies with a rich mosaic of non-office-based public leadership: watchdogs, moralists, dissidents, clergy members, revolutionaries, social entrepreneurs – they are all there. Some rely on personal charisma to build momentous social movements, while others effectively exploit the moral capital of already established non-government institutions to perform civic leadership work. Some work alongside existing office-holders and regimes, while others operate in stark opposition to them. Some self-consciously craft a public persona in the limelight of democratic deliberation and political controversy, but others self-effacingly accomplish significant feats of public service unseen by the larger public but keenly welcomed by beneficiaries and followers (Barker *et al.* 2001; Kane 2001; Elkington and Hartigan 2008; Kane *et al.* 2008).

Civic leadership comes to life in explicit relation, and opposition, to the power of political and administrative elites (Kane 2001). It has several distinct and not necessarily complementary roles to play. It brings societal needs, wants and ideas to the political stage, it monitors critically the political establishment's responses to these signals, and it harnesses societal self-government by engaging in the direct delivery of public services, with or without government support.

Monitoring and evaluating: the watchdog role

Many non-governmental organizations act as watchdogs over government, complementing, correcting and extending the work of 'official' watchdogs such as competition agencies, ombudsmen and auditors' offices. Human Rights Watch and Amnesty International assess and publicize governments' records of legality, fairness and decency in dealing with their citizens, particularly those who disagree with them. Greenpeace and a wide range of local, national and international groups do the same with respect to governments' records on protecting the environment and animal species. In free societies, the list of such informal watchdogs is long, extending into a wide range of domains of government intervention.

What tends to be distinctive about such civil society groups is the use of publicity – these days extending to the capacity to make waves on the internet – as leverage in dealing with government. Many of the established commercial and policy interests prefer to operate 'behind closed doors', where they can try to extract concessions from governing authorities. They share with watchdogs the potential to bite, but they tend not to share the potential to bark, preferring discreet lobbying for their constituents' interests over exposure and confrontation in the service of a wider public interest. For civil society watchdogs, their public bark *is* their bite: they contribute to public leadership by drawing public attention to the strengths or weaknesses of government action. They also demand that politicians pay close attention to the electoral support that such organizations can mobilize for or against them. Public interest groups can do much to generate their own publicity but ultimately are dependent on the power of the mass media to carry their message. The leadership available to public interest organizations comes down to the power over opinion formation – using publicity to shape and manage elite or public opinion in ways that support their cause (see Box 2.2). This requires not just a good grip on the cold facts of whatever aspect of corporate and/or government performance they seek to shadow but also the ability to create and sustain attentive publics.

BOX 2.2   Civic 'watchdogs' at work: tracking cyber espionage

State-sponsored attacks that block websites and shut down mobile phone networks are being used increasingly to disrupt the work of civil society at times when their input could be critical to political or social processes. Well-meaning groups working in the developing world also risk endangering the very individuals and communities they seek to help if they fail to get up to speed on information security in the digital era.

Rafal Rohozinski, founder of the Ottawa-based think tank SecDev Group, collaborated with a team of cyber sleuths burrowed in the Citizen Lab in the basement of the University of Toronto's Munk Centre for International Studies. For 10 months, the researchers tracked an electronic espionage ring they dubbed GhostNet, before bringing it to light in March 2009.

By the time the researchers lifted the lid on GhostNet, the covert intelligence-gathering operation had compromised almost 1300 computers in 103 countries. It was active for close to two years before abruptly shutting down two days after its existence was revealed in *The New York Times* on March 29, 2009.

Almost one-third of the affected computers were 'high-value' targets, located in foreign ministries, embassies, news organizations, international organizations, and NGOs. They included the offices of the Dalai Lama, the Russian embassy in Beijing, foreign affairs ministries in Iran and Indonesia, the Indian diplomatic service, and the Asian Development Bank. Computers were infiltrated for an average of 145 days, and for as long as 660 days. Though the researchers were at pains not to name culprits, the main servers from which the operation was run were located in Hainan, China.

Source: Haggart (n.d.). Reproduced by permission of the International Development Research Centre.

Challenging and exhorting: the advocate role

Watchdogs are typically defensive, barking when they sense a threat to the values they are committed to protect. But civil society organizations are often far more proactive, being vocal also when they sense that others might be roused to help form a useful public coalition to generate a desired response from a cautious government or public authority.

By definition, public advocacy involves the use of 'voice', often to push the interests of quite vulnerable or marginal groups. Advocacy refers to many forms of policy leadership, only a few of which need to have any public display or notice. That is, the voice exercised by effective advocacy groups need not be a one heard in public. Many governments or public authorities prefer to listen to external advocates in private. This preference for secrecy is itself evidence of the power of those advocacy groups to get the ear of ruling powers, and often rests on prior campaigns indicating the clear potential for wider public mobilization of the sort feared by ruling authorities. Leading advocacy groups involves planning campaigns, building networks and making tactical judgements that are not unlike those made by professional politicians.

BOX 2.3   Using fame as moral capital: celebrity leadership

Many of us care about refugees and displaced children. Tens of thousands of us spend considerable amounts of time and money on improving their lot. But few of us have been as effective in bringing, and keeping, these issues on the agenda of political elites and institutions around the world as Angelina Jolie. She has developed into a formidable agenda-setter, a tenacious lobbyist, a grand benefactor, and even a hands-on civil-war mediator (in Sierra Leone in 2005). A regular fixture in the last few instalments of the Time 100 list, Angelina Jolie is no longer just an actress and a celebrity figure; she has come to be seen as a public leader.

In fact, she is a public leader *because* she is a hot Hollywood commodity. She deftly uses her famous name, physique and acting qualities to gain clout in the world beyond Hollywood to advance the causes she has come to embrace ever since filming in Cambodia. She understands that a celebrity is not just someone hounded by tabloid journalists but also 'an individual whose name has attention-getting, interest-riveting and profit-generating value' (Rein *et al*. 1987: 15). Possibly inspired by Audrey Hepburn, one of the pioneers of humanitarian activism in Hollywood, but succeeding on a much larger scale than Hepburn ever contemplated, Jolie represents a paradigmatic example of 'star power' at work in the world of international politics (Cooper 2008: 32–5). She and other 'celebrity diplomats' such as Bono, Bob Geldof and George Clooney know that 'celebrity sells' (Pringle 2004), but instead of selling watches, cars, deodorants and beers they have chosen to 'sell' humanitarian and other political messages.

Star power defies conventional accounts of public leadership. It enables a form of leadership driven by fame, admiration and dramaturgy, rather than by election, representation, and accountability. It is leadership by those who are well-known, not necessarily leadership by the well-qualified. In an era of boundless mass communication worldwide and 'entertainment culture' merging seamlessly with 'high culture', star power feels a lot more potent and 'in tune' than does electoral power. Unless, of course, the two are aligned, with one reinforcing the other, as when Oprah Winfrey supported Barack Obama's fledgling presidential campaign, setting in motion a much wider and politically magnetic 'love in' between A-list celebrity activists and the autonomous 'star appeal' of the articulate young candidate (for further reading, see Marsh *et al*. 2010).

A common element of all effective advocacy by external groups is the threat of public leadership through the exercise of 'moral authority', typically involving 'moral capital' (Kane 2001) – credibility and public trustworthiness – of the institution, organization or indeed the person (think of the spate of celebrity advocates such as Bono, and see further Box 2.3). To build, sustain and yet also use that type of capital judiciously requires continuous and prudent leadership regarding the use of 'voice' (about what, when, where, how?), the mobilization of public emotion, and the controlled demonstration of public support. Also, leading public advocacy groups or campaigns inevitably includes making judgement calls about which, out of many pressing issues or injustices to prioritize, when to accept compromise solutions, and whether to declare particular battles lost or to persevere against all odds.

Front-line delivery: the provider role

Civil society leaders, particularly those who run community non-profit organizations (NPOs) are actively engaged in shaping and delivering services to those who need them and who are not, or insufficiently, cared for by government. Sometimes they also work in tandem with government, tendering for contracts for service delivery that government wants done but for various reasons does not want to carry out itself. In recent decades, the widespread privatization of social services and the contracting out of service provision to non-governmental organizations have created a new situation for the state as well as for non-profit organizations (Smith and Lipsky 1993). As a result of privatization, competition between non-profit and for-profit providers has gained momentum. In that situation, NPOs have been forced to restructure themselves and to re-evaluate their organizational and management strategies in order to enhance their distinctive competence and competitiveness. Competition has caused NPOs to modify their strategies, pricing, and marketing policies significantly.

This has introduced a strategic leadership dilemma. Leaders of non-profit organizations face the tension between engaging with their constituents as political activists and serving them as clients (see Box 2.4 and Table 2.2). The more passionately they perform advocacy and watchdog roles, the more likely it is that they will collide with government elites (Schmid 2009). As service providers, resource dependencies may encourage them in the direction of pragmatic, co-operative stances towards government elites. As competitors in a market not just for philanthropic donations but also for government contracts, they are forced to introduce 'cold' managerial practices in traditionally 'hot' mission-driven organizations. Both of these developments come at a price. Moving closer to government and adopting managerial princi-

---

BOX 2.4   The contingencies of non-profit leadership

There is no one-size-fits-all to civic leadership. Civil society groups and organizations can pursue very different missions and develop distinct modes of organizing. The professionalized, predominantly transactional form of leadership common in corporations and public bureaucracies fits well with the more established non-profit organization whose main mission is focused on service provision with a sizable budget and work force, regularly engaged with government in contracts or partnerships. Embedded as these organizations are in a managerial paradigm, they need to recruit and socialize their leaders on that basis. Schmid (2009) argues that in many Western countries, government policies with regard to public service provision have seen the demise of classic subsidization of NPO activities and a rise in the use of contracting, competitive tendering and partnership agreements. The classic NPO service provision organizations have had no choice but adapt their own modus operandi to these regulatory impulses. This has placed a premium on improved management capacity as well as 'professionalism' in their leadership.

However, as Table 2.2 shows, this logic of leadership is optimally suited to only part of the non-profit sector. It is populated not just formal and well-established organizations, but typically also counts numerous more informal groups and nascent (but often short-lived) organizations. Whereas for some, such as the Salvation Army or the Red Cross, the emphasis is first and foremost on providing services to those in need, others, such as Amnesty International or Greenpeace, are primarily focused on influencing public opinion and government policy by publicizing, protesting, and lobbying. Given a group or organization's place within this continuum (which may in fact evolve over time), different types of leadership styles and skills become important.

TABLE 2.2   *A contingency model of non-profit leadership*

Organization structure Mission/focus	*Informal*	*Formal*
Civil society (advocacy)	*Type I* Grass roots activist group: Democratic-participative leadership	*Type II* Advocacy and lobby organization: Activist-diplomatic leadership
Service provision (delivery)	Emergent, fledgling service provider: Entrepreneurial leadership	Established professional service provider: Transactional leadership

Source: Adapted from Schmid (2009).

ples both constrain the aura of independent partisanship that forms the moral capital they need to be credible advocates in the eyes of their constituencies. The non-profit and social movement literatures are replete with studies describing the civic leadership conundrum of purity versus pragmatism: civic leaders may choose to 'dance with the devil' in order to do some tangible good, but at the risk of being seen to have 'sold out' and loose their credibility as a result (Baraket 2008; Shergold 2008; Stutje 2012).

The tools of public leadership

Now we have a sense of what public leadership is, or ought to be, about, we can turn to the questions of its craft: how does one 'do leadership'? What tools do political, administrative and civic leaders have at their disposal? And if students of leadership want to observe it in action, what sorts of behaviour and relationships should they be looking at?

There can be no exact, complete and universal answer to these questions. Different leadership jobs entail different institutional 'scripts' for leader behaviour – being prime minister comes with quite a different repertoire from heading up Amnesty International or a tax authority. Even being prime minister in different types of political systems (presidential versus parliamentary; majoritarian versus consensual) implies significantly different roles, and thus behaviours (Strangio *et al.* 2013). Different cultural settings place different expectations and boundaries on the exercise of leadership (Wildavsky 1989; House *et al.* 2001, 2004; Javidan *et al.* 2006; Hendriks and Karsten 2014). Different situations call for different types of leadership interventions – economic prosperity versus adversity; peace versus war; technical versus adaptive problems (see further Chapter 5). And, perhaps most important, rooted in their personalities and life experiences, different individuals have different understandings of what 'leading' entails and develop different styles of doing so. So, as so often in human endeavour, 'it all depends'. But we can at least gain a sense of the broader toolkit from which they all draw their instruments – for example, survey studies of public office-holders asking them how they perceive their roles and how they operate (Marsh *et al.* 2010); up-close archival and observational studies of public leaders at work (Weller 1983; Preston 2001; Rhodes *et al.* 2007; Rhodes 2011) and the numerous (psycho)biographies of political and civic leaders (see George and George 1956; Erikson 1958; Wildavsky 1984; Brown 1991; Caro 2012) and the less numerous biographies of administrative leaders (see Caro 1974; Lewis 1980; Rowse 2002). So, let me distil from this rich body of insight five essential 'tools' with which people aspiring to exercise public leadership can perform the work that it entails.

Attention Most public leaders have extremely busy lives, driven by a multitude of responsibilities associated with their roles and incessant demands on their time from their associates, constituents, allies, rivals, the media and other stakeholders. It can be hard for a minister, a parliamentarian, a senior public servant or a social movement leader even to keep up with what the system throws at them in terms of day-to-day paperwork and meetings, and all those things their staff tell them they must read, attend, argue and decide about. One thing is certain: if in the face of this incessant daily onslaught they don't make clear choices about what they really want to achieve, and therefore which matters and people to pay more or less attention to, they will probably not be able to exercise effective leadership over any aspect of it.

Allocating attention purposefully is a *sine qua non* of leadership (Goleman 2013). This has a qualitative as well as a quantitative dimension. The latter can be tracked neatly by, for example, a diary or 'shadowing' studies. It is about how much time leaders put their bodies and minds to different potential actors, issues and arenas, why they do so, and how this allocation of attention changes over time. Interestingly, studies in this vein suggest that senior office-holders may well have an inaccurate picture of what they do actually spend their time on, even though they have clear ideas on how they would *like* to spend their time (Noordegraaf 2000; Fleming 2008).

Whether or not they are accurate in their self-assessments about it, what leaders spend their time on is going to determine in no small measure what they are going to achieve. By ignoring certain areas they effectively hand over the stage to other actors and forces; but in those they do attend to they at least give themselves a fighting chance to make their mark. Much will depend on how many issues they can attend to effectively at the same time, and how well they spend the time they have allocated to each.

The qualitative aspect of allocating attention is about the leaders' drive and ability to be truly 'present' when they are in meetings, or read or think about particular subjects (Sinclair 2007). Many witness accounts by people who have worked for 'great' leaders mention their laser-beam-like ability to work their way through piles of papers yet infallibly focus on and retain those parts that are truly essential to the issues they want to prioritize or know they can only ignore at their peril. Others who have been in conversation and meetings with them mention their ability to give people the impression that they have the leaders' full attention, even though the interaction is brief and fleeting, buried in a life packed with dozens of interactions every day. Descriptions of this process are often quite physical – such as a leader's eyes and body radiating 'involvement', 'desire to know', 'suspension of disbelief' and 'respect' (see also Scharmer 2009). This quality of attention was immortalized in the novel *Primary Colors* about a very Bill

Clinton-like Southern governor who rose to become the president of the United States. The novel opens like this:

> The handshake is the threshold act, the beginning of politics. I've seen him do it two million times now, but I couldn't tell you how he does it, the right-handed part of it – the strength, quality, duration of it, the rudiments of pressing the flesh. I can, however, tell you a whole lot about what he does with his other hand. He is a genius with it. He might put it on your elbow, or up by your biceps: these are basic, reflexive moves. He is interested in you. He is honored to meet you. If he gets any higher up your shoulder – if he, say, drapes his left arm over your back, it is somehow less intimate, more casual. He'll share a laugh or a secret then – a light secret, not a real one – flattering you with the illusion of conspiracy. If he doesn't know you all that well and you've just told him something 'important,' something earnest or emotional, he will lock in and honor you with a two-hander, his left hand overwhelming your wrist and forearm. He'll flash that famous misty look of his. And he will mean it. (Anonymous 1996)

However spontaneous or meticulously organized (the budding politician Richard Nixon had staffers track down the birthdays of the wives of all relevant constituents and associates and made sure they were sent congratulatory postcards on the day), this quality of attention is a crucial factor for leaders in building personal rapport, and thus support for themselves. But it can also be a hierarchy-shattering device that empowers subordinates and others to really 'open up' in the presence of the leader, thus improving the leader's information position.

Commitment Allocation of attention is closely linked to another crucial leadership tool – commitment. It is very difficult to exercise leadership on a particular issue or in a particular organization if one does not really care very deeply about it. This is where a leader's values are translated into behaviour. Conveying commitment provides leaders and leadership teams with an orientation to a purpose, and helps them articulate and dramatize that purpose for the benefit of others. Subordinates, followers and adversaries alike constantly monitor, query and test leaders about what it is that drives them and what they really want to achieve. Commitment is hard to fake: people who monitor leaders systematically see through their ad hoc whims or lofty statements of intent that are not backed up by actions. Stakeholders sense if leaders are committed to certain causes by observing whether they are willing to speak up about them even when doing so is not necessarily popular; make tough decisions to advance them; and prepared to run risks in being held accountable for their actions with regard to them. Eliciting commitment in others is hard to do if one does not display it oneself – not just in words but also in deeds; in other words, in the pattern in one's behaviour over time. This is how leaders convey the values they really hold and the norms they really want to abide by. Effective leaders do so self-consciously, and integrate the signalling of commitment explicitly into their behavioural repertoires. Less effective leaders may either not have that type of inner compass and commitment, or leave too many people guessing for too long about the nature and extent of their dedication to their cause.

Conflict management   Leadership is about engaging with change: getting groups and systems to respond to changes in the world 'out there' that they really cannot afford to ignore. Bringing the need to adapt and change to groups and systems that are not necessarily aching to embrace them is hard work. It is definitely risky, not least to the leaders' own popularity and authority among their constituents (Heifetz and Linsky 2002; Williams 2005). Leadership often involves taking people and systems out of their comfort zones, questioning their long-held beliefs, breaking taboos, shattering myths, exposing hypocrisy, or simply making it clear to them that it will not be possible to go on as they did before – not necessarily because you as a leader say so but because the world around them has changed and the old conditions on which 'business as usual' was based are gone or will soon be a thing of the past. What once 'worked' or was 'good enough', is now obsolete and no longer acceptable.

Leadership is thus about 'teaching reality' (Hargrove 1998). Teaching reality is about the art of provocation. Provoking people and systems is a necessary step towards getting them thinking, reflecting, learning and ultimately being creative and constructive about changing what they think, what they value, what they do and how they operate. It *sounds* perfectly sensible, but to actually be the one rocking other people's boats is one of the most daunting aspects of leadership. This is particularly so if leaders cannot or will not match this rocking of the boat with a set of ready-made solutions and an alternative future status quo that people will find appealing and only need to sign up to. Teaching unpleasant realities to people without offering solutions is going to disappoint those who see leaders as people who protect them and give them direction. Leaders therefore need the capacity to disappoint people at a rate they can stand (Heifetz and Linsky 2002). Challenging the status quo is going to generate conflict with those who find it comfortable, and thus are motivated to keep it in place. When to instigate such conflict, how to regulate its level, duration and manifestations, and finding ways of capitalizing on its functions while preventing its dysfunctions (Coser 1956) are crucial but delicate tools of public leadership. The great civic leaders of the twentieth century – Mahatma Gandhi, Martin Luther King, Nelson Mandela – were masters of it (Kane 2001). But it is not coincidental that two of them paid for it with their lives. Exercising such leadership is risky; conflicts generated by or centred on a leader can become overheated (Heifetz and Linsky 2002). Eschewing conflicts completely or keeping them small is a natural inclination, and doing so might be an effective way to perpetuate one's office-holding, but it comes at the price of forfeiting leadership.

Rhetoric and performance   The most basic instruments that leaders have at their disposal are their words and their physical presence. Gone are the days when leadership amounted to making a heroic speech before leading one's armies into battle – from the front, but the essence of the process has not changed. Leading as we understand it in today's democratic public spheres is not about 'the' leader calling all the shots, mustering their hard power to hire, fire, make unilateral decisions, issue orders, strike bargains, wield carrots and sticks, and expect full compliance. The leadership of today is not entirely devoid of such 'hard' power, but it hinges equally, if not more so, on 'soft' power: the powers of persuasion, inspiration and mobilization. Rhetoric – the art of crafting persuasive arguments – is therefore as essential as in the days of Ancient Greece and Republican Rome, when the demos and the senate had to be persuaded before they were willing to have public resources committed to the projects favoured by the rulers of the day. As Uhr (2014, in press) puts it:

> Rhetoric is a very real communicative power performed by leaders to persuade or influence others. In some cases, rhetoric is manipulative, with leaders using clever skills to mislead opponents or sometimes even their own supporters. Yet in other cases, rhetoric can be used freely and fairly, when competing leaders openly participate in a public contest to determine who deserves the higher public trust. Leadership provided by independent brokers can help interested communities test the claims of competing political leaders. Trust is usually ranked according to the leaders' credibility, which is judged in terms of *who* they are ('are they really so representative?') as well as *what* they say ('does she really believe that?').

Analysts of rhetoric, beginning with Aristotle, have considered some combination of three modes of argument and evidence as the secret of effective persuasion: the *ethos* or character of the advocate as it is presented to the audience by the advocate and chosen witnesses; the *logos* or chain of reasoning provided by the advocate and witnesses; and the *pathos* or emotional content and bond constructed by advo-cates with their audience (Thompson 1998). In addition to the words and delivery of these words, dramaturgy – the staging of their commu-

BOX 2.5   What rhetoric can do: Churchill's war speeches

After the Second World War, in UK radio and television programmes about the 1939–45 period, many interviewees expressed a fierce, highly emotional and 'attached' allegiance to Winston Churchill. The memory, at least of those interviewed, was that they would have done anything for the war effort *because of Churchill's speeches*. The emotion was partly related to them imagining him seeing them as heroes (who would 'fight on the beaches', as he expressed it).

What was being expressed was a willingness to die because of dramatic radio broadcasts in a crisis situation. Crucial in explaining this is the drama of the relationship between speaker and audience, its emotional character (Willner 1984). It is clearly not a one-to-one relationship. There is only one speaker, and it is he (here Churchill) who rhetorically invents 'our island' (which 'we' shall defend). Churchill also creates, or at least evokes, the qualities of the audience too; but there is something emotionally shared by those subscribing to the relationship. It is that each person, through sharing an imagined and emotional relationship to Churchill, also shares with others, and that each is 'held' by the other in their mutual emotion *vis-à-vis* Churchill, and this is dramatically reinforced by their physically sharing the same crisis situation (for further reading, see Gaffney 2014).

nicative performances is also a crucial tool available speakers: think of Joseph Goebbels' meticulous choreography of Adolf Hitler's hallmark speeches, or Al Gore's clever use of Hollywood-style scripts, props and techniques in the film version of his *Inconvenient Truth* call to arms concerning climate change.

Patience (and timing)   In popular fiction, leaders tend to be depicted as (wo)men of action: they are driven, know what they want, pursue their aims relentlessly, make swift and bold decisions, engage their opponents head-on, and thus 'get things done'. Life as a public leader is rarely like that. Public leadership is a form of politics. Politics is the art of the possible, and very often not all that much is possible at any given point in time. In public life there is plenty of day-to-day drama but in the absence of triggering events there is rarely sustained pace and movement. Things take time. Reluctant minds need to be trained on issues that leaders want to raise. Divergent stakeholder definitions of the issues at hand need to be aligned. Budgets need to be available. Proposed new policies must not conflict with existing laws and regulations. The political numbers need to be there. The money needs to found to pay for them. Organizations need to be adjusted to implement them. Staff need to hired, moved and trained. It is very difficult to obtain momentum for the imposition of large and swift policy changes, even if they are primarily symbolic gestures. The legacy of existing policies, funding streams, administrative routines and the coalitions of stakeholders that have sprung up around them is practically impossible to erase in one fell swoop (Rose and Davies 1994; Mahoney and Thelen 2010), unless there is a crisis under way (Baumgartner and Jones 2009; Boin *et al.* 2009).

So what leaders need in their toolbox is a realistic sense of time, timing and pacing of their efforts. Seizing the moment when it presents itself is one such tool (Ignatieff 2013: 34). But that tool can only be wielded effectively if a leader is also a master at waiting, observing, keeping his/her powder dry, and patiently laying the groundwork for change long before the change is to take full effect. Frederickson and Matkin (2007) draw an analogy between leadership and gardening: the art of practising patience, working with the seasons (that is, changes in the public mood, or the budgetary or operational environments), making small changes instead of big moves, and waiting to see them take effect before making more changes. An effective leader is in there for the long haul and has the patience as well as the sheer physical and mental stamina to see things through even when others have lost interest or moved on.

Conclusions

This chapter has self-consciously deployed a functionalist perspective on public leadership. It does not begin with the people commonly understood to be the leaders and then started wondering what they do and to what effect. It began at the other end, by asking what 'stuff' needs to happen for polities (communities, cities, regions, issue areas, professional fields) to come alive and stay afloat in a way that is not routinely produced by the formal governance institutions of those polities. It is there that the work of public leadership exists, and that the notion of 'tools' – the instruments leaders as craftsmen deploy to do their work – becomes pivotal.

We have seen in this chapter that the work of leadership is manifold, and that leaders can draw on – and therefore need to be aware of and be able to handle – a wide array of tools to perform that work. Yet leadership work is also messy. The job seldom comes with a clear-cut role description. Leadership cannot be fully prescribed by or contained in the formal institutional designs that envisage and circumscribe the roles of public authority figures. The three sub-spheres of the 'public' discerned here – political, administrative and civic – have a way of overlapping in reality. Whether they like it or not, sometimes holders of political offices will find themselves deeply engaged in administrative leadership work. Likewise, very few top-level public servants can completely avoid taking part in political leadership processes, if only because of the strategic and tactical advice they provide to their political masters. Also, many civic leaders engage not just in advocacy and watchdog work, but play fully-fledged policy-entrepreneurial roles. And to the extent that their civic activism comes in the form of heading sizeable movements or organizations, they will also have to exercise administrative leadership. It is therefore important not to be naive about the labels 'political', 'administrative' and 'civic'. They denote institutionally and analytically separable spheres of action, which in reality are often closely intertwined.

The work of public leadership is also comprehensive. Every polity needs it to be performed continuously, even though it only becomes visible and dramatized episodically. But, taken together, the eight 'chunks' of public leadership work constitute such a daunting challenge that it would be naive even in micro-polities such as towns or societal sectors to expect all this work to be performed by a single leader or even a leadership team. This would be normatively problematic. The politics–administration dichotomy, the *trias politica* and its logic of checks and balances, and the separation of state and society did not become staples in thinking about good governance by chance: public power and authority need to be dispersed and controlled lest even the wisest and most benevolent all-powerful leaders will succumb to the inevitable corruption of that power (Kane *et al.* 2009).

But also, the requirements of doing all this work and the range of tools that need to be mustered to do it well are such that it is impossible for any single leader or leadership team to do all of it all the time. It is another important reason to avoid the trap of thinking that polities are like vessels led by a single captain 'on the bridge' or 'at the helm'. The public leadership required to set and keep polities 'on course' is performed in a dispersed, distributed fashion.

If we want to understand public leadership we shall therefore always need to wonder *whether* it happens (are each of these eight functions being performed at any point in time?), *where* it happens (in which arenas, on which stages, in which back rooms and in which networks?), and *who* is making it happen, without assuming that constitutional and administrative hierarchies provide us with ready-made answers.

Chapter 3

Leading with Authority

Follow the leader?

Imagine you are a senior public servant in the Ministry of Human Services, Families and Multicultural Affairs, heading up the latter division. A key plank in your divisions work is the Celebrating Communities programme, which subsidizes ethnic community organizations in areas such as adult and religious education, neighbourhood development and social work, as well as funding long-term research to build up the knowledge required to carry out evidence-based policy in this relatively novel and complex area of public policy.

The recent parliamentary elections brought a dramatic victory to the new National People's Party (NPP). On the wings of an economic crisis and palpable public discontent about the blessings of multiculturalism propagated by the governing coalition in the face of high unemployment and high crime rates among its mainly Islamic immigrant population, the electorate was drawn towards the NPP's populist platform of ultra-nationalism, economic redistribution and anti-elitism, it shot from 13 to 57 seats in the 180-strong lower house. The NPP became a key partner in the next governing coalition.

Your new minister is from the NPP. He has no parliamentary experience, no leadership experience, and no public sector background. What he does have is strong convictions and loudly voiced opinions. He does not mince words in his first encounter with the department's senior ranks: 'Celebrating Communities is rubbish. I want it terminated. And I want its budget to be diverted to a new, Strong Nation programme, based on an assimilationist view of dealing with immigrant communities.' He makes it clear that he does not want to argue the point, nor delay its implementation: 'I am the minister, I decide, and you do as you're told.'

Is the minister exercising leadership? And, more important, do you do as he says, even if this means the complete destruction of policies, datasets, and relationships that have been built up painstakingly over the previous decade, and which a future government may well wish to support? Are you entitled to keep arguing the case? To mobilize support among your colleagues at the department, or in other departments? To talk to other ministers in the new government who are known to be opposed to such a radical policy reversal? To brief beneficiaries of the current programme with a view to mobilizing them to encourage public opposition? To buy time by highlighting rather than working to circumvent legal and other obstacles to the abrupt termination of current projects and funding streams? What if during the next few months the minister proves to be not only a tenacious fighter for his policy convictions but also a nasty bully who attempts to run the department based on mistrust and by means of intimidation and manipulation? Are senior public servants to serve the representatives of the government of the day, no matter what they want and how they conduct themselves? Or are they to exercise some independent 'stewardship' of larger, long-term public value considerations, including the interests of serving future governments?

This opening case example reminds us that there is a distinction between 'getting things done' by exercising leadership and by pushing people around. If the relationship between office-holders (or self-appointed 'leaders') and non-leaders is primarily or exclusively rooted in coercion and fear, no leadership is being exercised – just power-wielding. People only exercise leadership in so far as and for as long as – their positions and interventions are accepted as legitimate by others. This acceptance lies at the heart of what I call leadership authority. Leaders with authority are being seen, believed, trusted, identified with and followed by a sufficiently significant segment of the community in which they operate. They can get to this point in a whole variety of ways. To be able to see that requires a change of perspective: understanding the reasons why followers support their leaders.

Regardless of how they achieve it, the level of authority leaders enjoy at any point in time determines their ability to exercise leadership. Machiavelli observed long ago that one learns a lot about the quality of a leader by looking at the people he surrounds himself with. Who belong to the 'inner circle' of aides and counsellors to the leader? How did they reach their positions, and what keeps them there? Are they leaders in their own right, or does their current status and power derive only from their proximity to the key decision-maker at the very top? Are they personally beholden to the leader, or can they think, speak and act independently without fear of sanction? Machiavelli suggested that wise and strong leaders gather weighty and accomplished people around them. Weak leaders, in contrast, select people who they believe will not threaten their authority: vassals, of mediocre talent and limited ambition.

In this chapter, I explore the nexus between authority and leadership. Taking a relational perspective on leadership, I distinguish between different forms of authority that leaders may acquire. I examine the forms and challenges of 'followership'. The chapter culminates with a heuristic tool for assessing the authority of leaders and suggests how it can be used to think about the ebbs and flows of their leadership capital over time.

Leadership as relationship

Understanding leadership, in other words, involves grasping the 'dynamic interplay of wants, needs, motives, values, and capacities of both would-be leaders and their potential followers' (Burns 2003: 16). Some leader–follower relationships are characterized by fierce, unconditional, enduring loyalty, in which people will continue to follow their leader regardless of the direction he or she takes and the ways in which he/she uses his/her power. Followers may revere leaders as saints, whose beliefs, values and deeds they admire deeply and have earned them an unshakeable moral authority. Or they may see them as saviours, a force of courage, prudence and creativity when times are tough and uncertain, and no easy solutions are available to curb the followers' existential fears.

Other leader–follower relationships are much more cerebral, contingent and ephemeral, with the latter only accepting a leader's authority for as long as he/she feel that the leader offers them the best possible deal from a field of other contenders for their support.

If we want to understand leadership, we need first to understand the human components that make up the relationship – not just the personal characteristics of the comparatively few people who aspire to and achieve public leadership roles, but also the conditions, needs, resources and states of mind of the many that don't but who grant the authority to particular elites to lead them effectively. It is the needs and moods of their constituents that shape leadership possibilities. It is, for example, extremely unlikely that a leader with the political programme and rhetorical style of Adolf Hitler would have succeeded in eliciting mass support within thoroughly democratic cultures such as England or the USA, even in the depths of their Depression experiences. In contrast, as Daniel Goldhagen has asserted controversially, Germany, with its deeply ambivalent attitude towards its fledgling democratic Weimar Republic and its pervasive nationalist myths, were given exactly the kind of leadership that the bulk of them wanted. While this particular claim may be historically inaccurate and sociologically unconvincing, few will dispute that history, economy and culture conspired in Germany at that point in time to create a reservoir of discontent, fear, desperation and resentment among significant sections of the German population, which the Nazi party and its leader were able to tap into.

Why people follow leaders matters. According to Graham Little (1985, 1988), publics at different times and to differing degrees seek either visionary inspiration, safety from danger, or collective solidarity from their political leaders. Leaders and leadership groups that instinctively grasp or are able actively to appeal to these largely subconscious public moods and emotions, will be followed – provided their leadership agenda and style match these underlying states of mind effectively. Little's trichotomy, rooted in the psychodynamic work of Alfred Bion (1961), also mirrors to some extent the famous typology offered by Max Weber, who similarly discerned three fundamental authority postures:

- *Tradition-based authority* – constituents accepts leaders as legitimate holders of high offices, obtained through historically rooted cultural practices, such as hereditary monarchy, or selection by 'respected elders'. The core of the traditional authority claim is: follow me, because you have followed my predecessors.
- *Charismatic authority* – constituents follow leaders because they view the leaders as morally pure, heroic and wise, with fully charismatic leaders revered as god-like saviours who command the total submission of their followers. The core of the charismatic authority claim is: follow me, because of who I am and what I am able to do. This is not necessarily a good thing. On the contrary, James M. Burns rightly reminds us that, 'at best, charisma is a confusing and undemocratic form of leadership. At worst, it is a type of tyranny' (Burns 2003: 27). In the case of charismatic leadership, constituents become fully formed 'followers' whose loyalty is unconditional, indeed 'blind' (Davis and Gardner 2012; Avolio and Yammarino 2013).
- *Legal-rational authority* – in the third authority relationship, constituents ascribe legitimacy to leaders because they have made a conscious decision that the method by which these leaders are selected and held accountable is in the best interest of the community. The selection methods as such can vary. They can be democratic (as in the case of political leaders) or technocratic (as in merit-based bureaucratic hierarchies), but they are adhered to because they are felt to 'work', including the ability to constrain and sanction individuals in leadership positions.

Modernization has seen the rise of legal-rational authority at the expense of the other types, a development by and large applauded by Weber, who saw reliance on traditional authority as having a stifling effect, and pure charismatic authority as being potentially dangerous and inherently unstable (as it is totally dependent on the physical and mental well-being of the charismatic individual). Yet, in practice, pockets of traditional privilege continue to exist in contemporary organizational and public life. Also, especially in times of adversity, fear and conflict, there remains even in high-modern Western societies a romantic longing for 'more charismatic' personalities than the disciplined, cautious, bland professional bureaucrats and politicians who tend to rise to the apex of public power.

Does authority presuppose some form of hierarchy to back it up? Not necessarily. In fact, some of the most intriguing forms of public leadership are those in which the authority of leaders is not rooted in any asymmetry of power and resources at all. One of the most inspiring writers on leadership, Ronald Heifetz (1994), calls this 'leading without authority'. Heifetz's innovative work explains that these leaders lead by using a mixture of persuasion, confrontation, process management and empowerment. But it also becomes clear from his work that they can only do so to the extent that their interventions are accepted as legitimate by the people they seek to influence, even though they have no formal (or even informal) powers to impose anything on anyone. So they may not be 'in charge' but they still 'have authority'.

In fact, most contemporary social psychologists and sociologists would support the claim that leadership is to a very significant extent in the eye of the beholder, – for example, those who 'follow' (comply with, believe in, support) leaders. Understanding public leadership likewise requires an understanding of the 'bond', the psychological 'contract' between constituents and their leaders, and within that, the emphasis being more on the former than the latter. The relational approach, of which Weber's work on authority and political leadership forms a classic and enduringly relevant example, is highly relevant to the understanding of key forms of civic leadership, such as social movements, which often begin as informal groups with little formal hierarchy, in which it is moral rather narrowly 'political' capital that counts (Kane 2001). In such movements, authority flows to the most committed, most articulate and most courageous individuals before or beyond any formal structures. The relational perspective is also a much more productive way of understanding the special case of charismatic leadership than the quixotic quest by personality theorists and management scholars to isolate the traits and skills of individuals that make them bound to be seen as 'charismatic' regardless of the social and situational context (see Box 3.1). In the process of making charismatic leadership palatable or even highly desirable, these scholars water down the original Weberian notion to almost any form of leadership that involves generating a high degree of enthusiasm and zeal among followers (Conger and Kanungo 1987 and 1998; see also Box 3.2).

The relational perspective shows that 'followers' in many cases do much more than just that. Followers are not simply *subjects*, to be steered at will by those placed above them in a chain of authority controlling all the levers of power. Though unequal power is a fundamental characteristic of leadership processes, the degree of felt 'power

BOX 3.1   Alternative roads to gaining a warrant to lead

Inheritance and tradition – obtaining leadership by near-automatic conferral. This may occur literally through blood lines, as in monarchies and family-owned firms; or metaphorically, as when a pre-designated 'heir apparent' succeeds a powerful and respected incumbent leader.

Archetype: the leadership transition from Tage Erlander (leader of the Swedish social-democratic party and prime minister from 1945–68) to his long-time right-hand man Olaf Palme (party leader, 1968–86 and prime minister 1968–76 and 1982–6, when he was assassinated).

Success and performance – building a reputation for achievement by visibly demonstrating qualities deemed necessary for effective leadership in the cultural environment in which the leader operates (for example, physical strength and military cunning; exemplary professional competence and integrity; rhetorical dexterity and the capacity to inspire; conciliation capacity; ideological purity; policy vision; moral courage).

Archetypes: chief executive succession planning mythology; Mahatma Gandhi and Martin Luther King.

Insurgency and struggle – revolting against and successfully overcoming ineffective, unpopular or otherwise 'spent' *anciens régimes*.

Archetypes: Napoleon Bonaparte's accession to power in post-revolutionary France, Lenin's in Soviet Russia, Mao's in communist China, Sukarno in post-colonial Indonesia, and in a much less brutal but morphologically similar way, Nelson Mandela in post-apartheid South Africa.

Being there and ingratiation – making sure one is an indispensable operator within the right circles in what may be a contentious environment of shifting alliances at and around the top, while all the time avoiding the making of powerful enemies. When other, initially more conspicuous yet also more contentious candidates go in to bat against one another and self-destruct in the process, the loyal 'organization man' in the second tier may come to be seen in a different light.

Archetypes: Harold Holt's succession of long-serving Australian Liberal Party prime minister Robert Menzies (1949–66); John Major's accession to the Conservative Party leadership (and the British prime-ministership) in 1990.

distance' between leaders and non-leaders can vary considerably across organizations and communities, with different cultural predispositions towards hierarchy, inequality and rules (see, for example, Wildavsky 1987, 1989; Hofstede 1997).

Nor are non-leaders mere *sheep*: in all except the most brutally repressive or extremely sectarian cult-like settings, constituents are in a position to observe, weigh, test, and bestow differential degrees of loyalty on leaders. In democratic polities, followers are institutionally empowered to select and indeed 'deselect' leaders periodically – thus determining their leaders' fates as much as incumbent leaders are striving to shape those of their followers (Keohane 2010).

Of special relevance to public leadership is the idea of followers as *audiences*, in what is essentially an indirect, mass-mediated form of social drama. Most constituents never get to speak to their prime minister, president or even their local representative. They learn about their leaders' goals, qualities and achievements vicariously: through media coverage and word of mouth. Sitting at the top of a sprawling formal or imagined hierarchy, public office-holders therefore need to use every means at their disposal to get through to their constituents – who may not necessarily be attentive audiences for their messages to begin with – to substantiate their authority claims and actually exercise leadership. The more literally 'public' the office a particular leader holds, the more relevant it is to understanding their leadership as a form of self-presentation through rhetoric, dramaturgy and ritual, directed at various types of audiences that make up their authority-granting environment.

Followers moreover are active co-shapers of the leadership relationship. As Burns has pointed out, virtually all forms of leadership have a transactional quality, with followers granting their loyalty to leaders on the basis of a quid pro quo of one kind or another. Followers can therefore also be seen as *bargainers*. This is most clearly visible in democratic elections, which are all about horse-trading. But it is also a vital element of the relationship between ministers and public servants within government departments: though entitled to expect bureaucratic loyalty by virtue of their formal position as democratically mandated office-holders, the reality is that bureaucrats can 'do loyalty' to markedly different degrees. Whether they do their utmost to further the minister's cause depends upon the extent to which they are satisfied that the minister is keeping his/her part of the 'bargain' – by effectively delivering budget and other critical resources, building winning political coalitions, providing a sense of direction to their activities, and protecting them in the face of public criticism and political scapegoating (Savoie 2003; Hood and Lodge 2004).

A follower's dilemma: coping with bad leaders

The hypothetical case in the opening section of this chapter presents a contemporary bureaucrat's version of the age-old dilemma of followership: what to do if the authority figure proceeds imprudently or indefensibly? From a relational perspective on leadership, the phenomenon

BOX 3.2   Followership comes in a range of shapes and sizes

There have been many attempts to get a handle on followership – not quite as many as there have been efforts to typologize leaders, but still a wide array of efforts has been made – few of them grounded in systematic empirical research, and most often based on either the lifelong practical experiences of the author or deductions from theoretical premises. In recent years, there has been an upsurge in writing on followership, much of it in the 'management guru' vein (Hollander 2008; Chaleff 2009; Kellerman 2008). Chaleff's (2009) helpful typology discerns the following:

Implementers – they usually form the majority of any organization's membership. They 'get on with their jobs' and busy themselves doing and completing tasks, not questioning the leadership of the organization (other than through occasional quips, gossip and complaints at the coffee machine).

Partners – these individuals have the skills and attitudes to make them want to be seen as equals to the formal leaders, and as co-creators of leadership. When the formal leaders are responsive to this need, this type of follower will respect the leaders' position and support them. A strong and positive partnership can develop. If formal leaders are dismissive of the ambitions of this type of follower, they will gain their enmity and risk eliciting obstructive and rebellious behaviour.

Individualists – these people prize their sense of independence. They don't like to be reminded that they operate in a hierarchy. They like to do as they see fit and do not make great followers in the traditional sense. Sensible leaders will harness their drive, strong-mindedness and entrepreneurial instincts. Less sensible leaders may end up estranging and marginalizing them, and lowering the dynamic potential of their presence within the organization.

Recourses – these are the most literal form of 'follower': people who tend to lack the requisite intellect, imagination or courage needed to do more.

➡

of 'bad' leadership (Kellerman 2004) is a baffling one: why do people so often and for such a long time tolerate leaders who pursue morally abhorrent objectives or proceed in damaging or self-defeating ways to get others to achieve their goals? If we accept that followers are indeed to be understood as more than mere subjects or sheep, why don't they rebel when they find themselves confronted by bad leadership?

➡

Like many writers in the management field, Chaleff jumps freely from analysis to prescription. In the latter vein he proposes that followers need five forms of 'courage' in dealing with leaders:

The courage to assume responsibility. Courageous followers assume responsibility for themselves and the organization. Their values ground and guide their behaviour, and their internal compass comes from their understanding and ownership of the common purpose.

The courage to serve. Courageous followers assume additional responsibilities to unburden the leadership and serve the organization. When convinced of their wisdom, they are prepared to publicly defend their leaders and the sometimes difficult choices they make. They are passionate in pursuit of the common purpose.

The courage to challenge. Courageous followers, however, also give voice to the discomfort they feel when the behaviours or policies of the leadership or the larger group conflict with their sense of what is right. They are willing to speak out, risk marginalization and 'turn up the heat' on the actions of leaders and groups when they feel this is appropriate.

The courage to participate in transformation. Courageous followers are prepared to champion the need for change when they believe in its purpose and form. They examine their own need for transformation and become full participants in the change process as appropriate.

The courage to take moral action. Courageous followers are prepared to draw a line in the sand when other efforts fail to dissuade leaders and colleagues from inadvisable, problematic courses of action. This may involve refusing to obey a direct order, taking an issue further up the line or to the outside world (that is, whistle-blowing), or even opting to leave the organization. Their commitment to the common purpose justifies and sometimes demands such action.

For further reading, see Chaleff (2009).

These questions have intrigued social scientists ever since the publication of the Milgram experiments on obedience to authority, published around the time of Adolf Eichmann's trial in Israel for Nazi war crimes in which he justified himself by saying he was only following orders. Milgram (1974) found that an overwhelming majority of subjects in a laboratory experiment continued to administer what they believed to be painful, dangerous and ultimately lethal shocks to a peer when instructed to do so by a researcher as part of an alleged scientific study into the effects of punishment on learning performance. Ethically controversial, the experiments generated worldwide debate, extensive replication and above all pessimistic conclusions about human abilities to differentiate between legitimate and illegitimate commands given to them by authority figures, and act accordingly (Meeus and Raaijmakers 1985).

Decades after the initial Milgram study, social psychologists Herbert Kelman and Valerie Hamilton revisited the territory. They were, among other things, interested in why some of the people in the various permutations of Milgram's experiments disobeyed. Why did they, and only *they*, feel empowered to rebel against evil authority? The two psychologists eventually proposed an empirically grounded trichotomous typology of authority relationships, complementing Weber's essentially top-down perspective with a bottom-up perspective rooted in the psychology of the followers. According to Kelman and Hamilton (1989), people follow:

- because they fear the consequences of not doing so (*compliance*);
- because they feel a strong personal bond with the authority figure who is asking them to follow (*identification*); or
- because they substantively agree with what they are being asked to do (*internalization*).

They demonstrated that only the latter category retains the moral autonomy and psychological strength to stand up bad leaders and bad hierarchies. They will only do what they are told when and in so far as they themselves reach an autonomous judgement that the request is sensible and justifiable. The other two categories tend to externalize the moral judgement, relying either on the prevailing institutional hierarchy in which they are embedded or the personal judgement of those they have accepted as their leaders. Kelman and Hamilton further argued that these propensities towards authority are part and parcel of our personality structures, and that the proportion of people with an internalization-based followership ethos was likely to be comparatively small, though not insignificant.

However, it is unlikely that follower psychology alone can explain the persistence of bad leadership or complex phenomena such as torture (Kelman 2005; Zimbardo 2007). Eschewing psychological determinism, Padilla *et al.* (2007), for example, argue that 'followers of constructive and destructive leaders share similar motives. What distinguishes them is the control exerted by the leader, their independence from the leader, and their vulnerability to bad leaders in destructive settings – factors that are inseparable from the contexts within which leadership takes place. In constructive leadership settings, the followers are freer to disagree, more involved in determining the goals, and more able to affect the leadership of their organization, even if only indirectly. By contrast, in destructive settings, followers are more dependent on leaders, do not participate in defining the purpose of the enterprise, or contribute fully to the achievement of organizational objectives'.

This is in line with the small but growing literature on 'toxic', 'poor', and 'bad' leadership (see, for example, Janis 1989; Kellerman 2004; Lipman-Blumen 2006; Helms 2012): leadership – good and bad – is produced, sustained and destroyed in a triangular interaction between leaders, constituents and environments (the latter consisting of both situational as well as socio-cultural and institutional features shaping constituents' needs, emotions and resources *vis-à-vis* leaders). Trying to prevent leadership excesses therefore requires work on multiple fronts: vetting leadership candidates, holding leaders to account, and empowering non-leaders to retain their moral autonomy and resist illegitimate commands and undue hierarchical pressures to obey them.

The ebbs and flows of leadership authority

The relational perspective on leadership teaches one fundamental lesson: authority is a precious, precarious and finite leadership resource. In a leader's ideal world, he or she acquires significant levels of authority from day one in office, manages to expand it throughout their tenure, and wields it as much as possible for the full duration of their term in office. In the cynical world of the disaffected citizen or organization member, the reverse is the case: those in charge are never to be believed, trusted or indeed followed. In reality, the authority to do leadership work in their organizations or societies ebbs and flows. It takes time to acquire and accumulate (mostly, anyway). It can only be wielded every so often. And it declines when the impression takes hold that the leader in question is 'past his peak', 'has reached her sell-by date', or when formal term limits come into view and the inevitable lame duck period sets in as termination of the leader's tenure becomes not only certain but proximate. No matter how powerful and revered they once may have been, there comes a time when other actors begin to outwait incumbent leaders, and start talking ever more openly about the fact 'everybody' is doing so. Whatever the precise trigger and mode, the incumbent eventually disappears from the scene.

Understanding leadership therefore involves studying (the dynamics of) leaders' levels of authority. Leadership tenures – whether formal, office-based or informal and emergent, as in spontaneous and ephemeral social movements – follow roughly three developmental stages: acquiring authority; expending versus consolidating that authority; and losing it (Breslauer 2002: 13). Every leadership relation evolves through these stages, sooner or later, though not necessarily in a linear let alone a predictable fashion. Key variations between leaders occur in the levels of authority they enjoy and the nature and relative duration of the stages. Getting into leadership positions is one thing, but then to be able to consolidate and leverage them to 'make a difference' is quite another. If leadership is about 'teaching reality', about 'regulating distress' among followers and the publics in order to encourage them to do the often painful 'adaptive work' involved in forging behavioural and social change, then it is hardly surprising that experts depict leadership as a 'dangerous' enterprise in which 'staying alive' as a leader is difficult (Heifetz and Linsky 2002).

Exercising leadership involves risking one's political capital, laying one's authority on the line. And it is risky: generating momentum for changes that really matter is challenging, often time-consuming and potentially 'career-limiting'. Remember how quickly the near-euphoria following the election of Barack Obama to the US presidency turned into impatience and almost into derision less than a year into his term in office, when he had engaged with some of the toughest issues around (health reform; the Middle East conflict; the Afghan war), yet had few, if any, concrete 'runs on the board'? So, how do leaders go about consolidating their authority? Box 3.3 provides some classic possibilities.

Leaders vary widely in their ability to gain and retain authority throughout their tenures. It is tempting to ascribe this wholly to their personal skills and performance, but in reality, institutional (formal powers; informal norms), political (constellations of actors and coalitions) and situational (issue agendas, the mood of the public) factors play a major part. Particularly in combination, they at the very least co-determine how deep and broad is the authority that leaders come to enjoy, and for how long it lasts.

Most leaders initially acquire authority by inspiring the members of their organizations through a rhetoric of vision, hope, liberation and struggle. The bond with their constituents can, however, wane when the word is out that the leader does not 'walk her own talk' in actually dealing with staff, or when he or she takes unpopular decisions that contrast sharply with the visionary rhetoric of the initial grand design. Early assessments of the evolving Obama presidency present it as a case in point of this dynamic: a dealer in hope during the campaign who became mired in the mazes of divided government and ended up disappointing many of his most ardent initial followers (Renshon 2011) – but they nevertheless re-elected him in droves as the radicalization of the Republican Party and its unconvincing presidential candidate Mitt Romney gave them nowhere else to go.

BOX 3.3 Pathways for consolidating leadership authority

Constructing narratives of hope
Napoleon once called leaders 'dealers in hope'. Part and parcel of becoming a leader in the modern era is to embark on 'listening and learning' encounters throughout the relevant community and constituencies, and use these to weave an appealing story about the nexus between the leader and the group(s), as well as the past, present and achievable future of the system as a whole.

Archetype: Bill Clinton's first presidential campaign, with its unprecedented and effective use of 'town hall meetings' providing the candidate with close-up contact with groups of citizens highlighted his high level of emotional intelligence and allowed him to position himself as 'one of us'.

Purging and stacking the power base
Incrementally or radically removing known opponents or sceptics from crucial positions in the hierarchy, and replacing them with people known to be loyal to the new leader and/or the new regime's policy vision.

Archetypes: Stalin, Mao and their successors in the Soviet Union and China; indeed, most authoritarian rulers in one-party states.

Taking opponents to the brink
Tackling key unresolved controversies head on, leveraging the recently acquired leadership mandate, daring opponents of one's position, vision or policy platform to resist, and challenging constituents and authorizers who sit on the fence to 'take it or leave it'.

Archetype: Tony Blair's 'New Labour' party reform crusade shortly after being elected party leader in 1994, when Labour was 15 years into unelectable opposition.

Targeting beatable enemies
Mobilizing support within one's own group by identifying as targets 'out-groups', ideas or policies that are already unpopular, stepping up antagonistic rhetoric and taking conspicuously aggressive steps against them.

Archetypes: most dictatorships.

Leaders can lose authority in a whole range of ways. Quite often they get themselves into trouble by picking the wrong battles at the wrong time. Some leaders' erratic behaviour alienates even the most loyal or conformity-minded subordinates (Chaleff 2009; Courpasson and Thoenig 2010). Some underestimate the forces – and the value – of dissent among their constituencies (Banks 2008). Some take on enemies more powerful than themselves, become embroiled in bruising dogfights and may be forced into humiliating backdowns and backflips that leave their public prestige in tatters. For example, when taking office after eleven and a half years of Liberal Party government, the incoming Australian Labor Party prime minister Kevin Rudd called tackling climate change 'the greatest moral challenge of our time'. This message resonated strongly with the drought-battered electorate that put him into office. His visible policy activism in a range of areas stood him in good stead politically. Rudd rode a wave of popularity. But within 18 months, after the Senate had twice blocked his government's emission trading scheme legislation, he simply abandoned the effort to take a stand on climate change altogether. He then had to withstand a profound backlash that this U-turn, and the lack of spine it suggested, triggered among broad segments of the Australian population. When he subsequently imposed a unilateral 40 per cent 'superprofits tax' on the country's most prosperous industry, the mining sector, he picked a fight with an opponent with both the means and the determination to destroy his political capital. A very public war of words (and of nerves) ensued. It brought his government's poll ratings to unprecedented lows and his personal approval ratings were in free fall, forcing him to the negotiating table and further undermining his leadership credentials. And once the commentariat had made up its mind that Rudd's leadership style were at the heart of his government's problems, no display of skill and stamina in other areas of public policy – for example, steering the country recession-free through the depths of the global financial crisis, or delivering a historic parental leave scheme – was able to restore his political fortunes. His own party removed him before he could contest the next election.

This is a particular dramatic scenario, but at the end of the day virtually all leaders' authority will decline to a point where they have to go. Leaders leave office (for example, by going before being pushed) with or without residual authority. Depletion of political capital is not a necessary condition for leadership termination; for example, when it is imposed by legal term limits, personal considerations, or a force majeure. However, when it is strong and sustained, it is very much a sufficient condition. Deprived of authority, leaders can perhaps cling on to formal positions for a time, but they have effectively lost the ability to exercise leadership when/if any want to follow them. Depletion of leadership capital can be sudden or gradual. It can be self-generated or imposed by exogenous factors (see Box 3.4).

Assessing authority

With so much riding on it, it becomes relevant to be able to assess the state of a leader's authority in a way that is reliable yet parsimonious,

BOX 3.4   Pathways for losing leadership authority

Violating crucial systemic norms
Other than in totalitarian states and dictatorships, democratic leaders cannot 'get away with murder'. If their espoused views and public and private behaviour conspicuously violate legal norms and core beliefs of the groups they seek to lead, their authority will begin to dwindle. They might compensate for this by becoming more repressive, but in the long term this only compounds the problem, as democracies rightly pride themselves on their institutionalised ability to 'throw the rascals out'.

Archetype: US president Richard Nixon's demise over Watergate.

Consistent non-delivery
Leaders who want to survive and thrive cannot afford to disregard the bottom line. However well-intended, decent and likeable they may be, leaders that are seen to fail to produce tangible positive results – delivering key election promises; achieving performance agreement targets; improving shareholder value; and improving the lot of grassroots clients and supporters – cannot last. Fairly or unfairly, they become the scapegoats for blame.

Archetype: US president Jimmy Carter (1977–81), who came to office promising to deliver clean (much wanted after the Watergate trauma) and smart government but got caught out by the stagflation of the era, oil shortages caused by the power-wielding of the OPEC cartel, and a humiliating seizure of US embassy staff in Tehran, none of which his administration seemed capable of addressing effectively.

Making powerful enemies
Whether through hubris or lack of judgement and restraint, leaders sometimes get themselves into fights with people and interests they cannot afford to set aside. This will induce at best failure to achieve results, and at worst, rally one's own opposition.

Archetype: US president Woodrow Wilson's (1916–20) confrontational mode of pursuing Congressional ratification of the Versailles Treaty.

Mismanaging crises
Proving to be unprepared, disorganized, uninterested, ineffectual or callous in the face of major disasters and other emergencies. While such episodes of high-visibility, high-consequence failure need not be fatal when leaders have a solid pre-crisis capital stock, but they may fatally wound already low-capital leaderships.

Archetypes: Russian president Putin's perceived aloofness during the Kursk submarine, Moscow theatre and Beslan school hijacking dramas (each resulting in marked, though temporary, credibility problems); US president George W. Bush in the wake of hurricane Katrina (which along with the escalating war in Iraq, shattered public support for his presidency).

relatively precise yet able to register the fluidity of authority. Up to now, however, despite centuries of writing about it, the notion of authority has not delivered any such tool. In this section of the chapter, using an analogy from the world of finance and economics, we conceive of political authority as 'capital', thus opening a different set of connotations and methodologies.

Leadership capital is 'a broad term that has cultural, social, and symbolic aspects' (Nepstad and Clifford 2006) but analysts agree that, one way or other, at its heart are social, indeed public, judgements about individual skills, abilities, advantages and 'achievements' (Sørensen and Torfing 2003; Davis and Seymour 2010). It has been described as a combination of a person or group's perceived 'competence, integrity and capacities for leadership' (Renshon 2000: 200).

Leadership capital thus provides a measure for what one might call the 'licence to operate' a political actor enjoys from his 'authorizing environment' (Moore 1995). Having a healthy 'stock' of political capital confers on a leader the power to persuade and motivate as well as compel. The Leadership Capital Index (LCI) is a diagnostic tool for tracking the strength of leader's political mandates. It allows analysts to spot key variations in the nature and aggregate volume of a leader's warrant to act over time and issues. Three core components of leadership capital can be discerned: skills, relations and reputations (see Figure 3.1 below). *Skills capital* refers to attributed abilities of the leader; for example, their cognitive, physical, communicative and managerial capacity (Greenstein 2009; Theakston 2011; Bennister 2012; Daleus 2012; see also Kaarbo 1997; Preston 2001; Post 2005; Cronin 2008; Nye 2008; Hermann 2014).

What really matters here are not these skills per se but the way they are *perceived* by followers and the wider 'authorizing environment' (Moore 1995), in other words by the actors and institutions whose support is essential for leaders to maintain the ability to lead. The composition of these authorizing environments and the relative weight to be placed on the perceptions and opinions of different groups within it varies across systems, roles and situations. A head of government, for example, may face an authorizing environment in which cabinet colleagues, the armed forces, media owners and editors, regional party barons, key industrialists, trade union bosses and voters in marginal seats all play an important part. It is up to the analyst to decide the weight of the various opinions.

Relational capital refers to the loyalties that leaders mobilize. As we saw earlier in this chapter, why people follow, or at least accept, leaders matters a great deal in shaping the leaders' authority and influence (Turner *et al.* 2008). Social psychology and sociology provide a rich reservoir of insights regarding the composition, social categorizations and identifications, and leadership expectations of followers and constituents. These are key to understanding the nature of the psychological contract that develops between them and their representatives (Cronin 2008; Haslam *et al.* 2010). This contract extends beyond the circle of party members or movement followers. It can also be usefully applied to capture the relations between leaders, the media and the wider electorate (Davis and Gardner 2012).

Leadership relations differ in the kinds of psychological contract that underpin them. Burns (1978) picked up on this in making his classic distinction between transformational and transactional leaders, but by now there are many other salient distinctions (Reicher *et al.* 2014). The 'visionary', transformational leader first and foremost hopes to gather capital through a mobilizing story of ideals and aspirations, and is prepared to risk the political costs of ideological opposition to it and of delivered realities falling short of evoked expectations. In contrast, pragmatic, transactional leaders depend primarily on acquiring capital through technical competence and tangible achievements at the risk of leaving a vacuum of meaning and identification for their political competitors to fill. This divide between types of leadership styles and psychological contracts they forge with followers and authorizers cuts across holders of similar offices. Compare, for example, George W. Bush and Barack Obama, or the two most recent Popes, Benedict XVI and Francis.

The third component is *reputational capital*. Leaders' words and deeds are constantly monitored and assessed. Followers, observers and critics alike all try to distil a 'narrative' about what a leader 'is really like' from the pattern of that leader's behaviour and its observable impact. For each leader, such a narrative emerges, and, despite being only partially shaped and controlled by the leader him/herself, this forms the core of a leader's reputation. Such a narrative increases the leader's political capital when it meets two conditions: its normative core is seen by the observer as appropriate for the times; and the gap between perceived promise and observed performance is limited (or accepted as having been caused by exogenous, temporary circumstances). Effective reputations are coherent believable narratives in which a leader's life story, espoused philosophy and observable in-office behaviour are widely deemed to be in alignment.

Much of the data required to perform an LCI analysis of a particular leader is available from public sources, such as election results, opinion polls and the parliamentary record. Some of the data is likely to be an aggregate or composite of numerous views. For example, assessment of the various 'skills' (s_1, s_2) indicators can be based on biography and examples drawn from the media or academic assessment. Where data is limited or unavailable, it may be that other proxies are used, such as approval rating for trust.

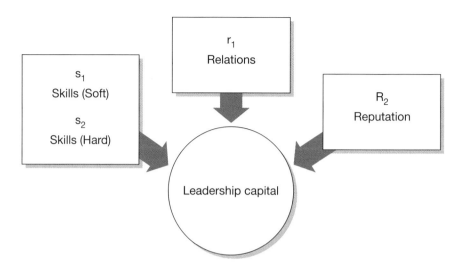

FIGURE 3.1   *Components of leadership capital: skills, relations and reputations*

The LCI thus offers a composite portrait of the shifting mix of skills, relation and reputation that can strengthen or weaken a leader. The scoring system will also help to draw out the nuances of a leader. The LCI will reveal, for example, a leader who may have communication abilities but be a poor manager. It may also show apparently strong leaders who win elections but are crippled in their legislative programs by poor party unity, which may in turn affect the passage of legislation.

Trajectories of leadership capital

Given the complex array of factors that determine a leader's authority, it is worth looking a little more closely at how such authority might evolve over time. Two dimensions are pivotal: the level and duration of the authorization leaders receive from their key constituencies. Observing these and deploying the mechanisms for acquiring, consolidating and losing authority presented above, I shall conclude this chapter by suggesting a number of ideal typical leadership capital trajectories one can associate with particular types of leaders.

Strong brands

Leaders of this type typically enter office with solid levels of support, for example because the previous leader has lost all credibility while the new leader has run an effective campaign against him or her, or

TABLE 3.1 *The Leadership Capital Index (LCI) of a political party leader*

Criteria		Measurements
s_1	01 Political/policy vision	1. Completely absent 2. Unclear/inconsistent 3. Moderately clear/consistent 4. Clear/consistent 5. Very clear/consistent
s_1	02 Communicative performance	1. Very poor 2. Poor 3. Average 4. Good 5. Very good
s_2	03 Personal poll rating relative to rating at most recent election	1. Very low (<–15%) 2. Low (–5 to –15%) 3. Moderate (–5% to +5%) 4. High (+5% to +10% 5. Very high (>+10%)
s_2	04 Longevity: time in office	1. < 1 year 2. 1–2 years 3. 2–3 years 4. 3–4 years 5. > 4 years
s_2	05 (Re)election margin for the party leadership	1. Very small (< 1% of relevant electors, that is, caucus, party members) 2. Small (1–5%) 3. Moderate (5–10%) 4. Large (10–15%) 5. Very large (> 15%)
r_1	06 Party polling relative to most recent election result	1. Very weak (< –10%) 2. Weak (–10% to –2.5%) 3. Stable (–2.5% to 2.5%) 4. Strong (2.5% to 10%) 5. Very strong (>10%)
r_1	07 Levels of public appreciation of leader	1. Very low (0–20%) 2. Low (20–40%) 3. Moderate (40–60%) 4. Strong (60–80%) 5. Very strong (80–100%)
r_1	08 Likelihood of credible leadership challenge within next 6 months	1. Very low 2. Low 3. Moderate 4. High 5. Very high
r_2	09 Perceived ability to shape party's policy platform	1. Very low **2. Low** 3. Moderate 4. High 5. Very high
r_2	10 Perceived parliamentary effectiveness of leader	1. Very low 2. Low 3. Moderate 4. High 5. Very high

because the leaders are (s)elected on the basis of a formidable reputation in prior leadership positions. Once in office, they manage to consolidate this support firmly. They remain largely immune to negative feedback about their behaviour or the outcomes achieved under their leadership. They leave office with strong reputations and with their key support base largely in tact (see the almost horizontal authority line in Figure 3.2). Key examples include US president Dwight Eisenhower ('I like Ike'), the D-Day mastermind and war hero who turned into a seemingly laid-back father figure of a president who could do no wrong in the eyes of the public; Ronald Reagan, the 'Great Communicator' whose endearing performances and frequent bloopers belied a cunning conviction politician who did not shy away from twisting arms and bending rules if it suited his aims; and the inimitable Nelson Mandela, whose 27 years in prison had honed rather than destroyed his capacity for reconciliation with enemies past and present, and who almost single-handedly prevented South Africa from descending into civil war prior to and following the end of apartheid's death struggle.

Meteors

These leaders typically rise to public prominence 'from nowhere', recruited as relative, often deliberate, 'outsiders' to the system in which they subsequently occupy a peak position. In combination with an unorthodox, 'refreshing' style, this enables a very rapid and steep ascendancy, as their hitherto disempowered but now energized followers place high hopes upon them, and their novelty value makes them the willing objects of benevolent media coverage. The leadership romance thus begun does not last long, however, as their very unfamiliarity with the rules of the game of their new role – or a deliberate unwillingness to abide by them – leads these leaders to disappoint, become mired in controversy, and lose authority quickly and incontrovertibly (see Figure 3.3). Classic examples include US president Jimmy Carter;, former wrestler turned state governor, Jesse Ventura;, and many business or community sector leaders elevated to high political office.

Misfits

Misfit leaders are tragic figures, in various ways. They obtain leadership by default, often after long, hard and damaging internal power struggles. By the time they finally prevail, they are tired, tainted and controversial. They never really 'take off', and their leadership is doomed from the start, as their road to leadership has undermined their authority claims (see Figure 3.4). They may also obtain leadership

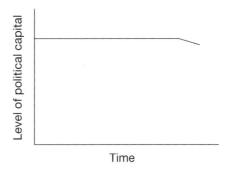

FIGURE 3.2 *The leadership capital trajectory of rock-solid leaders*

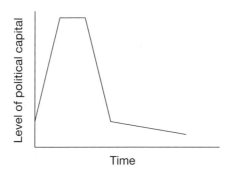

FIGURE 3.3 *The leadership capital trajectory of meteoric leaders*

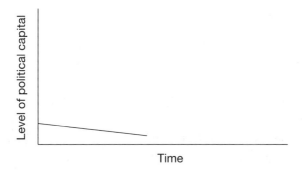

FIGURE 3.4 *The leadership capital trajectory of misfit leaders*

on a downward slope on the business cycle – in other words, at a time when the corporate or political ship they seek to captain is capsizing. Think of leadership succession struggles in very long-serving, 'tired' governments or in bitterly divided opposition parties trailing badly in the polls. Victories in these settings are decidedly Pyrrhic: the public has seen too much ugliness for too long, and just switches off from the successor. Examples abound: William McMahon's ignominious 1971–2 prime-ministership at the tail end of the 'Menzies era' of Liberal Party rule in Australia; former Treasurers Paul Martin's and Gordon Brown's painful stints as prime ministers of Canada and the UK, respectively, following years of open rivalry with their erstwhile partners/predecessors Jean Chretien and Tony Blair.

Other examples are so-called lateral appointments, in which a chief executive from sector/organization A is implanted into the leadership of an organization in sector/organization B, often as a result of political or board desires to forge cultural change and innovation in the latter. These are high-risk modes of managing succession, in that the new leader typically starts out with a low level of authority. The appointing powers may be enthused about their potential, but more often than not the organization members are sceptical if not outright critical at the prospect of an 'outsider' coming in over their heads to tell them what to do.

Cases of a situation going pear-shaped quickly and decisively are not hard to find. A classic example constitutes the formation of the first Dutch coalition government led by prime minister Jan-Peter Balkenende in 2002. Coming into government was the brand new party of the recently-assassinated right-wing populist Pim Fortuyn, which none the less had obtained 19 per cent of the vote and was an indispensable partner in a centre-right coalition. Deliberately recruiting their ministers from outside 'politics as usual', its three senior ministers included a Chamber of Commerce executive, a successful self-made entertainment entrepreneur and a professor of economics. The latter two were at loggerheads with one another almost immediately, and within a matter of months their row escalated to breaking point. The government was dissolved, and in the January 2003 elections that followed, the party's vote was reduced to a little over a third of its previous result just seven months before.

Fading giants

When the British Conservative Party MPs finally rebelled against Margaret Thatcher, one of them allegedly remarked that 'the problem with great leaders is that they don't know when to go'. This tendency is not confined to 'great' leaders, as many leaders do not leave until well after their authority has all but evaporated. The classic manifestation is the founder-owner chief executive officer (CEO), or the founder-leader of a social movement or political party: they reign over organizations that are literally their own creations and in which generally weak (in)formal checks and balances exist. As their years at the top accumulate, and they fall prey to the performance-compromising effects of sheer longevity (in terms of: physical and mental health, moral fibre, good judgement, or reflexivity), they risk becoming liabilities rather assets to their organizations. To the extent that they do reach this situation, who is going to tell them? And what if they refuse to listen? They tend to be firmly entrenched in the trappings of the leadership role, surrounded by an inner circle of supporters who owe their own positions and influence to them.

The result of this scenario is often not a pretty sight: a long and painful decline in the authority of leaders who soldier on, clinging to their own idea of being indispensable and acting in often formulaic ways, surrounded by increasingly hypocritical and desperate followers (see Figure 3.5). When the end does come, it is often in the form of a 'palace coup' or a barely face-saving, not quite pre-emptive 'voluntary' resignation, leaving the inner circle and the true believers from the olden days orphaned and vulnerable to culling efforts by successors. Often, the retiring leader of this type cannot really bring him/herself to do just that, brooding conspicuously in the background and taking pot shots at the new powers that be (even if the original leaders have hand-picked them for the role).

Pointed examples can be found among political leaders. A notorious case is West German Christian-Democratic leader and chancellor Konrad Adenauer's crippling five-year struggle to postpone his succession by the younger and much more popular finance minister, Ludwig Erhard. Adenauer only got the job at 73, and his political capital started eroding seriously when he was 82, yet he did not give in to pressures from within his party to step down until he was 87).

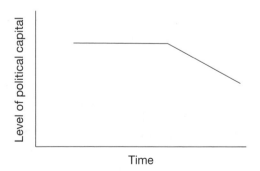

FIGURE 3.5 *The leadership capital trajectory of fading giant leaders*

Likewise, in the Australian Labor Party alone, three of its post-war leaders' authority trajectories closely followed the atrophy scenario: Herbert Evatt (1949–60), Arthur Calwell (1960–66) and Gough Whitlam (1966–80). Whitlam, for example, was a flamboyant, though narcissistic, leader who made Labor electable again after decades in the political wilderness, and led an ambitious and initially successful reforming government from 1972. He was controversially sacked as prime minister in November 1975 by the Governor-General after a chaotic year of increasing scandal and political standoff about supply with the opposition- controlled Senate. Whitlam thought he would be vindicated by the electorate, but the opposite happened: Labour was routed by voters in an historic landslide win for the Liberals. Mortally wounded politically in the world outside, he continued to dominate his party and to chase a redemption, which Australian voters were clearly not prepared to give. It took a second ignominious defeat in 1977 for him to get the message, leaving behind a party in tatters.

Comebacks

The authority trajectory of the comeback leader is double-peaked. They rise to leadership, suffer seemingly crippling defeats or setbacks, yet manage to rebuild their political capital, and re-establish their leadership credentials (see Figure 3.6). François Mitterand epitomizes this leadership type. A prominent French social democrat MP in the 1950s, he lost his parliamentary seat in 1958, bounced back to become the left's unsuccessful presidential candidate against Charles De Gaulle in 1965. After this loss he managed to run again for the left in 1974, when he lost narrowly to Valéry Giscard d'Estaing, only to bounce back again to obtain the presidency in 1981 and be re-elected in 1988 – not only surviving but thriving in periods of the centre-right's dominance of the legislature and cabinet. US president Bill Clinton – who was even nicknamed 'the comeback kid' – is another archetype, whose 'Teflon'-style ability to bounce back from scandal and electoral setbacks time and again helped him prolong his lease on the leadership. The story of comeback leaders is invariably one of iron-willed stubbornness, chameleonic qualities of personal and political reinvention, and deft blame-avoidance manoeuvres.

Sometimes plain and simple fortune is the sine qua non of the story. Take the cases of German chancellor Helmut Kohl and New York mayor Rudy Giuliani. Both were long-serving leaders who were firmly on an atrophy trajectory when a truly seismic event occurred on their watch. The crisis of the day then brought out the best in them, their performance was widely admired and helped to lift their almost depleted authority to higher levels than they had ever reached before. In Kohl's case, the deus ex machinea was the opening of the Berlin

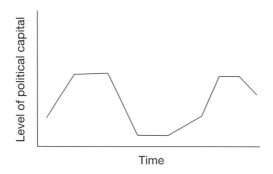

FIGURE 3.6　*The leadership capital trajectory of comeback leaders*

Wall in 1989, presenting him with a golden opportunity to become the architect of German unification (Maier 1997). As noted earlier, in Giuliani's case, his galvanizing response to the 9/11 attacks turned him into a world-wide hero, who thereby obtained a new lease on his political life.

Chapter 4

Leading with Others

Two-term US President Richard Nixon resigned in disgrace in 1974, cornered by revelations that he had authorized and subsequently covered up political espionage against his political opponents. Despite being an intensely controversial politician throughout his career, the public outrage and disenchantment that the relentless media coverage of the scandal generated was too much even for Nixon to handle. He bowed to the pressure, and spent the remainder of his life trying to regain public respect. Quite successfully so, in fact; when he died 20 years later, all his successors attended, and the eulogies at the funeral and in the media spoke highly of him. Nixon's attempt to re-establish his reputation rested largely on his stature as an international statesman, boosted by the foreign policy accomplishments of his administration – ending the Vietnam War, making a historic approach to Mao ('Nixon goes to China' is now a generic terms for leaders achieving a breakthrough by making a move that seemingly goes against all they stand for and their constituents expect them to do), nuclear arms limitation treaties with the Soviet Union, and bringing a noticeable thaw in the Cold War.

Nixon was rightly proud of these achievements. But the leadership that brought them about was not his alone; it was the product of political teamwork between himself and Henry Kissinger, the national security adviser and later foreign minister of his administration. Theirs was a leadership tandem of epic proportions. Both were fiercely ambitious, ruthlessly opportunistic and chronically suspicious, if not paranoid. They never did like, nor did they ever fully trust, one another. There was plenty of jealousy, fear and loathing in their interpersonal relationship: 'The political bruiser and the Harvard intellectual: these men should have loathed each other, and indeed they did. Nixon snidely dubbed Kissinger 'Sir Henry', called him a 'crybaby', a 'dictator', and suggested he put himself into the care of a psychiatrist. He also called him, to his face, 'my Jew boy'. Kissinger, who described his own behaviour in Nixon's presence as 'obsequious excess', referred to him behind his back as a 'madman', a 'drunk', 'unfit to be president' and 'the meatball mind' (Saunders 2007).

But their policy visions gelled, and they shared a penchant for bold initiatives, bypassing normal channels, outflanking bureaucratic and Congressional opponents, and secret operations. Nixon and Kissinger were both self-serving characters with grandiose dreams of recasting world affairs. This *amour-propre*, and their cynicism – about other people's motives, about scruples, about democracy even – roped them together as 'rivals who could not satisfy their aspirations without each other' (Dallek 2007). They both knew that each needed the other to put their grand plans into practice. Nixon looked up to Kissinger, the brilliant international relations professor with his grand designs and enigmatic public persona; Kissinger had in Nixon a keen learner, a constraints challenger and an intuitive strategist who had the political clout and risk-taking propensity required to achieve the foreign policy breakthroughs he envisaged. Kissinger used flattery and ruthless tactics of bureaucratic politics to outflank the State Department, the Central Intelligence Agency (CIA) and the Pentagon to become effectively Nixon's point man and confidante in security and foreign policy matters. When they worked in tandem, the whole was much greater than the sum of the parts (Dallek 2007).

Politics makes for strange bedfellows. And so can leadership, as the Nixon–Kissinger example plainly illustrates. But the leadership literature for the most part has overlooked this. I have been struck by the chasm that exists between the bulk of leadership theory and the day-to-day practice of public leadership as I observed it and heard it discussed. That chasm concerned the penchant for leadership scholars to portray leadership processes – despite many protestations to the contrary – fundamentally in terms of 'a leader and the rest'. In the minds of most leadership scholars, the epicentre of leadership is a person, and leadership can be understood by examining the mind, motives, moods, choices, words and acts of that person. Admittedly, the field has moved beyond a simplistic fixation on 'great men', the people at the top, and their competencies. It has started to acknowledge the importance of separating authority figures from leaders, and allowing for the possibility of leadership being exercised 'from below', by a person without a formal mandate or role. Also, most sociological and social-psychological theories of leadership have given equal weight in the leadership equation to the minds, motives, moods, needs, identities and loyalties of a leader's constituents. They urge us to understand leadership in terms of relationships (Chapter 3 of this book has covered much of that ground). But even so, most relational theories of leadership still work on an image of leadership consisting of one (the leader) and many (constituents, followers, the group from which the leader emanates, the organization, the party, the nation).

In leadership practice, however, I see the line between the one and the many being blurred. In many political and organizational settings the norm is not one of individual dominance by the head of government or CEO but of collective decision-making and collective responsibility at the top. The notion of cabinet government is probably the most conspicuous example. Although much is made of the alleged 'presidentialization' or 'prime-ministerialization' of many traditionally cabinet-centred governments, there is also plenty of evidence to suggest that actually very few prime ministers can really 'call the shots' all or even most of the time *vis-à-vis* their cabinet colleagues and front-benchers, particularly in coalition governments (Dowding and Dumont 2009; Strangio *et al.* 2013). Likewise, in many public agencies and not-for-profit (NFP) organizations, there is a governance structure in which the CEO is at best a primus inter pares – the first among equals. She might have some added weight in setting the group's agenda and being the group's public face, but where the individual cannot and will not have her way on issues in which a significant proportion of his/her colleagues disagree (Alvarez and Svejenova 2005).

I also see people who, at the front of the stage of political or organizational life, are being scripted and cast as 'the leader' being deeply embedded in symbiotic and even dependency relationships with their 'advisers' at the back of the stage. The 'real authority' may in fact lie with people who are technically subordinate to the designated leader. Furthermore, one can often see the actual work of leadership in organizations being performed not just by one but by several leaders at the same time beyond the formal collegial structures (Gronn 1999, 2002, 2009). In many governments and organizations the real locus of institutional leadership is in some informal duo ('tandem') or clique ('inner circle') of key players with complementary interests, skills, power bases and energy levels.

And finally, in the real world of complex social issues and equally complex institutional arrangements for their governance, more often than not problems are framed, attention is prioritized, decisions are made and action taken not in hierarchies with clear-cut vertical authority structures but in networks where 'no one is in charge'. Stuff only happens when technically autonomous groups, organizations, levels of government or public and private actors 'join up', co-ordinate, align their words and deeds – in short, collaborate. In such network settings, much of traditional leadership theory is pretty well irrelevant.

In this chapter, we venture into the world of 'we'-leadership as opposed to that of 'one and many'. We shall tackle two manifestations of 'we-processes' in turn: leadership as teamwork; and leadership in shared-power settings.

Leadership as teamwork

Leaders have always needed assistance and consequently there is a very old and now sizeable literature on advice-giving and advisory systems to heads of government going back to Machiavelli (Goldhamer 1978).

Traditionally, much of attention was focused on the delicate art of advice-giving: how to 'speak truth to power', when doing so may be unwelcome and therefore compromise the position of the adviser at the leader's court (Meltsner 1988).

In parliamentary systems much of the relevant research falls under the rubric of (prime-) ministerial advisers and offices, with a key issue being the balance between personal staff, the government bureaucracy, and external streams of policy advice to ministers (Campbell and Wyszomirski 1991; Bakvis 1997; Tiernan 2007; Rhodes and Tiernan 2014). Or it ties in with the broader issue of the balance of power in parliamentary systems; for example, raising the much debated spectre of 'presidentialization' of the prime-ministership, among others by the expansion of the advisory capacity in prime ministers' departments (Poguntke and Webb 2005; Dowding 2013).

In presidential systems, particularly in the USA, the literature focuses on two areas: the design and management of advisory systems to serve the needs and style of their chief clients, as well as to enhance the quality of presidential decision-making (Johnson 1974; George 1980; Walcott and Hult 1995; Patterson 2000; George and Stern 2002; Hess and Pfiffner 2002; Hult and Walcott 2004; Mitchell 2005; Walcott and Hult 2005); and leaders' actual performance in cases where presidential decision-making really matters, particularly foreign and security policy (Janis 1982; Burke and Greenstein 1989; Haney 1997; Hoyt and Garrison 1997; Preston 2001; Kowert 2002; Yetiv 2003; Pfiffner 2005) down to the level of highlighting the nature and predicaments of particular advisory roles in the White House make-up, such as Chief of Staff (Walcott *et al.* 2001; Sullivan 2004) or national security adviser (Daalder and Destler 2011). Numerous scholars are interested in the structure of advisory *systems*, as demarcated by formal and spatial boundaries, such as *Number 10* (Kavanagh and Seldon 1999), or *The White House Staff* (Patterson 2000). This helps them to understand the institutional dynamics of the power game surrounding leaders, but not to track its actual (crisis) performance in particular historical cases. Others are more focused on the advisory *processes*, largely denoted as the operation of 'inner circles' ('kitchen cabinet', 'war cabinet') of 'principals' around a president or prime minister (Preston 2001). These studies analyse advice-giving in terms of small-group dynamics (Garrison *et al.* 1997; 't Hart *et al.* 1997; Redd 2005; Garrison 2007).

Rod Rhodes has taken the argument a step further and posits that even today senior political executives (a head of government, a cabinet minister, a US-style secretary) can be thought of as being surrounded by a 'court': a coterie of public officials, political assistants, executive assistance, and other liked and trusted associates, all of whom seek to offer support and advice to the leader while at the same time are often also looking after their own personal or institutional interests. Relationships within the court can vary a great deal – from leader to leader, but also from time to time or even issue to issue – in terms of how access to the leader is structured, the level of cohesion and agreement between the various courtiers, and the degree of formality, hierarchy and openness of relationships. In his work on life at the top in British executive government, Rod Rhodes talks about 'the departmental court' that exists in every ministry:

> Every department has a central secretariat made up of several private offices and shared support units. However, this label is misleading; the central secretariat is better described as a 'departmental court'. This phrase draws attention to the beliefs and practices of the court, to the court politics surrounding ministers and senior civil servants, to the competition between ministers, and to the tensions between the court and the rest of the department and between civil servants and special advisers. (Rhodes 2013: 323)

These observations align closely with the findings of the US-based research on advisory systems and process dynamics in presidential systems. In fact, they echo those of contemporary observers of rulerships throughout human history. Whether we look at Roman historians, Shakespearian plays or memoirs of cabinet ministers and presidential aides, we see not simple leader–adviser and/or departmental hierarchies at work, but instead see a complex and variable mix of personalities and relationships. It makes sense, therefore, to interpret and assess these executive courts through a group-dynamic lens as well as a leadership lens. In some of my earlier work, this is what I spent much of my time doing ('t Hart 1994; 't Hart *et al.* 1997). From it, I distilled various logics of thinking about courts, cabinets, committees and other elite groupings in public life. Each provided a distinct interpretive frame for making sense of and evaluating how they operate.

The court as think tank   A key reason for working with groups and teams in organizations in the first place is that if they work well as a unit, they are demonstrably superior to individuals when it comes to processing information about novel, complex and unstructured problems – the types of problems typical of high-level policy-making. A common task for policy-makers and managers is to interpret events and trends in their environment, and make decisions to adopt or modify their policies and actions based on these interpretations. To this end, they use committees, working groups, project teams and staff units.

The group as think-tank metaphor zooms in on the dynamics of group information processing: the ways in which the group arrives at a common representation of events, the extent to which during the deliberations group members come to share with their colleagues information available to the individual members, and the process by which groups make inferences from the information available to them and develop a composite picture of its implication for past, present and future policies.

The process by which groups solicit and interpret information as the basis for policy adjustments may be less than optimal. As a result, important events may go unnoticed, serious threats may be played down, potential alternatives to the present policy are not examined, and latent opportunities pass by unexploited. Such flaws in the process of group perception, and, literally, group thinking, can have catastrophic results, since, in the real world of business, government and collective endeavour disaster is always a single bad decision away (see Box 4.1).

The court as sanctuary   Advisory groups can also be an important source of psychological gratification, for their leaders and members alike. In many cases people join groups because they want to: it may be advantageous or prestigious to do so, or it may provide them with a sense of identity and belonging. In well-functioning groups, members provide one another (and the leaders) with invaluable emotional support. They are drawn together by bounds of joint socialization, party loyalties, personal friendships, joint enemies and a common fate. Membership of the court – the inner circle, the sanctum of power – can provide the members with the security and comfort they seek. These typically derive from the individual's knowledge that here is a group of trusted and liked associates who share his world view, values and concerns, and who have a first-hand understanding of the predicaments he is facing. Any inner doubts he may have about certain issues or parts of his performance can be held at bay by the confidence and approbation of his peers.

The positive effects of a supportive group climate on the task performance of their members should not be underestimated. Yet research shows that there is a risk that maintaining such group sanctuaries may have insidious effects on the policy-making process. There may be a thin line between advisers offering emotional support and becoming sycophants to a dominant leader. If consensus and mutual support becomes the norm, an absence of critical thinking and self-reflection may take hold. As a result, leaders and group members may be led to overestimate their own effectiveness, morality and integrity. They may also underestimate the abilities of rivals as well as the salience of risks and vulnerabilities associated with the group's preferred course of action.

The court as arena   It would be a mistake to think that the differences of interests, opinions and values with regard to the policy issues that leaders need to attend to somehow stop at the door of the executive

BOX 4.1   Groupthink: 'teamwork' going astray

Inspired by reading his daughter's high school essay on the Bay of Pigs invasion fiasco, Yale psychologist Irving Janis's (1982) study of 'groupthink' has become one of the most influential psychological contributions to the study of decision- making in politics, management and the professions. Janis challenged the then dominant view in theoretical and applied social psychology that group cohesion always results in better performance. He maintained that under certain conditions and when a group engages in stressful decisional tasks, strong group cohesion can in fact contribute to defective decision-making, which in turn may lead to a policy disaster. He defined groupthink as a mode of thinking that people engage in when they are deeply involved in a cohesive in-group, when the members' strivings for unanimity override their motivation to realistically appraise alternative courses of action. He also stated that groupthink refers to a deterioration of mental efficiency, reality testing and moral judgement that results from in-group pressures.

Janis identified eight main symptoms of the groupthink 'syndrome':

- an illusion of invulnerability among group members;
- the use of rationalizations to discount warnings and other negative feedback;
- a shared belief in the inherent morality of the group;
- stereotyped views of members of opposing groups;
- self-censorship on the part of group members so as not to 'make things difficult' for the group or its leader(s);
- an illusion of unanimity;
- self-appointed 'mindguards' within the group who act to shield the group from information challenging its premises or decisions; and
- direct pressure put on any members of the group who do articulate doubts or dissent *vis-à-vis* the assumed consensus.

elite group. They don't. Dealing with difference and conflict is one of the chief challenges of managing court processes. Ignoring or suppressing them can produce the kind of unhelpful consensus-seeking described above; but not reining them in when they risk undermining the quality of the deliberative and collaborative process is equally dangerous. Certainly in the world of politics and business, many groups assume the characteristics of 'arenas' – stages for the enactment of conflict and negotiation between members who think of themselves as 'stakeholders' or even as rivals first and as 'colleagues' only a distant second. In many inter-agency meetings within government, for example, agency representatives to the group meeting are merely acting out their organizational roles as set out in their agency's pre-arranged briefs, and are not necessarily interested in making these groups actu-

Janis analysed high-profile US policy fiascoes such as the escalation the Korean and Vietnam wars by presidents Harry S. Truman and Lyndon B. Johnson as well as the Watergate cover-up by president Richard Nixon. In each instance, the group dynamics in the inner circle around the president were found to be a root cause of the defective decision-making that drove these polices. Since then, symptoms of groupthink have been detected in a host of policy fiascoes worldwide, such as British policy during the 1956 Suez crisis (Verbeek 2003), the 1980 Iran rescue mission tragedy (Smith 1984), the Enron corporate scandal (O'Connor 2003) and the 2003 US decision to invade Iraq (Badie 2010).

In Janis's original formulation, three types of antecedents are likely to trigger groupthink: the group is highly cohesive; there are structural faults in the organization in which the group is embedded, serving to neutralize potential checks and balances on and within the group (such as group insulation from the rest of the organization, a lack of norms requiring methodical procedures for group deliberation, and a lack of a tradition of impartial leadership); and the group is acting in a provocative situational context generating a high degree of stress among the members of the group. Groups that are affected by groupthink are likely to display a series of decision-making defects such as an incomplete survey of alternatives, failure to re-examine the preferred choice as well as initially rejected alternatives, and a poor scrutiny of information. Combined, such decision defects set the group up for choosing, and rigorously sticking with, decisions that are unrealistic and often morally questionable.

Though its theoretical and empirical claims have been open to challenge and amendment (for example, 't Hart, 1994; Turner and Pratkanis, 1998; Baron, 2005) the bottom line is that the notion of 'groupthink' highlights the dangers involved when leaders do not organize, protect and utilize diversity of expertise, values and beliefs in the inner circles that surround them and the collegial teams of which they are a part.

ally work as teams. Consequently, in many cases, bargaining and compromise formation, however tenuous, contrived and implicit, rather than all-out conflict tend to be characteristic of what goes on in these committees. The key question is how this clash between divergent perspectives and interests, mixed motives and tactical role-playing affects the group's deliberation process and outcomes.

This raises the issue of power. Who control(s) a group's agenda, decisions and actions? In most groups, and despite public protestations to the contrary by all concerned, members have unequal status. This goes much further than the truism that there is always a certain leadership in any group, whether appointed or emergent, and individual or collective. Most groups have a complex, finely tuned informal hierarchy that shapes the interpersonal relations between their members. Group leaders can be people who are formally 'the boss' – the CEO in a company's management board; the prime minister in a cabinet; the dean in a faculty executive, for example. They can also be group members whose expertise, experience, drive, values and skills are recognized as authoritative by other group members regardless of their formal status in the group. Whether formally or informally established (and the two types can co-exist and even conflict within one and the same group), leaders can exert great influence over the composition of groups, the framing of issues, the rules of interaction prevailing in the group, and the substantive choices the group eventually makes. They can shape the very purpose and nature of group deliberation. It is interesting to observe, however, that just as the leadership team as a whole sometimes exerts little actual control over the conduct and implementation of policy, so do team leaders over the behaviour of the team. Much depends on whether they observe the limitations placed on their power by the group's role structure. Though it is commonly held that leaders enjoy considerable 'idiosyncrasy credit' (Hollander 1979), empirical research on power in high-level management teams suggest that this is only true up to a point. The obligation to act within the bounds of a senior role does not decrease as one assumes higher positions of authority; a senior role may grant more discretion as to how it is enacted, but there are normative constraints to even the highest level positions. Even chief executives must exercise power within the norms of authority, unless they are prepared to become de facto dictators (and some are) – thus robbing the group of much of its capacity for smartness, reality-testing and integrity – or to risk revolt among their colleagues, which could see them not just cut down to size in terms of political capital and thus their ability to lead the group effectively, but also to be removed from their positions completely (as the literature on CEO and party leader succession amply demonstrates; see, for example. 't Hart and Uhr 2011).

The court as ritual   However, the power game within and around a court or management team can also be less overt and brutal – but no less consequential. Roger Hilsman once observed the following about John F. Kennedy's style of managing the decision-making process:

> Kennedy said: And now we have the 'inner club.' He meant that we had together the people who had known all along what we would do about the problem, and who had been pulling and hauling, debating and discussing for no other purpose than to keep the government together, to get all the others to come around. (Hilsman 1965: 6)

In complex organizations, high-level group discussions may not always be what they seem. Many such groups are part of the formal structure of the organization. In government, they may even be rooted in law or the Constitution. Yet that does not mean that, for this reason alone, they are actually performing their stated tasks. Like Kennedy, many chief executives and senior policy-makers have found it expedient at times to conduct an important part of their business using informal groups and settings, while leaving intact the formal system. When this is done on a more regular basis, a dual structure of policy-making develops. The formal system of committees and cabinet meetings remains important primarily for symbolic reasons: it reinforces deeply rooted organizational norms and constitutional myths about how collective decisions ought to be made, it provides a platform for marginal actors and dissenters to articulate their positions, and it allows key players to make certain statements for the public record. In sum, it provides an essential source of legitimacy for the policies and actions of an informal, more closely-knit inner circle – where the real decisions are made.

At the personal level, the management style of the chief executive is crucially important. For example, leaders may feel uncomfortable in formal group settings; they may have a low tolerance for conflict among their advisers and colleagues; or a strong need for emotional support in handling difficult issues. All of these personal factors will encourage them to gather a relatively small circle of trusted and like-minded associates around them, and to minimize their reliance on the more sizeable, heterogeneous and potentially conflictual formal bodies. Other leaders are more comfortable in these settings, and will even want to avoid inner circles.

There are also forces inherent in the collective decision-making process itself that drive this process. Especially in more established groups working together over a long time, a good deal of interaction is displaced by anticipation, with group participants preferring to compare notes and work out common positions in informal subgroup meetings before the plenary session. As a result, the plenary session of the group can become a mere show, covering ground already decided upon elsewhere (in the 'inner circle'), while the real arguments and causes of action remain in the dark to a good many of the group's members who are excluded from the relevant inner circles.

Leadership style and court dynamics

The degree to which each of these logics of group dynamics apply to any given court or other leadership team varies, as does the importance of the role played by leaders as a variable affecting the characteristics of the group process. For example, in the case of presidential inner circles, especially in the US context, policy-making groups tend to be more cohesive and loyal to the leader than those of parliamentary systems of cabinet government, particularly those with coalition cabinets, where a prime minister can sometimes be construed as first among equals (Baylis 1989; Blondel and Muller-Rommel 1993). The same probably holds true for the courts surrounding nascent social movements encouraged by charismatic founders/leaders, as opposed to the more formally structured elite interaction that may occur at the apex of older, more established civil society groups such as Amnesty International. In the more informal, leader-centred groups, many of the classical malfunctions resulting from excessive (desires for) group cohesion are more likely to occur. In the latter, centrifugal forces are more marked as a result of the conflicting interests of well-established baronies within the organization, turning the elite group into more of an arena where bureaucratic politics is more likely than 'groupthink' to be the name of the game (Preston and 't Hart 1999).

Institutional structures provide certain incentives and rules of the game for players, but a significant role should always be reserved for people, specifically senior political leaders (presidents, prime ministers, governors, mayors), who, like corporate CEOs (Jackall 1988), interpret, manipulate and alter the rules of the game of the 'top team' to suit their personalities, leadership styles and whims of the moment (Preston 2001; Kowert 2002). For example, Preston (2001) found that leaders with a high *need for power* (see also Chapter 1) preferred formal, hierarchical advisory system structures designed to enhance their own personal control over the policy process. These leaders tended to centralize decision-making within tight inner circles of trusted advisers, and to insist on direct personal involvement and control over policy formulation and decisions. Their policy preferences tended to dominate both the policy deliberations within advisory groups and the nature of the final policy decisions. In contrast, leaders low in the need for power preferred less hierarchically structured courts and required less personal control over how they operated. Their known policy preferences tended not to dominate their court's deliberations. As a result, the input of subordinates played a greater role in policy-making. Unlike the leaders low in the need for power, leaders high in the need for power were found to have assertive interpersonal styles in which they would actively challenge or seek to influence the positions taken by their advisers; further, these leaders were also more likely to override or ignore the conflicting or opposing policy views of subordinates.

Similarly, the personality factor of *cognitive complexity* – a person's level of appetite for rich and varied information before reaching a decision – also shapes how senior executives structure and manage 'their' courts. High-complexity leaders were far more sensitive than others to the external policy context as well as to the existence of multiple policy dimensions or perspectives on issues. During policy deliberations, they also engaged in broad information search routines that emphasized the presentation of alternative viewpoints, discrepant information and multiple policy options by their advisers. Such leaders focused substantial discussion within their advisory groups on future policy contingencies and the likely views or reactions of other policy actors in the environment. In addition, they were less likely than leaders low on cognitive complexity to use simplistic analogies, 'black-and-white' problem representations, or stereotypical images of their opponents during group deliberations. Complex leaders were less decisive and more deliberative in engaging with their advisers.

Finally, the *prior policy experience or expertise* of leaders has a significant impact on their leadership style, the nature of court interactions, and how forcefully leaders assert their own positions on policy issues (Barber 1972; George 1980; Hermann 1986). Hermann (1986) noted that past experience provides leaders with a sense of which actions will be effective or not in specific policy situations, as well as which cues from the environment should be paid attention and which are irrelevant. Relative to leaders with little policy experience, leaders with prior experience are more likely to insist on personal involvement or control over policy-making. Further, experienced leaders with expertise in a policy area are far less likely to rely on the views of advisers or to use simplistic stereotypes or analogies to understand policy issues and situations. Such leaders are more interested in gathering detailed information from the policy environment, and they use a more deliberate decision process than do their less experienced counterparts (Preston 2001).

The exact nature and extent of the impact of leader personality factors on group structure and process is, of course, variable and situation-specific. In some cases, the styles of leaders and their individual characteristics may encourage or actively instigate conflict within their court or the collegial body in which they operate. An example is US president Franklin D. Roosevelt's deliberate use of a competitive style in the way that he managed his court and reached policy decisions. FDR created overlap and ambiguity among his advisers which encouraged them to actively advocate in and around meetings with the president. The advisers ended up in perennial battle and acrimony, but FDR thus became the central node in a rich and redundant network of expertise, opinion and partisanship, giving him a full picture of the issues and interests at stake and motivating everyone to seek to maintain positive relations with him in order not to lose his ear (Johnson 1974; George 1980). He used the same philosophy in staffing key public agencies, such as the now-legendary Tennessee Valley Authority, where he orchestrated a creative conflict between its three hand-picked but very different leaders, which contributed much to the eventual transformative success of its unprecedented regional development effort (Hargrove 1994; Burns 2003).

In other situations, the characteristics of leaders may eliminate, or at least mitigate, the group pathology of turning courts into divisive arenas by introducing more collegial advisory systems that reduce the kinds of conflicts found in the competitive model, while still gathering immense amounts of information from the environment (see further, Preston and 't Hart 1999; Preston 2001; Dyson and 't Hart 2013). John F. Kennedy's intensely studied and often-praised handling of his court during the Cuban missile crisis is often cited as a case in point. Kennedy, having been a victim of groupthink early in his presidency during the Bay of Pigs fiasco, was determined to avoid premature consensus when he was presented with the vexed issue of what to do with satellite information about a Soviet missile site under construction in Fidel Castro's Cuba. Resisting his initial impulse to strike back immediately and hard, he took time to reach a carefully considered decision instead. He split his court into two separate groups that were both tasked with considering the options available and making recommendations. He spent relatively little time in any of the group meetings, to avoid his advisers second-guessing his preferences and tailoring their views accordingly. He thus created the conditions for almost a week of rigorous behind-the-scenes court debate in which all options were canvassed and scrutinized, eventually settling for a naval blockade of Cuba, an option that had the big advantage of sending a clear signal to the Soviets but leaving them a lot of time and flexibility to realize the seriousness of the situation and consider their options. This created a window for finding a joint, negotiated resolution in ways that bombing or invading Cuba would have made impossible (Janis 1982; Lebow and Stein 1994).

Leadership in shared power settings

Imagine you are to be the head of a high-profile new task force on obesity, installed by a newly elected government. This blue-ribbon body is to be composed of senior representatives from academia, government, business and civil society (for example, not-for-profit organizations in health, education and social services). Your committee's task is to advise the government on a 'whole-of-society approach' to what has come to be thought of as the 'obesity epidemic' during the election campaign, where the topic emerged as a major theme alongside the management of the economy and law and order issues.

The sense of urgency around the issue increased considerably after three events occurred more or less simultaneously. First, there was the broadcasting on the eve of the campaign period of *Oversized Nation?*, a penetrating documentary series effectively dramatizing the fate that befalls many obese people: daily physical discomfort, chronic health problems, social isolation, an endless regime of bad food and bingeing, low self-esteem and/or depression. The series powerfully emphasized how disjointed and costly, yet largely counterproductive the current policy regime with regard to obesity is. Second, the so-called 'Tragic Josie' YouTube suicide video caused a national shockwave. Josie, a 34-year-old supermarket worker, had struggled with obesity since early childhood. Clearly obsessed with body image, and after many years of disappointing therapies and failed attempts to turn her life around, she killed herself, leaving behind a husband and two children. The video statement provided a harrowing account of her life, and the lack of effective resources available to help her. The video was quickly picked up by the mainstream media and created an enormous amount of public debate. Finally, in the run-up to the election, several scientific reports were published documenting a rapidly rising incidence of obesity and an exponential rise in the net social costs associated with it.

The tabloid press in particular presented the assertion that 'our country has become the fattest nation on earth' as criticism of the government's much-vaunted election plan for a 'public health revolution'. Amid endless talk about systemic reforms, successive governments had let the obesity issue slip and allowed it to escalate into the full-blown social crisis it had now become. Polling showed that this critique struck a chord within the community (regardless of the fact that within the scientific community there is ongoing and intense debate about the definition of obesity, its alleged health effects, and the most appropriate intervention methods). In the election, one candidate announced that, if elected, he would 'fight obesity first' in the area of health policy, instead of getting mired in the 'big-ticket' but highly intractable issues such as funding agreements and systemic reform. Another candidate announced that the issue would be at the top of her government's agenda, promising to 'turn the trend around' within 18 months.

Now that your party has won the election, the time has come to deliver on that promise, and your task force is the crucial vehicle chosen by the incoming government to do so. But the very definition of the issue is contested. Experts disagree on where being overweight stops and obesity starts, but perhaps even more on the issue of just what kind of a problem it is, what its social costs are, and where they have the most impact. Within the public sector, there is a serious lack of co-ordination between various jurisdictions and disciplines, largely a result of entrenched territoriality among various government stakeholders and the persistent conflicts of values and interests concerning the definition and ownership of the obesity issue that these bureaucratic silos exacerbate. Moreover, successive governments have been known to shelve proposals for regulatory intervention in the area of food sales and advertising put forward by health departments.

In contrast, many individuals and groups within not-for-profit agencies in the public health, social services and educational sectors have been sounding the alarm for years. The NFPs have argued unsuccessfully with governments for a more proactive, preventative approach – leaning harder on the fast-food industry, for example. At the same time, even the most active NFPs have experienced problems of their own in advocating a tough position. Some children's hospitals have fast food restaurants prominently integrated into their architecture, unable to resist the lure of foundation money. And when local government health and education departments team up to try to insist that only healthy food can be sold in school canteens, they more often than not are met by a revolt from parents and caregivers associations who rely strongly on fast-food sales for their income streams.

Finally, within the business community there has been a fundamentally ambivalent attitude to the issue. Employers have become ever more aware of the financial burdens that the 'obesity explosion' imposes on the workforce. Some industries, particularly diet, fitness and sports companies, see the issue as a business opportunity, and a number of gyms now offer 'fat-buster' memberships. But at the same time, a considerable number of firms, particularly in the food industry resist legislation which, they argue, would impose high compliance costs and take responsibility away from families.

You as a respected academic head this task force, which also comprises a former government minister, a former head of the Cabinet Office, the CEO of the Council of Food and Grocery businesses, and a CEO of a high-profile NFP organization working on eating disorders. Putting aside the formal terms of reference, the new health minister tells you that the action plan your group is to hammer out must allow for all of the three sectors –to commit to effective, drastic and mutually reinforcing sets of actions. It must not antagonize the business community. It must not simply dump more tasks and expectations on already highly pressured institutions such as local governments, schools, GPs, hospitals and social services without providing them with additional resources. Given the complexities, urgencies, stakeholders and constraints, how do you go about your job in leading this task force?

This scenario, though fictitious, captures the day-to-day realities of contemporary public policy-making much better than the alternative scenario that is implicit in most 'leadership' accounts of the way in which governments operate and public problems are tackled. Many actors have a stake across all sectors of society. It involves competing values. It involves the public interest, but it also goes deeply into what many consider to be the private sphere of individual lifestyle choices. There is disagreement about the very definition of the problem and the kind of evidence that is relevant for diagnosing it and selecting possible remedies. No single actor, inside or outside of government, is able to 'lead' in the conventional way; that is, by deciding authoritatively on a set of solutions to be implemented. If there is to be any chance of reducing obesity and/or the various obesity-induced burdens, there has to be close consultation and agreement between many parties, none of whom is 'in charge' of the entire issue, let alone capable of undertaking effective preventative or remedial action under its own steam.

This is not a world in which classic approaches to leadership can be expected to work. This type of nagging, complex social problem will not be solved by relying on one or a few players at the top of the tree to understand the problem, develop a vision, propose a set of solutions and subsequently use their authority, charisma and other power resources to build support for their policies and forge their implementation. There are simply too many too-diverse players, and too many 'veto points' on the road to effective action. No single person or body has the ability to command or cajole all the others into line. Addressing complex social problems such as obesity is much more like 'negotiation' and 'learning' than it is like 'decision making' and 'implementing'. It is not simply about persuading others to follow. Instead, it is about seducing others to embark on a joint process of exploration, trust-building and mutual accommodation. Getting such processes under way and seeing them through requires a different approach to leadership.

The logic of collaborative governance

For thousands of years, the notion of leadership has been connected inextricably to that of hierarchy. Clans, tribes, cities and states were thought to need clear direction from the top (or the centre). The functions of leadership were typically expected to be performed by one or a small number of authority figures. While over time different practices evolved for endowing particular individuals with such authority (from physical force and courage to inheritance, to election and representation), in only very few cases (for example, anarchistic communes or nascent social movements steeped in egalitarian ideals) was there any question that somebody needed to be 'boss'.

The advent of large and complex organizations served only to reinforce the importance attached to hierarchy as the core foundation for the exercise of leadership. Again, the principles upon which hierarchies were founded evolved – with the rise of professionalism and performance over tradition and tenure – yet the basic principle of leadership being expected and exercised from the top down remained firmly intact. In extreme conditions, such as disasters or battlefield situations, the formal hierarchy might break down and give way to informal, situational forms of leadership exercised by people who were capable of dealing with the demands of the moment rather than those highest up the ladder. But even so, the locus of leadership remained clear and focused on a single leader or a small coterie.

In recent decades, the dominance of government and its institution-alized hierarchy as the main driver of public leadership has begun to wane. This has happened not because the egalitarian ideals of the 1960s have, after all, won the battle of public ideas, but because the nature of the most challenging problems faced by contemporary soci-eties has changed. Today, the issues that are really crying out for 'lead-ership' are all about complexity and borderlessness: urban stress, cyber crime, climate change, refugee flows, obesity epidemics, religious fanaticism, alcohol and drug abuse, problem gambling, child traffick-ing, genetic engineering, resource depletion, global poverty, prolifera-tion of weapons of mass destruction and so on.

These are complex problems because they involve a large number and diverse range of stakeholders, values and interests. They entail irreducible uncertainties or conflicts about the nature and scope of the problem as well as the likely impacts of alternative ways of tackling it. They cannot be solved by known, affordable and easily managed response modes, but instead require novel, untried, risky solutions. Borderless problems defy the ways in which we usually categorize issues and organize responsibilities and resources for handling them. They transcend the boundaries of particular organizations, policy sectors and government jurisdictions, and often also transcend the problem-solving capacity of the state sector and require the involve-ment of the corporate and community sectors. Some also have very long-term ramifications, which challenge conventional time horizons employed within politics and government. Getting all these actors together has proved to be difficult, and quite often decision-makers are left with fragmented responses to systemic problems such as obesity, ageing populations or climate change (Linden 2010:15).

The inexorable rise of such 'wicked' problems (Head and Alford 2013) has confronted public policy-makers and professionals with the high and steadily increasing degree of interdependence between them-selves and other actors in the same issue area. It has forced us all to break open the mental, organizational and political silos and monopo-lies that have dictated the ways in which we governed ourselves for so long. In response, we have seen the rise of what Manuel Castells (1996) has called the 'network society', in which connectivity and interdependence are the name of the game. We either learn to harness and integrate the knowledge, resources, values, and interests of actors across a range of domains, sectors and indeed nations, in dealing with such problems, or we face the adverse consequences of our inability to effectively govern the world we have created.

As Rhodes (1997) and many others have documented, there has been a significant shift in the modes of collective problem-solving employed by contemporary societies. Governing is now about 'adhocracy', 'policy networks', 'consultation', 'partnerships', 'community involvement', 'deliberation' and 'internationalization', to name but a few of the alternatives to the hierarchy of government that have emerged over recent decades. They all represent ways of social problem-solving, in which the logic of the empowered few persuading or compelling the many to adopt their proposed course of action has made way for mechanisms that are flatter, more inclusive and more negotiated – in short, polycentric, interactive governance instead of unicentric, hierarchical government (Torfing *et al.* 2012).

In polycentric governance, three things occur. First, the state is coming to terms with its own internal complexities. Its constituent parts realize that none of them can credibly afford to ignore any of the others in tackling key social issues. Contemporary state actors therefore invest heavily in 'corporate governance', 'co-ordination', 'joining up' and 'whole of government' (Christensen and Lægreid 2004). Equally, if not more importantly, the state and its agents no longer self-evidently claim to sit atop of 'society'. Instead, they acknowledge that businesses and community organizations are necessary and indeed more pivotal components than they themselves in tackling the issues of the day. Finally, state actors reconsider the idea of sovereignty, and invest significantly in intergovernmental as well as supranational forums for aligning their actions with those of other states and regions. In a fully polycentric setting, it has become impossible, if not irrelevant, to tell 'who's in charge around here', the special powers and responsibilities of 'the' state notwithstanding (see Bell and Hindmoor 2009).

This raises a pivotal question: how is leadership exercised in such a world? The move from hierarchy to interdependency as the crucial organizing principle of social problem-solving does not in itself obviate the need for any of the key functions of public leadership identified in Chapter 2 to be performed. But it drastically changes the ways in which leadership authority can be acquired, used and lost (see Box 4.2), and it also changes the types of specific challenges faced by leaders. In this world of networks and partnerships, collaborative leadership is the name of the game. It is about organizing consensus and enabling joint action between interdependent actors rather than about showing the way to underlings and followers.

The work and the tools of collaborative leadership

Horizontal governance thus comes into play – and is only worth the considerable effort required to get and keep it under way – when all, or at least most, parties are convinced that 'going at it alone' simply will not work. As Bryson et al. (2006: 46) put it, 'public policy makers

BOX 4.2   Governments versus networks: different rules of the game

The world of government	*The world of networks*
Bounded entity	Multi-party system
Authority	Interdependence
Pyramid	No one in charge
Formal position	Added value
Mandate	Trust
Orders	Agreements
Sanctions	Reciprocity
Compliance	Diplomacy
Subjects	Partners

are most likely to try cross-sector collaboration when they believe the separate efforts of different sectors to address a public problem have failed or are likely to fail, and the actual or potential failures cannot be fixed by the sectors acting alone'. If one or more key players are not convinced that they are in fact condemned to co-ordinate and collaborate, their commitment to horizontal governance will not be strong enough. They might opt out, obstruct or remain passive when commitment is needed. For a whole range of actors to come to acknowledge their interdependence at about the same point in time is no easy feat.

Many actors – professionals, politicians, community organizers, entrepreneurs – often believe strongly in their own established ways of tackling challenges. Their history, their pride, and their values tell them just to try harder within their preferred mode of problem-solving. It often requires a crisis of sorts to raise the salience of the issues (as in the obesity case presented above), and highlight the inherent limitations of everyone's past efforts to come to terms with them. But it always also requires leadership work to bring actors from across jurisdictions, specializations and sectors to sit around a table in a setting where they begin to explore their overlapping needs, interests and resources in novel ways. So let us rethink the work and the tools of public leadership for collaborative settings.

Despite small differences in terminology, there is a remarkable consensus in the fast-growing literature about the nature and dynamics of collaborative processes in the public domain (Chrislip and Larson 1994; Goldsmith and Eggers 2004; Agranoff 2007; Ansell and Gash 2007; O'Leary and Blomgren-Bingham 2009; Goldsmith *et al.* 2010; Linden 2010; Archer and Cameron 2013). Collaboration can be thought of as a multi-stage (Morse and Stephens 2012) and/or cyclical process (see Figure 4.1). Its key currency is trust, and the key dynamic is the process of building (or losing) it. In short, engaging in collaboration implies that the actors that take part in it:

- identify and readily acknowledge their mutual interdependencies with respect to the issue(s) on which they all seek to make progress;
- start and sustain a process of systematic exchange of operational (about 'cases') and strategic (about their respective ways of working and the incentive structures that sustain them) information;
- dedicate themselves to the process of mutual engagement as well as to tangible outcomes that are to be achieved by aligning their actions with respect to the issue(s) at hand;
- discover, develop and negotiate 'rules of engagement' governing the way in which they interact with one another; and
- build and consolidate trust through positive feedback cycles and institutionalization of the collaborative process at the level of the network itself as well as within the routines and value systems of the participating parties.

Collaboration thus defined may develop at the 'front line' of public service delivery, with workers from different agencies moving towards more holistic forms of 'case-managing' complex clients. It may also spring up among departmental silos and baronies within government, which agree to mitigate their perennial infighting over 'turf' (budgets, mandates, autonomy, desirable work, public visibility, issue ownership and so on) and over the thrust of government policy. And it may be of a cross-sectoral kind, as in place-based compacts and agreements between governments and community organizations or public–private partnerships with the business sector. Figure 4.1 provides an overview of the dynamics of trust-building that are at the heart of collaborative processes.

All of this is comparatively easy to model, yet extremely hard to accomplish in practice. The obstacles to effective, institutionalized collaboration across institutional, organizational and professional boundaries are often daunting. This is where 'leadership' comes in. Collaborative leadership – or as it is labelled in Figure 4.1, facilitative leadership – in effect amounts to the art of creating momentum and sidestepping obstacles in the pursuit of joint action between parties that do not normally do so. It involves four distinctive 'chunks' of leadership work

Framing work: defining issues and identifying stakeholders   Going back to the main example at the beginning of this section, the leadership challenge here is to frame obesity in a way that engages – and does not distract, deter or antagonize – what you consider to be all the key stakeholders that would need to be involved for a joint approach to the issue to work. Defining obesity as an issue of personal choice

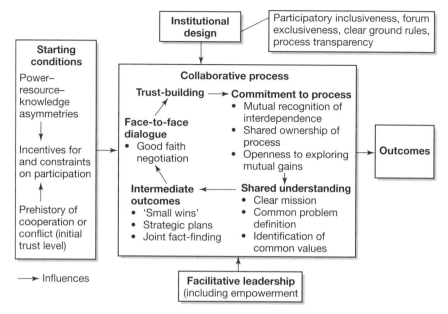

FIGURE 4.1   *The collaborative process*

Source: Ansell and Gash (2007), reprinted by permission.

and self-control obviously leads to a quite different agenda and set of parties around the table than viewing it as family health, food industry or urban design problems, respectively. The trick in framing problems so as to enable collaborative solutions is to think not of issues in terms of linear cause and effect flows but of issues being embedded in and being products of larger social or socio-technical systems (Checkland 1981; Chapman 2002). Doing so allows you to capture the underlying reproductive cycles and the institutional mechanisms that perpetuate the problem you are seeking to address. It also points you towards a much broader range of actors and factors, and more complex causalities, than would otherwise be taken into account. Creative use of systems thinking and a multi-disciplinary orientation to mining and mobilizing research documenting and interpreting the issue are part and parcel of the framing process.

Though framing can seem like a purely intellectual exercise, it has important ramifications: who and what you define 'in' and 'out' of the picture sets the scene for the collaborative effort that is to follow. It scopes the range of the values and interests that will be taken into consideration. The dilemma involved is that between inclusion and exclusion. The basic logic in collaborative work is one of maximum inclusiveness: one does not want to exclude powerful or otherwise important actors and viewpoints at the very start of the process. But for many wicked problems it can be both practically and politically impossible to bring all relevant considerations and stakeholders into a single collaborative frame. The numbers would become unwieldy, the ways of thinking too diverse, and the conflicts of values and interests too daunting. Nothing would get done. Think of the idea of international summits to tackle climate change: for months, years even, the world was led to expect that the 2008 Copenhagen Summit would produce major global policy breakthroughs. The reality of the conference process quickly showed the naivety of that idea. The Summit may have been useful for symbolic purposes and to inch towards progress in some areas, but given its nearly unlimited scope, limited duration yet its masses of state and non-state actors, it was bound to leave the true believers utterly disappointed. But at the heart of the rather predictable disappointment many felt lay an error of framing and scoping what the conference was supposed to achieve in the first place.

Seduction work: enlisting parties to a joint problem-solving process
Getting parties to the table is another sine qua non for collaborative processes to get under way at all. The facilitative leadership role here is twofold. One the one hand, there is a need to create a sense of urgency around the issue. In the example above, the sense of urgency arose as a by-product of media reporting and electoral politics. But it can also occur when pivotal players make a principled stance and commit publicly to addressing a particular tricky problem as a key priority, one for which they are prepared to make themselves accountable. This is what the newly appointed Police Commissioner of the state of Victoria, Australia – Christine Nixon – did when, in one of her first statements to her organization and the public of Victoria, she made it clear that she had three priorities for her leadership, and that one of those would be an issue all but ignored for a long time by Victoria Police but nevertheless was responsible for 40 per cent of all callouts – namely family violence. By doing so, and by appointing one of her most able assistant commissioners to 'fix it', she signalled to her organization that it would no longer be acceptable to treat 'a domestic' as second-rate police work that had to be dispensed with as quickly as possible. Moreover, as the first female police commissioner in the country with a strong record on women's issues in her previous jobs, her commitment was also a strong signal to the Human Services sector within the Victorian government as well as the dozens of not-for-profit women's groups around the state that ran shelters and family protection programmes. The signal she sent was that the police, a key gatekeeping organization when it came to signalling the occurrence of domestic violence, and the only one with a 24/7 around-the-year intervention capacity, was now under fire from their own senior executive to take a hard look at its own values and practices in this domain, and would

now be willing to 'play ball' with other parties to address this massive issue in a more productive way. A Harvard Kennedy School graduate and a devotee of Heifetz's (1994) adaptive leadership terms, Nixon deliberately 'turned up the heat' around the issue, and empowered Leigh Gassner, the designated assistant commissioner, to play a facilitative leadership role *vis-à-vis* the other parties in the domestic violence arena. Gassner went out and met all the stakeholders. These were tough meetings, where the community organizations vented their frustration and anger at the police's ingrained indifference and stereotyped, euphemistic views of what family violence was all about. Gassner, a quiet, soft-spoken man, mainly listened and did not try to defend his organization's record, or explain the legal and procedural constraints preventing it from acting more decisively. And he did not stop at one meeting; he and his team kept coming back for more, demonstrating resolve. By doing so, they won the respect of the community organizations. The police's triple-punch – Nixon's reframing of the problem and the raising of its stakes, followed by Gassner's active, humble, open and persistent outreach, and backed up by Gassner's well-informed and well-connected sidekick – worked: both the community sector and other parts of the Victorian government came to the table. Thus began a long and arduous process of joining the dots in Victoria's family violence response system that would greatly improve the chances of the victims (and to some degree also the perpetrators) of such violence getting the support needed to help them sort out their lives.

The case example highlights two things: the fact that no progress is made in tackling certain difficult problems often has much to do with profound disconnects between the various actors working on the issue; and that getting those parties talking to one another in more intense and productive ways is not something that can be made to happen by fiat. It requires a great deal of thought and a good deal of effort to overcome ingrained intergroup stereotypes, tensions and 'bad vibes'.

Process work: orchestrating and sustaining dialogues   Once participants have been enlisted, the facilitative leadership that is required is not unlike the work that mediators do in getting parties to move from their fixed positions and into new headspaces where working on joint solutions becomes the real focus of the effort rather than defending turf or venting frustrations (Moore 2003). The dilemma here is that really constructive dialogue is unlikely to really happen until the 'venting' has run its course – and that it is all too easy for the parties to stay in their defensive/ aggressive mindsets indefinitely. Leaving the orientation to self-interest and parochial institutional logic behind is intellectually challenging and can be politically risky for parties. It requires a leap of faith. The art of facilitative leadership is to help them make this

BOX 4.3   Managing collaborative processes: key tactics

Motivate participants
Find powerful ways of reminding participants of the stakes involved and of their mutual interdependence in tackling the problems that each of them faces (and seizing the opportunities that each of them discerns) in the issue area that is the focus of the collaborative effort.

Keep the conversation flowing
Orchestrate intensive and sustained communication between participants, but regulate the pace and depth of the interaction with a view to what parties can handle.

Make it possible for participants to 'move' and to 'learn'
Create 'off-line' venues with limited public visibility and constituency pressures, and nudge participants towards putting their established world views and institutional routines 'on hold' to make space for innovative 'objects of joint desire' and jointly designed trials and experiments.

Nudge parties towards shared understandings
Focus participants' minds on jointly formulating their expectations of what the partnership is (and is not) for, and what constitutes success in both the short and longer terms.

Take the time for relationships to build
Don't be in a hurry, be prepared to earn trust, expect setbacks. Collaboration is not a linear process. It is not heroic. If it had been easy to pull off, it would already have been done. It rather resembles the 'slow boring into hard boards' that sociologist Max Weber told us was the essence of political leadership. Trust is fickle. Quick wins may be hard to come by. In some cases, things may seem to get worse before they get better. Also, key individuals representing parties will rotate out of the collaborative process as they change jobs, and their successors may not share their commitment or do not have their clout as they turn up for the meetings.

leap regardless. This requires a high degree of emotional intelligence – understanding, respecting and empathizing with what's on the minds of the various parties – as well as a political nous for the mood of the participants' constituencies and the (im)possibilities for 'movement' this provides. It also requires a mastery of the psychology of multiparty meetings and the creative and timely use of discussion formats, scene-setting, breaks, third-party interventions, what-if explorations and other process management techniques. All these can be mustered to begin and build a process of the parties acquiring a better understanding of one another's positions and ways of working, which the literature suggests is a necessary condition for trust to emerge. Box 4.3

provides some process management techniques that are mentioned time and time again in the literature.

Consolidation work: institutionalizing momentum   Once parties are starting to exchange information and develop joint action, the need for logistical support and co-ordination will increase. At this point it becomes pivotal to persuade the parties to invest in joint support systems that are organized at the level of the partnership itself, rather than continuing to rely on the good offices of individual parties. Ideally, these are jointly funded and jointly staffed secretariats, which not only symbolize shared ownership but also have an exclusive focus (and an institutional self-interest) to keep the collaborative process going. By making sure the various stakeholders in the partnership second competent people to work in such interface units, further knowledge about and momentum for the joint effort will be built up among the partners.

Much of the collaborative governance literature is filled with good practice cases and exhortations to do the right thing. However, collaboration practice is often frustrating and fragile, as it not only takes two but in fact *all* parties in the process to tango. Not infrequently, some of those parties cannot or will not engage productively. Some will say they do, but then shy away from committing. Some will pay lip service to the process, but then actively work to undermine it. Some participants are personally genuinely committed but fail to deliver their more sceptical constituencies. It is useful to be alert to some of the key ways in which 'anti-collaborative leadership' might operate. These include:

- going through the motions: treating the process as a purely symbolic exercise;
- boxing collaboration in from the outset: restricting the mandate of one's delegates to the collaborative process;
- playing 'small-p' politics: engaging in blame games, leaking, flaunting one's veto power, breaking commitments; and
- exhausting momentum: abstaining from or actively impeding partnership capacity-building efforts.

Whose leadership?

Who can exercise collaborative leadership? The really radical answer is: just about anybody or any group who feels strongly committed to making real progress on complex issues that can only be tackled effectively if multiple actors co-ordinate their efforts better. Since in a formal, hierarchical sense 'no one is in charge' in network settings, there is no single natural authority figure that all actors look to for leadership. Moreover, there is inevitable conflict to be had, orchestrated, and made to work productively rather than destructively (Burns 2003: 186–98). In the obesity case, for example, the food or fitness industries, or even a great many morbidly overweight people themselves, would not necessarily expect the new government and its health minister to take ownership of the problem – and some might in fact actively resist it, depending on their perceptions of the issue, its causes, its ramifications and their own roles and responsibilities in it. In reality, it goes without saying that some actors are better positioned than others to exercise what Neustadt (1960) once so aptly called 'the power to convene' that is so crucial to facilitating effective conflict management and nurturing collaborative processes. Having the power to convene means that when you try to get a conversation going, other actors are unlikely to snub you in this effort. The US president, about which Neustadt was writing when he coined this phrase, constitutionally has relatively little scope for decisive, unilateral action outside the security policy realm. Presidents, operating in a system of divided government, need to build social and political coalitions for every major policy initiative they undertake. They cannot take the voting in both Senate and House of Representatives for granted. But what they do have is the moral authority of the office combined with their every move being covered intensively by the mass media. When the president invites you over for a 'summit' or some other multi-party forum, you go. It is as simple as that. Snubbing presidential invitations to at least talk is not something that even their most ardent opponents can persistently do without running the risk of being effectively stigmatized as being unhelpful, unresponsive, negative or self-serving.

But the convening work at the heart of collaborative leadership can also be undertaken by less formidable actors, who may not hold high office but have other things going for them that make other actors stop, listen and respond to them. These would be actors who:

- have a central and long-standing involvement in the issue;
- play a big part in the 'on the ground' delivery of policies and programmes in the issue area;
- possess or be able to mobilize resources that are vital for addressing the issue; or
- have strong moral or political capital *vis-à-vis* the issue.

According to the research, much collaborative leadership is actually exercised at the ground level, by passionate front-line workers or their supervisors, who see and feel on a day-to-day basis the limitations of conventional silo-like and bureaucratized approaches to complex issues. And, like all other forms of public leadership discussed in this book, it will often be exercised not by the single impassioned and self-appointed facilitator/mediator but by an informal 'tag team' approach

TABLE 4.1   *Fostering collaboration: political, administrative and civic leadership roles*

Political leaders	Administrative leaders	Civic leaders
Providing direction Articulating or supporting the ambition and the strategic vision underpinning the collaborative effort	*Removing roadblocks* Overcoming ingrained departmentalism and turf-war mentalities within own and other public service organizations, and reverse the onus of argument in favour of holistic approaches	*Harnessing expertise* Collating and amplifying grass-roots practical knowledge about how the system (really) works now and how it might work in the future
Relinquishing control Resisting the temptation to risk-manage the process and content of collaborative efforts		*Overcoming constituency reluctance* Show the need to 'dance with the devil', and show how it is done (that is, doing business with governments and corporations) to achieve genuine partnership
Buying time Taking a long-term view of the process and not distorting it with ad hoc, short-term interventions	*Empowering experts* Picking skilled subordinates and providing them with a mandate for experimentation with innovative, joined-up modes of policy development and programme delivery	
Providing cover Taking political responsibility for collaborative processes even when they are not (yet) producing concrete results	*Building capacity* Forging one's own organization's 'capacity to deliver' its part of the joined-up approach and freeing up resources for a network support unit	*Organizing representation* Arranging participation in the network of credible representation of the relevant clusters of community sector organizations

between different players each doing his or her share of the leadership work that is required. This was certainly the case of the transformation of the approach to family violence in Victoria, Australia, where Nixon and later Gassner were the ones exercising the initial power to convene, but where a good deal of the other leadership work was performed by Gassner's two very able off-siders, other Victorian government bureaucrats, and key platforms.

As important as institutional background and 'clout' with other parties is the skill set and 'value added' that collaborative leaders bring to the table. Table 4.1 suggests that political, public service and civil society leaders each have distinctive roles to play. For all of them, engaging in collaborative ventures constitutes a break with their own 'business as usual'. Politicians have to give up the role of 'deciders', who set directions at the outset and reserve the right to chart their own course when the 'crunch' comes of making authoritative policy decisions. Bureaucrats have to give up on being 'in control of the process'.

In the words of one highly experienced civil servant in this domain: 'Genuine collaboration ... requires public servants who, with eyes wide open, can exert the qualities of leadership necessary to forsake the simplicity of control for the complexity of influence ... [T]hey need to operate outside the traditionally narrow framework of government, which they have for so long worked within' (Shergold 2008: 21). Finally, civic leaders have to overcome their own and their constituents' reluctance to 'do business' with governmental and corporate actors whose values and modus operandi they and their constituents routinely spend a good deal of time and energy roundly criticizing, if not demonizing.

The message is clear: collaboration is not a panacea. It is a leadership domain whose operative principles remain to be studied systematically despite the ready availability of countless handbooks telling one how to do it and what personal competencies are required to be an effective collaborator (Linden 2010; Williams 2012). They make it sound easy. But in reality it is hard. It is not a quick route to 'doing more with less'. It is not a form of governing as a love-in; it rather resembles an orchestrated clash of personalities, styles and cultures. It is never a quick fix, and much more likely to be a long, hard slog whose gratifications are often delivered only over time – way past the next election, for example. To undertake it seriously requires unusual levels of wisdom, drive, an appetite for risk and persistence in the face of imperfection. But if we are serious about doing more than offering fragmented, patchwork, ineffective and inefficient responses to some of the most pressing challenges facing our societies, have we got any alternative?

Chapter 5

Leading in Context

Australian prime minister, John Howard (1996–2007), learnt the hard way that time and timing are crucial in achieving and exercising public leadership. He became leader of the Liberal Party at a time when it was internally divided, and much of the country rallied behind the popular Labor prime minister, Bob Hawke. Howard lost the first major elections under his leadership, and paid the price. He spent years in the political wilderness as a shadowy presence in the shadow cabinet, now run by his main rival. But Howard possessed a deep belief in his own capability to lead and an insatiable appetite for power. Riding out the rebuffs and derision, he never considered quitting. Instead, he waited in the wings. He never stopped campaigning, rebuilding connections with the grass roots and the party organization.

'The times will suit me,' he had said, characteristically, back in 1986, fresh into what would prove to be a disastrous first run as Liberal party leader, which ended in 1989. And yet he was proven right in the end. After years of working in the background, his gamble began to pay off. His immediate successors faltered, and his leadership rivals made mistakes. When the Labor government eventually ran out of steam, he knew he had a fighting chance. He regained the party leadership and achieved his coveted goal: to become the popularly elected prime minister of his country. He won four consecutive elections and remained prime minister for 11.5 years. Howard was a great waiter and a great opportunist, holding off on controversial moves in areas such as refugee policy and indigenous affairs until a triggering event came along that provided the sense of urgency and increased public acceptance of controversial reforms. Ironically, the one time he jumped the gun was when he had the legislative numbers in both houses of parliament to pass his long-coveted workplace reforms. It became the beginning of his political undoing, ending in ignominious defeat for his party and himself at the 2007 elections. His time had come, and gone. He had understood the first marker, and ignored the second. His reputation as a leader suffered as a result.

The moral of the story? Context matters for leadership. The backdrop against which they operate enables and constrains the ability of leaders to perform their roles. Conversely, sometimes leaders are able to mould parts of the context in which they and their successors find themselves. Reaching their historical moment and grasping the imperatives of the situation at hand are surely among the chief arts of leadership. They shape leaders' abilities to consummate the authority associated with these roles. When to push ideas, wage battles, confront or ignore opponents, address or neglect problems: considerations of need, opportunity, timing and momentum are crucial to leadership. Temporal dynamics such as the daily news cycle, the three- or four-year electoral process, and the more opaque and disputed recurrent 'tides' of public opinion and 'party realignment' are pivotal in shaping the considerations and behaviour of most actors. Given their importance in structuring public life, anticipating, using and perhaps even modifying the parameters of such cycles and the 'windows of opportunity' they present, constitute important avenues for exercising leadership (Kingdon 1984).

Some leaders are arguably simply better than others at grasping and using this importance of context. But that is not the end of the story. Every political system has had its share of politicians who were highly successful in one leadership role yet failed in another. Think of Jimmy Carter as a successful governor of Georgia, then a struggling and ultimately largely ineffective president, and then as a widely respected post-presidential peacemaker; or of Barack Obama, the highly charismatic campaigner of 2008 and the hemmed-in president whose pragmatism disappointed his erstwhile followers and failed to placate his Republican opponents.

There are also plenty of leaders whose effectiveness varied even within one and the same role, depending on the issue area or moment in which they intervened. German chancellor Helmut Kohl is a prime example of this: in the autumn of 1989, after seven years in the job, he seemed destined for a quiet life after two terms of domestic policy stasis; but after the collapse of the Berlin Wall in November of that year, he displayed hitherto unsuspected international statesmanship to secure the unification of Germany while simultaneously binding it closely to the European Union and in the process prolonged his hold on the office for another two terms (Zelikow with Rice 1995).

There is an entire cohort of government leaders who had the bad luck to be in office when the second oil shock and stagflation of the late 1970s happened. They ended up being booted out of office ignominiously, as none of them – whether they were from the left or the right – were quick enough on their feet to abandon the Keynesian paradigm of economic management they had all been socialized into accepting as the policy orthodoxy. It took their predicament of policy paralysis and deep fiscal crisis to bring to power an alternative set of leaders who were not bound by these conventions, and who eventually became epoch-making reformers (for example, Thatcher and Reagan; Hawke and Keating in Australia; Lange and Douglas in New Zealand).

These examples clearly suggest that even astute leaders are able to act in tune with their context only to some extent and only some of the time. What students and practitioners of public leadership alike need to know is *when and how* contexts shape leadership possibilities, and, conversely, when and how leaders are able to mould the contexts in which they operate. Going back as far as Plato's philosopher-king and Plutarch's *Lives of the Noble Greeks and Romans*, leaders have long been portrayed as 'heroes in history' (Hook 1943). The hero, however, has two faces: the wise, resourceful and tenacious individual who overcomes great odds to put his or her stamp on history (dubbed the 'event-making' leader by Hook), but also the tragic figure facing overwhelming forces stacked against him/her which at best limit him/her to a role as a 'trend follower' and at worst condemn him/her to the dustbin of history ('eventful' leaders, according to Hook). The 'event-making' hero type has been the subject of centuries of biography and hagiography, a robust and lucrative – people like to read about 'heroes' – tradition which continues to this day. Its traditional preoccupation with the drives, character, skills and deeds of the leaders in question, however, all too often seduces scholars of the genre into person-centric, reductionist accounts of complex historical processes.

Even early Greek writers were aware of this, and in their tragedies explored the opposite end of the spectrum, depicting would-be heroic leaders either prospering or perishing at the whim of the gods in the Pantheon. This emphasis on external factors – natural and metaphysical forces – prevailing over human volition was echoed in Christian historiography and political theory. In Augustine's theology, for example, the outcome of the central, history-shaping conflict between the City of Man (dominated by earthly politics) and the City of God (based on submission to the will of God) is preordained: the latter is bound to win.

Eventually, Machiavelli found a formula for folding the two opposing perspectives into one neat formula. He saw all of human life and history as being determined by only two forces: *virtu* (competent statecraft, or in today's parlance 'good leadership') and *fortuna* (chance, or, in other words, contextual influences). If leaders lacked the will or the competence to display statecraft, human affairs would be fully controlled by fate. Truly competent leaders should be able to tame fate considerably through effective foresight and robust pre-emptive action. He ends *The Prince* with a now notorious analogy: 'Fortune is a woman, and if she is to be submissive it is necessary to beat and coerce her' (*The Prince*, book XXV). Yet Machiavelli conceded that even the most competent rulers could perhaps only control half of their own fate and that of their subjects. So even the most competent rulers still need a degree of 'luck' to go down in history as successful leaders. Likewise, the potential impact of malevolent and incompetent leaders is partly shaped by circumstances (Lipman-Blumen 2006). In today's parlance: 'it depends' (Goodin and Tilly 2006).

Contingency approaches to leadership

Moving into twentieth-century scholarship, the person–context nexus was tackled most explicitly in organizational theory, which has seen various classic 'situational' and 'contingency' approaches become part of its staple diet of theories reviewed in all its textbooks (for example, Northouse 2009). Classic situational and contingency theories within the field of leadership studies all grapple with the issue of *which* matters most and *when*. Most scholars tend to come out on the deterministic end: situations shape leadership opportunities more than leaders are able to improve the odds of their success. Fiedler's (1967) classic model of leadership effectiveness, for example, surmises that a leader's orientation towards task accomplishment versus maintaining positive relationships with co-workers is more or less fixed. Therefore, particular types of situations – defined by low–high scores on their position power over others, structure of the task at hand, and the prevailing climate of leader–subordinate relationships – favour or disfavour leaders. The best prospects exist when leaders are 'in control', the task at hand is straightforward and they enjoy positive relationships with their team members; and the worst prospects when the reverse conditions apply. If one leader's orientation profile does not 'fit' the characteristics of the situation, failure is all but inevitable – unless, of course, the leader manages to influence one or more of the three context parameters in a game-changing manner. Fiedler was never really able to explain why he observed these correlations in the many studies he conducted, but this did not stop him from coming out with a strong prescriptive approach.

House (1996) sought to improve on Fiedler by adopting a more flexible approach. He allowed for the possibility that, despite each person having a preferred style type, individuals are actually able to display a range of different leadership behaviours, which they can vary according to their perceptions of the requirements of the situation. He also added follower characteristics (for example, their ability level, attitude towards authority, and need for affiliation, as well as for structure and their locus of control) to the 'variables soup'. Leaders in House's path–goal theory thus have to be masterful readers of multiple layers of context (task, authority, relationships, follower characteristics), and have the ability to rise above their own personality make-up to continuously adjust their leadership style to fit the exigencies of the context as they interpret it. That is a very big demand, and well beyond the grasp of most ordinary mortals (robustly testing such a complex, multivariate construct has – not surprisingly – proved elusive).

The elegance of contingency models of leadership bears the promise of clarity and of clear-cut 'if..., then...' analytical linkages and behavioural imperatives – stated with some provisos but nevertheless often worded strongly enough to be easily mistaken for contextual determinism. Such a stance is methodologically deeply problematic, and encourages a rush towards prescription that is likely to set itself up for disappointment. To contemporary students of organizations, management and leadership, their neat efforts at 'if..., then...' matching of types of contexts to leadership styles feels somewhat quaint and too good to be true. This has not stopped dozens of self-help books on leadership propagating their own idiosyncratic versions of contingency models, many of which stake their mostly prescriptive claims on limited empirical evidence; virtually none of them explicitly address political leadership.

Adopting a largely similar analytical strategy, a wide range of studies across a variety of disciplines emphasize variability in the properties of 'problems at hand' facing a particular government, policy sector or organization. This literature offers typologies based on, for example, the degree of complexity, ambiguity, controversiality, volatility and 'wickedness' of the issues and circumstances facing policy-makers and managers (Thompson and Tuden 1959; Lowi 1972; Hickson *et al.* 1986; Pfeffer and Salancik 2003; Grint 2010) and argues that they set different types of challenges for leaders and policy-makers. Much of this literature is quite prescriptive, either explicitly or in its implications: if leaders do not grasp the kinds of problem with which they are struggling and adjust their modes of problem-solving accordingly, things do not get done and they risk compromising their effectiveness and their positions.

Regardless of its determinism, an extraordinarily helpful specimen of such a problem-centred typological approach to leadership analysis is Ronald Heifetz's (1994) work on adaptive leadership. It is premised on the contrast between 'technical' and 'adaptive' challenges facing a group. Technical challenges are those where the nature of the problem is agreed upon, and potential solutions to it are well honed and uncontroversial, if still difficult to achieve in a practical sense. Think of dealing with an imminent risk of flooding after heavy rainfall, or of tackling a growing demand for public transport in a particular region. Adaptive challenges, in contrast, exist in contexts where there is fundamental uncertainty and lack of agreement about the nature of the problems as well as about ways to address the problems. In his 1994 book, Heifetz uses micro settings, such as patients of whom it is discovered that their illness is going to be fatal, as well as macro settings such as race relations in the USA in the 1960s. Today's adaptive challenges would include the debt crisis, climate change, ageing populations and mass migration.

In dealing with a technical challenges, Heifetz argues, leaders can basically do what is expected of them, namely to provide the protection, direction and order needed to mobilize people to take up and implement the optimal approach of dealing with the challenge at hand. Leaders lead from the front, develop the vision, sketch a road map, and persuade others to follow. The same approach will go nowhere when applied to an adaptive challenge. It would only reinforce what Heifetz calls 'inappropriate dependencies' from the community *vis-à-vis* the leader, which will turn ugly when it becomes clear that the leader does not really know either, or advocates a particular definition of the issue disputed by others. Adaptive leadership therefore amounts to giving the work of change back to the group, instead of falling into the trap of prescription from on high. It amounts to training people's attention towards to the conditions at hand, closing off all the escape routes, and providing an environment that persuades people to engage with the real issues and underlying differences.

Institutional rules as context

In a parallel universe, the so-called 'old' institutionalism in political science (Finer 1970; Rhodes *et al.* 2006) has long focused on describing and interpreting the formal architecture of party systems, electoral systems, executive government, executive–legislative relations and judicial review. This has, *inter alia*, yielded an interest in penetrating the way that these institutional parameters in various jurisdictions shape, and are being interpreted by, individual office-holders. This has resulted in a wealth of studies on party leaders, presidents, prime ministers, legislators, public servants and constitutional courts as political actors, exercising leadership under different institutional conditions by navigating and renegotiating the institutionalized expectations of their roles (Cooper and Brady 1981; Weller 1985, 2007; Blondel 1987; Peters 1990; Elgie 1995; Bevir and Rhodes 2003; Helms 2005; Rhodes *et al.* 2009; Rhodes 2011; Heppell 2012).

One strand of research in this vein examines the role of political party rules for selecting and ejecting leaders. Given the key role of party leaders in an era of growing 'personalization' of politics and voting, a range of scholars have begun to study the manner in which leaders are selected. Generally, parties have changed their rules since the 1990s, with the ostensible aim of increasing the influence attributed to rank-and-file party members at the expense of party elites and particularly the parliamentary party. The question is: do such rules and rule changes matter at all regarding who become leaders and how those leaders are able to operate?

The resulting body of studies examining the consequences of these rule changes comprised a range of in-depth case studies of individual parties over time as well as comparative and cross-national case studies covering a wide range of parties and large numbers of succession episodes (Heppell 2008; Laing and 't Hart 2011; Cross and Blais 2012; Quinn 2012). Its conclusions show that the longevity of party leaders as well as their relative autonomy in shaping their party's policy and strategy varies significantly depending on the kind of selection and removal regime they happen to encounter. Cross and Blais (2011: 147) observe:

> While the threat of removal by the extra parliamentary party has resulted in leaders leaving office, the difficulty in organizing this large and dispersed group, and the time involved in doing so, provides leaders with significantly more security than when the parliamentary caucus can depose them. Those removable by their parliamentary colleagues are the most vulnerable.

On balance, therefore, research into the effects of changes in party rules on leadership authority ultimately underpins Mair's (1994) hunch that, paradoxically, widening the selectorate has tended to strengthen the hand of party leaders, made them less accountable to their colleagues in the party room and the party hierarchy, and made them better placed to hold on to the top spot for a long time – as long as they nurture the mandate given to them directly by the rank and file members of the party.

The arrival on the scene of the so-called 'new institutionalism' in the1980s sparked a resurgence of attention for the rules of the political game – not just formal–legal but also normative–cultural and rational–tactical ones (March and Olsen 1989; Scharpf 1997; Peters 2005). Thus understood, such rules of the game are contextual in that they act as incentive structures constraining some and enabling other policy preferences and behaviours on the part of political actors. Studies in this mould find that contexts can be quite overbearing, limiting the scope for ambitious leadership. They tend to stress the prevalence of policy continuity as a result of 'path dependence' and 'inheritance' (for example, Rose and Davies 1994; Pierson 2004), and suggest that change occurs incrementally (Kay 2006; Mahoney and Thelen 2010). Others engage in a more culture-focused form of contextual determinism, arguing that the shared mindsets of the communities propel political leaders towards particular styles of leadership (Wildavsky 1984, 1989).

In its valiant attempts to capture the dynamic interplay between structure and agency, neo-institutionalism has, however, also sparked investigations of how and why certain leaders are capable of forging and sustaining non-incremental policy change, instigating institutional reforms (Moon 1995; Goldfinch and 't Hart 2003). To firm believers in the power of context and structure, findings such as these may appear somewhat startling, highlighting as they do the 'exogenous interventions of imaginative individuals' (Aldrich and Shepsle 2000: 41). To others, they are the very essence of political agency, in proud Machiavellian fashion: 'structuring the world so you can win' (Riker 1986: ix). Yet others sensibly return to the middle ground, asserting that leadership in politics matters but that it inevitably occurs 'in context', and that students of leadership therefore need to encompass both contextual and individual factors in their research designs without a priori according more weight to one or the other (Hargrove and Owens 2003).

Time as context

Most of us think about time as a *linear* sequence of past, present and future. The past is the realm of what once was and what took place. We access it by use of our memory, and conjure up images, stories and artefacts to evoke it. The present is the realm of the now: our lives and those of others as they unfold in the moment and at the moment. The future is the realm of expectations, of things that we know, hope, fear or guess might happen later. And we see them as connected: we act in the present, but we do so guided by our interpretations of the past and our expectations of the future.

Much of our personal and public life is organized around these distinctions. We save money now so that we have something to fall back on later. We plan. We 'factor in' or 'discount' parts of the future in the decisions we make now – about how to eat, exercise, where to live, what to study, which employment to seek. In most of this, we imagine life as a sequence of scripted stages: childhood, adolescence, adulthood, old age. We design public policies and institutions based on these distinctions, taking into account the relative size of the populations that will be living in one of these stages at various points in the future, for example.

Likewise, societies make organized efforts to remember – and forget – particular parts of their pasts in ways that suit their present-day needs and values. Recording, recounting and interpreting past performance has become part and parcel of life in public organizations, largely because of deeply held beliefs that doing so will enable them to perform better in the future. Organized forms of looking back come in many guises, such as evaluation, accountability, performance management or benchmarking. However, their driving assumptions and public justifications are largely the same, namely that thinking about the past helps us to modify our present arrangements and behaviour in order to achieve better outcomes further down the line.

The linear view of time, omnipresent though it is, does not exhaust all possibilities. Its chief alternative is the idea of *cyclical* time. Instead of thinking of time as a progression of finite (as in human life) or potentially unending (cosmological time) events and stages, the cyclical view stresses the idea of recurrence. Instead of stages, we talk about sequences: things still come and go, but they eventually come again, in an identical or highly similar form. Think of clock time, calendar time and nature's seasons. If we dig beneath the surface of the dominant linear script of how a human life unfolds, elements of circularity emerge: hormonal cycles, mood swings, the ups and downs in long-term intimate relationships. The same applies to social life. The ups and downs of economies as captured in the idea of 'business cycles' or 'waves' of alternating periods of economic buoyancy and sluggishness.

Many institutions in public life have been created explicitly around the idea of circularity. In the world of organizations and policy, budget, planning and reporting cycles stand out. In human resource management, there are periodic performance reviews and promotion rounds. In political life, the electoral and the daily news cycle are pivotal in shaping the considerations and behaviours of most actors. Given their importance in structuring public life, anticipating, using and perhaps even modifying the parameters of such cycles constitute important avenues for exercising leadership.

The third pivotal view of time is yet again different in that it dispenses with the idea of order, clarity and predictability that is present in the linear and the cyclical views. In the linear view we may not know precisely how long a particular phase will last, but we have the certainty that it will come to end at some point, never to return, and will morph into another. In the cyclical view we may not always know the precise duration of any particular sequence, but we know for sure that once it passes it will come again when the cycle repeats itself or the pendulum swings back again. The third view emphasizes *randomness*. Instead of order, chance rules. Instead of phases or sequences we have punctuations. Periods of relative stability are disrupted by 'events': surprises, shocks, big bangs, black swans. Things speed up during those periods. The pace of events seems to feed on itself, defying attempts of human or corporate actors to understand let alone contain it, and yet for that very reason at the same time handing the same actors major opportunities for reflection, change and innovation.

Even the random view of time can to some extent serve as a principle for regulating our lives. Luke Rinehart's famous novel *The Dice Man* depicts a bored psychiatrist who has made the decision to subject himself to randomness: when he faces a choice of whatever kind – from the mundane to the profound – he assigns alternative course of action to each of the numbers of the dice, rolls it, and lives with the consequences. This radically reduces the predictability of his behaviour, and, not surprisingly, lands him in a good deal of trouble with family, friends and peers alike. In contrast, the much admired ideal type of the

TABLE 5.1   *Types of time and their leadership implications*

	Time unfolds in...	Examples in the world of governance	Leadership virtues	Leader ideal types
Linear time	...progressive phases	Working days/weeks Scenarios Strategic plans Term limits	Memory Foresight Vision	Pioneer
Cyclical time	...recurrent stages	News cycle Budget cycle Electoral cycle Economic cycle	Anticipation Timing Endurance	Tactician
Randomized time	...bursts and lulls	Disasters/accidents Scandals/fiascos Elite rotation/ removal	Patience Preparedness Opportunism	Entrepreneur

Source: Adapted from 't Hart (2011a).

entrepreneur is fundamentally premised on the idea of time as randomness, the key entrepreneurial skill being the ability to both identify and exploit opportunities for profit or value creation when they come (and go), preferably before others do so.

In the world of public policy, the so-called public entrepreneur ideal type of leadership is much the same. Predicated on the idea that the world of policy and politics is fundamentally unpredictable, exercising leadership in order to transform public policies or grow public organizations becomes a matter of calculated opportunism. It is all about patience (not wasting energy and capital when the time is not ripe), preparedness (nurturing policy ideas and networks of like-minded actors so as to have a story and a coalition to back it up in case opportunities present themselves) and opportunism (moving into overdrive to forge policy change when events happen that allow the entrepreneur to connect ideas, actors and resources in ways that were hitherto impossible and may soon become infeasible again).

Table 5.1 summarizes the argument so far. Clearly, the three forms of time co-exist in the public sphere. They exist objectively, in the sense that clock time is omnipresent, many public institutions have established cycles in their governance arrangements, and shocks do happen unpredictably yet potentially consequentially from time to time. They also exist subjectively as social time, e.g. individual and shared beliefs about time. The latter implies that leaders and groups can and do vary in the conceptions of time they hold and upon which they base their behaviour.

These are unlikely to be simple either/or choices. It is more likely to be a matter of primary and secondary emphases. Hence, some public leaders are drawn most strongly towards 'the vision thing', a long-term view of where society is coming from and in which direction they want it to move. Yet many of them will be astute enough to realize that the struggle to turn vision into reality will partly take place in the context of the predictable rhythms of institutional cycles that shape the constellation of actors, resources, and authority with which they have to work. Likewise, the classical politician whose mindset is dominated by the news and electoral cycles may well realize the disruptive power of unscheduled contingencies. British prime minister Harold Macmillan, for example, famously observed to a journalist that 'events, dear boy, events' were the main forces thwarting his best-laid plans. And the essentially opportunistic entrepreneur, while being fundamentally attuned to the chaotic nature of political life, will still observe the realities of budgetary and policy cycles and try to turn those to their advantage too. It is therefore the mix of temporal beliefs and practices that matters in shaping leadership styles.

Moving beyond types of time, it is important to acknowledge two further crucial dimensions of social time, each of which also can be thought of in objective and subjective terms. The first of these is the *time horizon*. We can 'cut' histories and futures into slices of differing sizes. In linear terms, we may look back at events that occurred months, years, decades and centuries, all the way up to millions of years ago; and look forward on similarly varying time scales. Subjectively, historians typically offer different ways of narrating and interpreting the past, with disagreements about periodicity – did the country turn a corner and enter a new phase at time x or y? – being clearly a function not so much of the historical record but of their mental maps of what should be counted as important and less important benchmarks in the temporal trajectories of social systems.

In cyclical terms, the loops of the daily news cycle are extremely narrow, whereas economic cycles are measured in decades. Even within one type of cycle, key design differences can matter greatly. Market analysts are, for example, keen to track the economic implications of political systems that operate on three-year compared to four-year election cycles, and between systems that have fixed election dates compared to those where incumbent governments have the scope to choose election dates (Alesina and Roubini, with Cohen 1997). Students of international conflict likewise have found that 'aggressive behaviour is much more likely the further the leader is away from a possible election. As the election draws closer, the public's ability to constrain the leader increases, which induces pacifism in the leader. This dynamic is stronger in endogenous election systems, when the degree of public constraint is even higher than in fixed electoral systems (Williams 2007).

In terms of randomized time, the shape of 'punctuated equilibriums' may vary. Punctuated equilibrium (PE) refers to a mode of evolution of physical and social systems in which periods of relative stability are fundamentally disrupted by unpredicted and uncontrollable contingencies, which require actors to make adaptive leaps and forge some new equilibrium. PEs contemplated by observers and practitioners of public policy typically encompass a few decades at most, whereas paleontologists, seismologists and climate change scientists are keenly observing 'big bangs', stagnation and periods of incremental change on a wholly different time scale. To make politicians and bureaucrats see the relevance of thinking about environmental, energy and disaster preparedness policies in those terms has proved to be a key challenge for researchers in these professions.

The other dimension of social time that is crucially important for understanding public leadership is the so-called *ontological status* of time. How 'real' and how 'immutable' is time (Lauer 1981; Adam 1990)? One way to answer this question is to see time as a constraint: it is there, and we have to live with it. Whether in ordered (time as a constant) or more random (time as a contingency) fashion, things happen. Once they do so, they create a new reality, a new balance of forces that actors have to come to terms with, interpret and 'factor in' when deciding what to do next. The notions of 'organizational learning' and 'path dependency' are a clear illustration of this objectivist take on time. The former is premised on the idea that institutional actors can document, remember and draw policy inferences from their own as well as other pasts. If they do so sensibly, they will be more likely to devise better policies and practices for the future; yet if they opportunistically forget, distort or exaggerate lessons of the past, they set themselves up for failure when moving forward (Neustadt and May 1986; Brändström *et al.* 2004). At the heart of path dependency thinking lies the observation that social processes can become self-reinforcing, making reversals of events or past choices made by actors very difficult. Therefore, the specifics of timing and sequencing decisions or actions matter for the way in which public organizations and policies evolve over time. Through processes of stickiness (growing thresholds for reversing past decisions), social learning and amplification, large consequences may result from relatively small or contingent events (Lindblom 1979; Pierson 2004: 18). The entire structure and size of the state, and the nature of state–society relationships in different countries are cases in point.

The other main way to answer the question is to see time as a social construction, with not a physical but a mental phenomenon at its core. Time is what we make of it. In this view, politicians need not be slaves of the 24-hour news cycles, periodic opinion polls or the latest crisis – all factors known to induce a collapse of time horizons in makers of public policy. They always have a choice of time horizons. They can organize against the dominance of short-termism by making sure they have persistent inputs from institutions and advisers committed to longer time horizons. They can always model themselves on Zhou Enlai and take a very long-term perspective on things. He famously replied 'too early to tell' when asked for his view of the effects of the French revolution – but then again he ruled over a China without a free press or opinion polls.

Moreover, they have choices in how to structure the very temporal architecture of their professional lives. The higher up the hierarchy, the greater the ability to impose time frames on others, and to reset institutional calendars (though not unlimitedly so; within government many of the crucial temporal parameters are embedded in laws and even constitutions). As Goetz (2009: 187, citing Schmitter and Santiso 1998: 71) observes, decision-makers can 'learn how to manipulate time, that is, to turn it from an inexorably limited, linear and perishable constraint into something that could be scheduled, anticipated, delayed, accelerated, deadlined, circumvented, prolonged, deferred, compressed, parcelled out, standardized, diversified, staged, staggered, and even wasted'. Leaders can make time work for them; for example, by using delaying mechanisms such as inquiries and consultations in order to orchestrate 'crunch time' around sensitive public issues in such a way as to fit their political calendars. Likewise, in relatively new and still developing polities such as the European Union (EU), a fixed temporal order has not yet fully taken hold, and temporal considerations are therefore an integral part of ongoing institutional design and reform discussions (Ekengren 2002; Dyson 2009; Meyer-Sahling and Goetz 2009).

Time, in other words, can be seen as weighing in upon leaders, but also as a set of levers for exercising leadership. Pollitt (2008: 142) even talks about this in terms of a 'toolkit for time'. While conventional historians may abhor the very idea of instrumentalizing time in such a crude fashion, practitioners of public management and policy will recognize it instantly. For them, the difference between things going well and things being in crisis is defined by the very difference in the status and relative power of time. In times of 'business as usual', leaders 'own the time' whereas in crises 'time owns the leader' (Docters van Leeuwen 1990).

Placing leadership in time

In the world of government, leaders' fates are determined to a significant extent by their placement in what has been called *political time*. Political time refers to the ebb and flow of regimes: sets of basic values,

TABLE 5.2 *Leadership challenges as a function of political time*

Regime viability	*Ascending/High*	*Declining/Low*
Leader commitment to regime		
High	*Articulation*: Regime elaboration	*Preservation*: Regime reconstruction
Low	*Pre-emption*: Regime destruction	*Innovation*: Regime replacement

Source: Adapted from 't Hart (2011a).

ideas and policy propensities around which the polity and its governance are organized. Regimes are equivalent to paradigms in the world of science; adhering to a set of basic premises and commitments means buying into a whole range of derivative theories/policies. Paradigms and regimes both persevere as long as they are widely thought to possess problem-solving capacities. This is the case for as long as a dominant coalition of actors remains committed to tackling new challenges (thrown up by contextual changes or discrepant observations) with the paradigm's or regime's tools. Over time, as challenges accumulate and nagging crises stretch and outpace the adaptive capacity of the regime, support for it declines and the case for regime change becomes more compelling. A death struggle ensues, and sooner or later a new dominant coalition is formed around an alternative regime. The cycle then repeats itself.

The cycle is there, but it is not a mechanical process. At any stage of this developmental process, the actors in the system – be they scholars or in our case politicians and other key public stakeholders – have a fundamental choice to make: do they believe in, support and therefore seek to perpetuate the paradigm of the day, or do they wish to see it replaced with an alternative set of ideas and arrangements? The shape of the life cycle of regimes as well as the selection of their eventual successor also depends on the constellation of these choices, the skills and resources of the actors lined up on both sides of the argument, and the dynamics of the broader environment in which the regime operates.

Combining these two fundamental dimensions, US political scientist Stephen Skowronek (1993, 2008) developed a powerful theory of presidential leadership, which I suggest can usefully be modified to understand public leadership more widely across a broad range of other political systems and public policy domains. It is depicted in modified form in Table 5.2. Political time in the table is constituted by the pendulum movement along the horizontal axis of regime viability, i.e. its perceived problem-solving capacity. Both the key challenges leaders face and the authority they enjoy are determined by their placement in the two-dimensional space.

Let us begin with *articulation* leadership. This refers to a type of leader who is committed to the current regime, and who takes office at a time in which this regime is in the ascendant. The leader's fundamental challenge is to use this propitious alignment of forces to firmly institutionalize the regime in norms, customs, regulations, agencies and programmes. Such leaders are likely to enjoy broad support, as long as they convince the dominant coalition to which they belong that their proposed course of action serve this underlying purpose. Their job is to bolster the regime, to broaden the base, and to deepen its roots in the fabric of society to make it as difficult to reverse as possible. The key risk these leaders run is that of overstretch: to try to get the regime do more work than it can. It is one thing, for example, to use Keynesian economics to curb the fiscal and social effects of the economic business cycle (as Franklin D. Roosevelt did), but it is quite a few steps further to then use its key instrument of government-led spending programmes to address other types of social problems apart from economic boom/bust cycles (as his political relative Lyndon Johnson attempted to do with his Great Society programmes combating poverty, urban degradation and racial inequality). The latter amounts to taking a tested formula into unknown territory, one that has proved to be considerably less amenable to yielding benign and controllable multiplier effects. Articulating leaders who push their luck may end up being routed as megalomaniac, hubristic or overly idealistic.

The main challenge of *preservation* leadership is to rescue a regime that has begun to run into serious headwinds. Leaders of this category need to come to terms with the paradox of dynamic conservatism (Schon 1971), that in order to preserve the regime, some of its subsidiary ideas, policies and programmes need to be adapted to changing circumstances and to placate a growing number of sceptics and challengers. An example of this is the field of drug policy. Countries such as the Netherlands as well sub-national governments in Switzerland, France and other countries are committed to a regime that is premised on a public health rather than a law enforcement definition of the situation. They are consequently prepared to tolerate the controlled sale and use of cannabis and other recreational drugs classified as 'soft' – less harmful and less addictive – while continuing to lean heavily on the sale of 'hard' drugs, yet providing needles and even free drugs to 'hard drug addicts' so as to manage their health in the best manner possible and reduce the petty crime the addicts would otherwise engage in incessantly. This regime was well entrenched in the Netherlands in the 1980s and 1990s, but has since come under strong pressure from two sides: the overwhelming majority of fellow EU member state national governments who remain firmly committed to

across-the-board hard-line policies and who objected to Dutch excep-
tionalism; and changes in the manufacture of cannabis and marijuana
that have made them more powerful and therefore, so medical research
has begun to show, more dangerous to the health of users, thus undermining a fundamental premise of the public-health paradigm.
Successive Dutch governments therefore faced the challenge of reconstruction: either finding new coalition partners for the existing regime,
or being prepared to adapt some of its features in order to placate its
critics (Boekhout van Solinge 1999; Kurzer 2001; Garretsen 2003).

Preservation leaders need a fine eye for the layered nature of public
policy – the distinctions between stability and change in the settings of
particular policy instruments; the nature or mix of the instruments
themselves; policies in which these instruments are embedded; and the
underlying ideas and values that constitute the regime's core paradigm
(Rose and Davies 1994; Kay 2006). If they are solidly committed to
the latter, they can only save the day if they are willing to tinker with
the former three. In fact, they will need considerable creativity and
astuteness to do it. In doing so, however, they must stop well short of
unleashing a momentum that will undermine the very foundations of
the regime they are seeking to protect.

The main risk for preservation leaders is that of being overrun,
trying to fight battles on behalf of a regime that is beyond salvation.
When they do, they are likely to be regarded as 'out of touch', politically incompetent and anachronistic. Many government leaders holding office during or immediately following the latter half of the 1970s
suffered this fate: Jimmy Carter, Robert Muldoon (New Zealand),
James Callaghan (UK) and Malcolm Fraser (Australia), to name just a
few. In essence they all adhered to the post-war Keynesian interven-
tionist, welfare state paradigm but faced an economic environment
(stagflation) in which the money required to keep it going was in
increasingly short supply and tried and tested policy instruments no
longer seemed to work. All of them saw their governments end in division, disarray and voter repudiation. And all of them were succeeded
by radical reformers who were treated much more kindly by history.
Were they 'bad leaders'? Should they have seen it coming? Should they
have been more flexible in shedding their fundamental commitments
and hitherto widely taken-for-granted 'theories in use' about public
finance and public policy? Did comparable others do much better at
that same critical juncture? Don't say 'yes' too quickly. Rather than
bad leaders, they are better understood as tragic leaders, whose
moment in political time passed under the influence of forces well
beyond their control while they were still in the job.

If preservation leadership is an exercise in swimming against the tide,
innovation leadership, in contrast, is much more like sailing with steady
tail winds. It is potentially the finest hour for leaders, and it is fair to

say that most non-wartime leaders who are consistently regarded by posterity as 'great' leaders come into this category. It is a match made in heaven: the existing regime is mortally wounded, and the new leader is determined to get rid of it. In US presidential politics, think Roosevelt in 1932, and Reagan in 1980. Elsewhere, think Helmut Kohl and the collapse of the Berlin Wall. Think Boris Yeltsin and the end of communism. Think Nelson Mandela in 1994. Think also (and pause to reflect on) Benito Mussolini in 1922 and Adolf Hitler in 1933. Think, somewhat more reassuringly perhaps, Barack Obama as a presidential candidate in 2008 ('change we can believe in').

Innovation leadership revolves around the exploitation of existing regime crises. It is an exercise in political brinkmanship and in change management: highlighting the bankruptcy – economically, socially, politically – of the existing regime while offering a persuasive vision of a superior, feasible alternative. The job of innovation leaders is to kick-start a new regime, and build a new coalition around it. That job is made easier the more visible, enduring, painful and widely felt the problems of the existing situation. Innovation leaders therefore thrive on recession, civil strife, predecessors' fiascoes and scandals, and social instability. But what they also need is ideas, and the ability to sell them. Behind many cases of successful innovation leadership stands therefore not a single 'great communicator' such as Reagan or Obama, but in fact a much broader brains trust, some of whom may have been trying unsuccessfully for years, if not decades, to find minds receptive to their long-standing vision of an alternative regime. Milton Friedman is a prime case in point: his neo-classical paradigm was considered outrageous and irrelevant for more than a generation after he first formulated its key ideas. He spent long years at the margins of the progression and without supporters in Washington. But in Reagan and his inner circle he found a bunch of true believers, and in the hundreds of former Chicago students that ended up in powerful positions in their home countries and international organizations, he patiently nurtured a veritable army of true believers spreading the new regime around the world (Klein 2007), whose time came when the Keynesian order collapsed in the late 1970s.

The chief risk of innovation leadership is its failure to neutralize the 'rhetoric of reaction' of their opponents (Hirschman 1991) and galvanize sufficient support for a central alternative vision. Take climate change. Building on decades of research and advocacy by many scientists and politicians, Al Gore's crisis rhetoric was incredibly successful in convincing large numbers of people that climate change was real, dangerous and human-made. He also convinced many that deep changes were needed: to public policy, to the modus operandi of our economies, and indeed to our ways of life. But neither he nor any other leader was even remotely as successful in mobilizing similar levels of momentum for an alternative regime. With proponents of the status quo widespread and well-connected, climate change debates became bogged down in a nasty politics of fear on the one hand and heated exchanges about the benefits and risks of fairly arcane regulatory horse-trading. Despite ever more desperate warnings by scientists, in the absence of creative and coalition-building innovation leadership, the much-needed breakthroughs were elusive.

If preservation leadership can be tragic and innovation leadership is prone to generate resistance, *pre-emption* leadership is an exercise in political risk-taking that borders on a suicide mission. Pre-emptive leaders are committed to the destruction and replacement of regimes that are still seen as desirable and fungible by the dominant coalition. Skowronek (1993: 449) argues that most of them fail and are often chased from office – despised, friendless, and seen by their opponents as tainted politically as well as morally. He cites examples such as Richard Nixon, Woodrow Wilson and Bill Clinton.

This remarkable phenomenon raises questions. Why would anybody opt to become a pre-emption leader to begin with, if the odds are so strongly stacked against him or her succeeding? And why do such dangerous heretics make it all the way to senior leadership positions? Skowronek (1993: 449) argues that 'the distinctive thing about pre-emptive leaders is that they are not out to establish, uphold or salvage any political orthodoxy. Theirs is an unabashedly mongrel politics; it is an aggressive critique of the prevailing political categories. These leaders bid openly for a hybrid alternative'. In his view, pre-emptive leaders are 'third way' politicians, straddling existing ideological divides, explicitly renouncing both sides of these divides as extreme and trying to occupy an as yet undefined middle ground. In cultures where two-party contestation and 'winner takes all' principles are deeply rooted, third-way leadership is a dangerous occupation. Skowronek (1993: 449) continues: 'the characteristic risk of leadership of this sort is that in charting a third way the president appears to be wholly lacking in political principles. By exploiting the indeterminacy of his oppositional stance, he will be branded unscrupulous and cynically manipulative'.

While not disputing this interpretation of pre-emption leadership, I think there is an alternative type overlooked by Skowronek: pre-emption leaders as closet conviction politicians, ideological zealots who hide their true colours by tactical pandering to the middle ground, until they feel they have consolidated enough power. Australian prime minister John Howard had to wait for more than eight years before he could secure majorities in both House and Senate, but once he did so he wasted little time in making his biggest pre-emptive bid: to radically reform workplace relations in Australia away from its traditional collectivist principles towards an individualist concept. He knew this policy ran counter to majority sentiment, but he had the numbers to turn it rapidly into legislative reality, hoping that by the time the next election came around voters would have moved on. Unfortunately, they hadn't. Not only did they throw the Liberal Party out of government after 11 years, they also robbed Howard of his own seat (as only the second prime minister in history to suffer this humiliating repudiation).

These types of pre-emption leaders are contrarians, not shying away from opposing even a firmly established regime. They are driven to try policies based on non-mainstream values and beliefs. For them to be given that chance requires some form of exceptional circumstance to prevail in which voters or leader selectors, though still broadly supportive of the existing regime, are dissatisfied with one or more of its key policies, and/or with all of the regime-supporting leadership candidates. Think of times where public opinion is strongly concerned with deeply unpopular wars such as Vietnam and Afghanistan, or divisive policies from incumbents in traditionally sensitive areas such as health care, or pension or tax reform. Selectors in such circumstance may give their single-issue 'protest votes' to a candidate who gives them what they want in those particular areas, without realizing or temporarily discounting the radical (partly scary, partly infeasible) nature of the full package into which they are buying. When they do wake up, they will use every opportunity available to disavow and eliminate the candidate for whom they voted.

Despite inevitable criticism directed towards its schematic approach and potentially deterministic implications (see Laing 2012; Skowronek 2008; compare Brown 2014), Skowronek's theory has been acclaimed widely for providing broad explanatory narratives for the course of the presidential leadership throughout US history, inviting scholars to compare like with like among presidencies in terms of the political context faced by various office-holders rather than by roughly dividing US political history into two or three periods and assuming that no meaningful comparison is possible between presidents from these different eras. Recently, students of political leadership in parliamentary democracies have begun to explore the potential of his contextual theory of executive leadership for understanding the dynamics of prime-ministerial leadership ('t Hart 2011b; Laing and McCaffrie 2013).

Organizational life cycles as leadership challenges

The notion of regimes developing, blossoming, decaying and being replaced in long-range cycles is not unique to the world of politics. The dynamics of corporations as well as public organizations have been analysed in highly similar fashion (Selznick 1957; Quinn *et al.* 2006; Adizes 1999), and with similar implications for leadership. Without wanting to repeat what has just been said, let me briefly translate it from the macro stage of political and public policy to the smaller stage of organizational leadership. Rather than following common organic metaphors (Morgan 1986) of birth, growth, decay and death to demarcate organizational time, I take my cues from Selznick's (1957) influential ideas about the institutionalization of organizations (see also Boin 2001; Boin and Goodin 2007).

Selznick argues that formal organizations, created to accomplish particular tasks, can evolve into institutions: organizations that have become 'infused with values beyond the requirements of the task at hand'. In a fully developed institution, three features coincide: a coherent mission, a made-to-fit and well-inculcated 'technology' to achieve it, and a strong degree of internal and external support for both. Institutions have become what marketing experts call 'strong brands', evoking a high degree of loyalty from their members and clients alike. In the public sphere, institutions are organizations whose existence is widely applauded as being inherently desirable. They are 'taken for granted' and for that reason receive the benefit of the doubt. This in effect buffers them – at least much longer than the average organization – from the kind of voice and exit behaviour that tend to follow substandard or otherwise controversial agency performance. But while much is made of the spectre of 'permanently failing organizations' (Meyer and Zucker 1989), the reality in today's high-transparency, high-accountability public sector is that even the strongest public sector brands can get into deep trouble when they repeatedly and conspicuously commit errors or transgressions. What then ensues is de-institutionalization: the erosion of internal and external support for organizational missions and methods.

And thus a cycle of organizational development ensues: from creation (or reform) to institutionalization, to de-institutionalization, and to reform. The cycle should not be read as a catch-all straitjacket. Clearly, the pace, depth, and even the sequence of these developmental stages will vary greatly between organizations and sectors. Some organizations manage to reach long-lasting equilibria at high levels of institutionalization and have fairly stable missions and technologies – think of the judiciary and the fire services in most Western states. Others, like the UK National Health Service (NHS), manage to remain fairly highly institutionalized in terms of their brand and their public acceptance regardless of relentless and often highly unproductive efforts to tinker with their missions, structures and methods (Pollitt 2008). Yet others – such as the police – tend to vacillate more between higher and lower levels of institutionalization, and tend to go through waves of reform as a result.

Perhaps most important, not a small number of public organizations find it impossible to ever truly institutionalize. This may be because their mission is inherently controversial and internally inconsistent, because their technology is, or because the two are not effectively linked. Think of public agencies in areas such as social work, child safety, social security, parole, or even education. Their missions are complex and often fraught with value conflicts not resolved by the legislatures that set them up and fund them. Their professional paradigms are not universally recognized in the community. They have no black gowns, white coats or expensive offices to command respect. When their operations run counter to some clients' interests, they will not hesitate to dispute their authority. Clients think they know better. Also, their prime constituencies may be of low social status or political clout, thus making it difficult to obtain adequate amounts of top-level attention and funding. And they often have to serve multiple clienteles simultaneously who have opposing interests and priorities. Hargrove and Glidewell (1990) argue that leading an organizations that combines these features amounts to a (nearly) 'impossible job'.

Leading these different types of organizations during these various times in their developmental trajectories entails a series of challenges. And here the parallels with Skowronek's theory of political leadership appear. Table 5.3 clarifies this. It combines two of Selznick's three defining features of institutions (mission and technology) on its horizontal axis, and places the third one (internal and external support) on the vertical axis. This yields four distinct organizational 'states', each of which entails a set of strategic leadership challenges.

Institution-building leadership is about capitalizing on existing goodwill and political momentum both inside and outside the organization to craft a coherent and consistent mission, and developing robust methodologies for producing the (public) value the organization aims to create. Think of J. Edgar Hoover's first decade as leader of the then fledgling Federal Bureau of Investigation (FBI). His job was to capitalize on the will to combat the growth of organized crime to build his organization into a high-performing machine and into a public brand whose reputation and right to exist few would dispute. Other examples can be found in the EU, where the European Commission created more than 20 new arm's-length agencies between 1993 and 2009, covering a wide range of areas such as drug approval, health and safety at work, food safety, human rights, racism and xenophobia monitoring, plant species variety, vocational training. Given a mandate, a building and a budget, the directors of these new creations had to start from scratch to carve out a niche and settle the organization and its work into the already densely populated European bureaucratic space (Groenleer 2009).

Consolidating leadership occurs when organizations reach high levels of institutionalization. The challenge is to prevent complacency. Concretely, it is about maintaining and fine-tuning the organizational story and its technology in view of changes in its relevant environments

TABLE 5.3 *Leadership challenges as a function of organizational time*

Coherence and alignment of mission and capability	Low	High
Level of internal and external support for mission and capability		
Firm	Institution-building	Institutional consolidation
Weak	Fire-fighting	Reform

Source: 't Hart (2011a).

(societal, political, technological and so on). Think of Hoover's middle decades, when the FBI had become a formidable bureaucratic empire, but saw public concern for its original raison d'être (crime fighting) abate somewhat. Seizing upon the new public and political fear of the era, the Cold War obsession with communism, Hoover repositioned the agency and its modus operandi to incorporate this growth market effectively and thus strengthen the brand.

Reform leadership is called for when the institution's acceptance comes under threat, either because the organization's inherent performance has declined, internal disagreements have sprung up, or because it has not adapted its mission and modus operandi effectively to meet changing societal norms and expectations. Think of the criticism the FBI was beginning to achieve in the post-McCarthy era when the concern for communist infiltration of US society had all but abated and the issues of civil rights (and the excesses of the white backlash against it in the American South) and Vietnam started heating up. For a variety of reasons, Hoover's FBI was slow in adapting to this new environment. The agency's lack of effectiveness and particularly even-handedness in dealing with violent ultra-radicals on both sides of the tensions became a bone of contention. The leadership challenge was to demonstrate in words and deeds that the FBI had the capacity to transform itself to tackle the new agendas and the changing societal value sets these implied.

Fire-fighting leadership occurs when de-institutionalization is complete. The organization is fighting for its survival amid a clamour of voices disputing its relevance, its integrity and/or its effectiveness. The task is to get the organization off the front pages and out of the news bulletins. It is about surviving inquiries. It is about coping with efforts by political or bureaucratic superiors to micromanage the organization, or indeed to gobble it up. It is about (re-)connecting with key constituencies and the wider public. It is about leadership in what Mao once dubbed 'interesting times': a relentless pressure cooker of incidents, surprises, criticism, attacks and negative emotion. Think of Hoover's successors in the post-Watergate era. Or think of heads of 'impossible job' agencies, as identified by Hargrove and Glidewell (1990). Many correction, parole, police and child protection agencies fit the bill: saddled with internally conflicted missions, employing professional technologies that are essentially contested, working for low-prestige clienteles, and torn by intense conflict among their various constituencies. Leading such agencies often boils down to hoping to stay out of the news for a more than a few weeks at a time.

Conclusions

The contingency models of leadership reviewed here, and particularly the political time and organizational evolution models presented in the last two sections, are heuristic devices, not fully tested theories. They are elegant and thus tempting. Yet some caveats about them are in order. First, they should not be interpreted in a mechanistic fashion, neither by students nor practitioners of public leadership. Skowronek (1993) may flirt with the idea of regular long-range regime cycles in American political development, of roughly the same duration, but the evidence for this is contested. And even if his case survives scrutiny, it is unlikely to have any relevance for the regime rhythms of other polities. It is safer to presume that the overall pattern is cyclical, but that some regime cycles last much longer than others. Successive articulating and preservationist leaders who are both creative and lucky may in effect preside over extended periods of regime continuity. In contrast, if preservationists are inept, inflexible or confronted with unusual contextual adversity, regime demise and replacement may happen relatively quickly. Perhaps the clearest instance of this was the cascaded implosion of the communist states of Central and Eastern Europe within a few fateful months in 1989 and 1990.

Second, Skowronek analyses the American polity as one macro-level regime, similarly treats successive presidencies as units of analysis, and the person of the president as the one pivotal and immutable leader figure within it. This is not attuned to the diversity of sector-specific and even issue-specific temporal dynamics that chief executives and other policy-makers routinely confront. If one does allow for this diversity, a much more fine-grained picture of any given leader's stance and performance can be obtained. It takes us closer to the lived realities of leaders, where they chose to fight some but not all potential battles they face at any point in time.

However auspicious the match may be between the overall health of the regime and their political stance when they take office, few leaders are likely to be articulators every time and all the time. They inevitably also inherit nagging problems of declining performance and/or support in some issue areas or parts of the regime. Or despite being generally supportive of it, they are likely to find themselves in disagreement with particular policies and institutional features of the regime. Leaders can thus be articulators in one area, consolidators in another, and pre-emptors in yet another. For example, John Howard was an articulator in macro-economic and foreign policy, a reformer in areas such as gun control, and a pre-emptor in industrial relations and, during his final months, indigenous affairs (see Brett 2007; Errington and Van Onselen 2007; Kelly 2009). This is a daunting yet utterly plausible prospect, which they cannot hope to cope with successfully if they choose take on all these diverse challenges by themselves and in parallel. The diverse and dynamic nature of the leadership challenges the average senior executive faces clearly force them to prioritize and sequence their interventions, as well as to rely on others to do part of the requisite leadership work.

Moreover, leaders may develop and change during their time in the job. They may change their minds, or at least change their stances when they deem this to have become inevitable. As political chameleons, some of their commitments and choices will be attuned to the opening and closing of political opportunities over time, as cyclical regime time collides with the more randomized patterns of punctuated equilibrium that characterize most individual issue areas (Baumgartner and Jones 2009).

Also leadership, like public policy (Wildavsky 1979; Rose and Davies 1994), is partly its own cause. The very impact – intended or not – of leaders' own prior interventions in a regime may cause it to change, which will probably induce them to change their stances towards it. Likewise, articulators who stay on long enough to experience cracks in the regime's armour most probably evolve into consolidators. Pre-emptors who manage to make a dent in a once robustly supported regime, yet fail to destroy it, may fall back on more pragmatic reformist leadership aimed at changing it incrementally. Margaret Thatcher did this with respect to the NHS: having tried without success to get rid of it in favour of a market based model of health care delivery, she set about at least getting the NHS to operate in a more 'business-like' fashion (Moran 1999; Harrison and MacDonald 2008). Paradoxically, this may leave such pragmatic reformers only a hair's breadth away from preservationists who realize that, in order for the regime's core values to be protected, many of its structures and policies will need to be reformed significantly (Terry 1995).

Finally, changes of leadership stance within one office-holder's period in office may also be simple products of the taming and energy-sapping impact of life at the top itself. Initially energetic reformers and bold pre-emptors may deplete much of their leadership capital well before they leave office. They learn to tolerate and compromise more than they ever imagined at the outset of their careers. Some of the post-Stalin cohorts of Soviet leaders are a case in point: Nikita Khrushchev retained a burning ambition to innovate and reform throughout his tenure but had essentially exhausted his authority among the inner circle in the wake of the wild, lost gamble of the Cuban missile crisis – and was removed by a palace coup two years later. His successor Leonid Brezhnev was an energetic, hard-line consolidator who turned into a nondescript time-server through the sheer effects of old age. In the UK, Harold Wilson's agenda and style varied considerably between his first (1964–70) and second (1974–6) terms as prime minister: not only had economic circumstances become considerably grimmer by the time he returned to power, but he himself had also aged considerably and was in fact to resign prematurely midway through his second term, knowing he was in the early stages of Alzheimer's disease (though he did not state this reason publicly, triggering much speculation and conspiracy theories about the 'real' reasons behind his shock departure).

With or without these nuances, the models of political and organizational time presented above highlight the need for leaders to 'think in context, and particularly to 'think in time'. Harvard leadership scholars Neustadt and May (1986) explicitly recommended that they do so. In their view, leaders should not so much ask 'what the problem is' in the organization, polity or issue area they propose to govern, but rather 'what the story is'. Figuring out the story of where entities have come from, how they have evolved and where they might be heading allows leaders to situate the present in ways that conventional diagnostics often overlook. This encourages them to think about how they themselves – their values, beliefs, identities, skills, experiences and support base – fit in. Thinking in time by being aware of the long-term and dynamic nature of their political and institutional environments allows leaders to make better informed judgements regarding whether and where the times will suit them.

We should, however, go one step further and question whether all of this is only about leadership as 'reading' the proverbial writing on the wall. Do we assume, for example, that the leaders treat things such as population numbers, unemployment figures, poll ratings, weather statistics, treaties and contracts as being akin to physical realities – as things that exist in the world 'out there' and that cannot be willed away or enhanced by human sense-making capabilities? Or do we take the subjectivist position that even the most material, directly observable of phenomena – the condition of the polar ice caps, the size of tropical rain forests, streets of boarded-up houses, 2001 terrorist attacks on the Twin Towers – only assume meaning in the world of political leaders through the stories that they choose to tell or believe about them. As Hajer (1993: 44) famously argued: 'large groups of dead trees as such are not a social construct; the point is how one makes sense of dead trees. In this respect there are many possible realities. One may see dead trees as the product of natural stress caused by drought, cold, or wind, or one may see them as victims of pollution.' Just assuming contexts are what they are is therefore frankly implausible.

For example, across three major books and numerous articles on the subject, Heifetz provides little if any empirical evidence for the central typology of 'challenges' that underpins the entire edifice. Where does the 'technical' end and the 'adaptive' begin when different group members interpret the catalogue of issues facing it at any given time? What levels of (dis)agreement are needed to make them fall into one box rather than the other? Contingency scholars should explicitly address those issues rather than obfuscate them.

Another set of reflective questions is about the relative power of context over leaders. Can context factors really make or break the careers of leaders, or do they merely provide a more or less good 'fit' for leaders with certain policy preferences or operating styles? Many leaders of note appear to rise to become great influencers because of a strong, innate belief that circumstances conspire to lead them to greatness – even if their contemporaries at the time do not regard them as natural born leaders (Ludwig 2002). Context is never just 'out there'. It can also never be fully caught in analysts' elegant typologies. Things happening 'out there' are perceived and understood differently by political actors with different beliefs, roles, loyalties and vantage points. Context factors such as 'the economy', 'the Zeitgeist' or 'the geostrategic situation' are simply not given. They are assigned meaning in stories that are framed in particular ways – often with strategic intent – and are challenged by stories propagated by other actors. It is the course and outcomes of the ensuing meaning-making contests that are going on around them, and in which they often actively participate, that are pivotal in motivating political leaders to take notice of and act on contextual changes.

A key challenge for future studies of the leadership–context nexus is therefore to examine much more rigorously than has been done to date the constructed nature of this nexus. For example, under which macro-economic and political conditions can political leaders successfully 'talk up' or 'talk down' the national economy, and when do they lose the ability to do so (Wood 2007)? How do constraint-accepting versus constraint-challenging leaders respond to changes in their geostrategic environment (Keller 2005)? To whose stories about context do leaders listen? Which individuals and institutions are considered to be authoritative interpreters of economic, socio-cultural, historical, ecological and geo-political context by different political leaders and their inner circles, and how does this affect their policy agendas? How do broader governance traditions and cultural practices shape elite beliefs about the capacity of existing institutions to absorb demographic and socio-cultural changes in the population (Bevir and Rhodes 2010)? How do we get a solid grip on the possibility of mutual influence between context and leadership, whether operating in a modernist-empiricist or an interpretive epistemology? How can we ascertain reliably when the nature of influence is entirely unidirectional?

These questions should be at the forefront of any serious effort to remove the contextual analysis of leadership from the outdated shackles of contingency theory, avoid the false clarity of deductive typological reasoning, and provide us with more firmly empirically grounded insight into how public leaders notice, interpret, use and leave their mark on the various contexts in which they operate.

Chapter 6

Leading in Crises

The heat of crisis

Let us begin by looking at three government leaders who were faced with major emergencies and how they fared. In August 2002, some six weeks before the scheduled national elections, flooding of the River Elbe hit eastern parts of Germany. When the floods hit, Chancellor Gerhard Schröder's position as head of a coalition of Social Democrats and Greens was relatively weak, with his government lagging behind the Christian Democrats in the polls. Despite responsibility for the emergency response lying with the states (*Länder*) rather than the federal government, Schröder visited disaster-struck areas and quickly made available emergency funds to aid the relief and recovery effort. These gestures conveyed the impression of a leader who genuinely cared and was decisive when needed. His chief opponent at the election, Christian-Democrat Edmund Stoiber elected to stay away from the flooded areas, as he had nothing concrete to offer as opposition leader and did not want to be seen to be drawing resources away from relief operations. The public interpreted this as a critical lack of judgement. Stoiber – who was also the chief minister of the rich southern state of Bavaria – apparently had no empathy with the plight of the poor former East German population affected by the floods. The contrasting crisis leadership performances of the two election candidates were later shown to be a major factor in Schröder's surprise election victory a few weeks later (Bytzek 2008).

Moving over to Spain now: on 11 March 2004, a series of bombs were detonated on four trains just outside Madrid, killing 192 people and wounding around 2,000 others. The attacks came three days before the national elections. Prime minister José Maria Aznar's conservative Popular Party was ahead in the polls, despite Spain's participation in the unpopular war in Iraq. Aznar quickly blamed the Basque separatist group ETA for the attacks, but this judgement soon proved to be ill founded. All signs pointed to Al-Qaeda, thus linking the attack to Spain's participation in the war. A swift backlash was orchestrated through the social media. High-profile public demonstrations against the prime minister and his party took place all over Spain within 24 hours of Aznar's announcement. Three days after the attacks, the opposition Socialist Party, under José Luis Rodriguez Zapatero secured a historic and unexpected victory, paving the way for a Spanish troop withdrawal from Iraq (Olmeda 2008).

And in the United States in 2001, president George W. Bush had been less than eight months in office when the 11 September terrorist attacks on the World Trade Center and the Pentagon occurred. The crisis gave his presidency the sense of purpose and conviction it had been lacking, providing him with a strong narrative of 'us versus them' around which he could rally the nation in support of military action in, first, Afghanistan and later in Iraq. In managing the fallout of the 9/11 attacks domestically, Bush initially opposed an independent commission but subsequently reversed his position because of pressure from victims of the attack and their families. Bush was re-elected in November 2004, by which time sweeping domestic security reforms had been introduced – the flagship organization being the new Department of Homeland Security.

Nearly five years after 9/11, on 30 August 2005, Hurricane Katrina hit and devastated areas of Louisiana and Mississippi. The greatest havoc was caused in New Orleans, with the flood surge covering 80 per cent of the city in water, leaving more than 1,500 dead and many more homeless. The response by city, state and federal authorities to the flood was a fiasco: emergency aid came too late and was utterly deficient, with deadly consequences. At the time of the disaster Bush was seven months into his second term but already politically vulnerable because of declining support for the war in Iraq. His presidency never recovered. The subsequent inquiries were damning for all concerned. The main immediate casualty was Federal Emergency Management Agency Director Michael Brown, but support for Bush declined further amid accusations that his leadership was weak and out of touch on domestic issues. The aftermath of Katrina led to the adaptation of emergency management policies and practices across all levels of the federal system, though not on the scale of the post-9/11 security policy reforms ('t Hart *et al.* 2009).

These three examples remind us that even in otherwise prosperous, peaceful and stable communities business as usual can give way to critical conditions of disaster, conflict and breakdown of vital structures, beliefs and values underpinning public safety, security and prosperity. When this happens, 'un-ness' reigns: communities face unplanned, unwanted, uncertain and often deeply undesired prospects and choices. Crises act as pressure cookers: they arouse the interests and emotions to higher levels of intensity. The more threatening, surprising and acute they appear, the stronger the collective stress they elicit. They defy normal structures and routines of collective problem solving. They test the resilience of communities and their governments. They raise intense and awkward questions for the community, but particular for its public leaders: How could this happen? Why didn't we see this coming? Who is to blame? How do we move on from here? The three examples above therefore also show that crises are crucial performance tests for public office-holders and public organizations alike. These tests are consequential, both for leaders' political capital and for the policies or organizations they represent. Also, their success or failure in passing these tests depends as much on perceptions as it does on realities.

In this chapter, we look at public leadership through a situational lens. We focus on crises as one of the most pronounced, inevitable, consequential and yet ambiguous form of situational leadership challenge. We focus on two key questions. First, we ask how leaders prepare for and perform under the intense personal and political pressures generated by crises. However, we should not assume that crises are simply 'bad news' for leaders, with crisis management focused purely on damage limitation, both operationally and politically. Crises may also provide leaders with unique opportunities to discard old policies and commitments, kick-start new ones, reform public organizations, and reshape the political landscape by forging new coalitions. Hence a second pivotal question about crisis leadership is: how do leaders identify and use crisis-induced opportunities for policy innovation and institutional reform?

Crises: realities and perceptions

From a leadership perspective, a crisis can be said to occur when *policy-makers experience a serious threat to the basic structures or the fundamental values and norms of a system, which under time pressure and highly uncertain circumstances necessitates making vital decisions* (Rosenthal *et al.* 1989: 10). This definition covers many different phenomena that challenge public elites at various levels and throughout society to 'step up to the plate' and find ways to cope with unusually large, ambiguous and nasty challenges such as natural disasters, industrial accidents, financial meltdowns, major product failures, mass shootings, policy fiascos, terrorist attacks, hostage takings, major epidemics – the list is lengthy. Table 6.1 distinguishes between two different types of crises: *situational* crises that are the product of forces 'out there', and *institutional* crises, where the performance of public office-holders, organizations or governments themselves are seen to be the urgent problem. The examples presented in the introduction to this chapter show that the distinction between the two types is not iron-clad: situational crises such as a flood or a terrorist attack can highlight institutional flaws in foreseeing, forestalling and responding to critical risks. When this happens, the public spotlight and the leadership challenges move from combating exogenous stressors to facing up to endogenous risks and failures. Conversely, latent institutional prob-

TABLE 6.1   *A typology of crises*

Crisis type Manifestation	Situational	Institutional
Sudden	Classic natural disasters	Ineffective emergency responses
	Industrial accidents Outbursts of collective violence Terrorist attacks Pandemics	Emergency-exposed institutional failures (e.g. bank frauds or collapses) Public revelations of institutional fraud, waste and abuse
Creeping	Critical resource depletion Environmental degradation Demographic imbalances	Chronic policy failures Erosion of citizen trust in public institutions and office-holders Incremental degradation of public assets and infrastructure Policy or organizational paralysis by stalemates

lems in an organization or political system may be so debilitating that they eventually produce acute situational crises through negligence, mismanagement, bias or corruption in governments or regulatory and executive agencies that allow unsustainable risks and tensions to escalate. For example, what we now think of as the 'global financial crisis' began long before its acute manifestations; an underlying institutional crisis of norms, incentives and regulatory oversight had been disregarded for much longer.

Indeed, Table 6.1 highlights the fact that while a sense of urgency is characteristic of all crises, not all crises materialize abruptly. So-called creeping crises have a long onset, and part of the reason why some of them reach boiling point is because of protracted doubts and disagreement about the scope and seriousness of the threats they pose. Climate change, many would argue, is a prime example of a creeping crisis being allowed to escalate to an acute emergency (or, in this case, more likely a whole range of acute emergencies triggered by the cumulative effects of incremental climatic shifts).

In our definition, crises have three essential characteristics that need to coincide. First, a sense that core values or vital systems of a community are *under threat* (and may already have already been violated). Think of widely shared values such as safety and security, welfare and health, integrity and fairness, which become shaky or even meaningless as a result of (looming) violence, destruction, damage or other forms of adversity. The reality or the prospect of mass casualties, destruction of property, infrastructural damage or economic breakdown generates fear and bereavement. However, a deep sense of threat and loss also occurs when a community's core beliefs, traditions and values are being challenged or compromised from inside the community itself – for example, by the discovery that the very office-holders and institutions charged with managing the public's business turned out to be fundamentally inept or untrustworthy.

The magnitude of perceived threat cannot be calculated by counting the numbers of bodies, jobs or dollars affected. It is also a function of cultural expectations about levels of order, prosperity and security, which vary widely within and between different communities and polities, partly depending on existing levels of preparedness and prior crisis experience (Quarantelli 1998; Perry and Quarantelli 2005). The anthrax scare and the Washington Beltway snipers caused the deaths of relatively few people in the autumn of 2001, but nevertheless evoked widespread fear among the public and severely affected community life in significant parts of the USA for weeks. A flood killing 50 people may be a routine occurrence in Bangladesh, but would be considered a national crisis in Sweden or Canada.

A *sense of urgency* is also a key ingredient of crisis. Not every threat is viewed as being urgent. While experts and activists may worry and attempt to push their concerns up the political agenda, most political leaders do not lose sleep over problems with a horizon that exceeds their electoral business cycle. If leaders ignore or downplay the acute nature of potential threats – for example, the Bush administration's stance on Al-Qaeda prior to 9/11, levee protection in Southern Louisiana prior to Katrina, or climate change – the de facto message is: we have a potential problem but there is no crisis, so we can afford to take time in addressing it. Conversely, leaders and policy-makers can feel a great sense of threat and time pressure when they or their organizations become the subject of intense and critical media or parliamentary scrutiny, even when the issues involved do not necessarily hold major importance for actors outside that policy arena. Moreover, time pressure may be self-generated: in cases of conflict and negotiation, policy-makers who seek to pressure unions, demonstrators, terrorists or states by issuing an ultimatum also put pressure on themselves to 'deliver' the predicted punishment on time. When that deadline approaches with no solutions in sight, the sense of urgency may quickly become overwhelming.

In a full-blown crisis, the perception of threat is furthermore accompanied by a high degree of *uncertainty*. This uncertainty pertains both to the nature and the potential consequences of the developing threat: What is happening? How did it happen? What's next? How bad will it be? More important, uncertainty clouds the search for solutions: What can we do? What happens if we select this option? How will people respond? Again, uncertainty can be a characteristic of the situation at hand but it can also be produced or compounded by institutional responses to events. For example, when decision-makers consult various radiation experts on the risks associated with an accident at a nuclear facility, such experts may well disagree on the nature and depth of these risks, or on the measures that need to be taken. Remember the pervasive uncertainty around almost all of the above questions that lasted for months in the wake of the 2010 BP oil platform accident off the Louisiana coast. Even elementary questions such as 'How much oil is spilling into the sea every day?' could not be answered with certainty, let alone questions about the practical feasibility of a whole suite of stopgap measures that were attempted to stem the flow, all of which ultimately failed. The sheer duration of uncertainty despite the full range of assets of both BP and the US government being brought to bear on the problem contributed to the image of importance and malaise that destroyed BP's brand credibility (and its financial position, if not its very survival as an independent company) and significantly damaged the Obama presidency. A similar scenario unfolded in Japan in March 2011 when the Fukushima nuclear reactor complex sustained major earthquake damage, triggering radiation releases and reactor cooling problems that even as late as two years after the event were not fully understood or contained (Heineman 2011; 't Hart 2013).

Crises are the combined products of unusual events and shared perceptions that something is seriously wrong. However, no set of events or developments is likely to be perceived fully uniformly by members of a community. Perceptions of crisis are likely to vary not just between communities – societies experience different types of disturbances and have different types and levels of vulnerability and resilience – but also within them, reflecting the different biases of stakeholders as a result of their different values, positions and responsibilities. These differential perceptions and indeed accounts of a crisis set the stage for crisis leadership (see Figure 6.1).

When confronted with potentially critical contingencies, leaders may adopt fundamentally different postures. We distinguish here between:

- Denial that the events in question represent anything more than an *unfortunate incident*. This stance is likely to produce a downplaying of the idea that the events have any political or policy repercussions. This is precisely the stand that government leaders and monetary authorities in Western countries outside the US took when the 'mortgage crisis' gathered pace and started to engulf US financial institutions. Before the collapse of Lehman Brothers Holdings Inc. in September 2008, both the private perceptions and public attitudes of

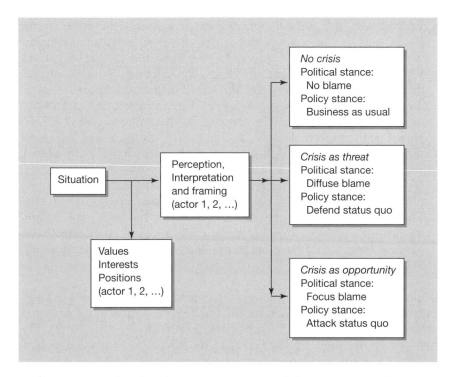

FIGURE 6.1 *Identifying crises: perceptions and their political implications*

Source: Adapted from Boin et al. (2009), p. 84.

most leaders was that the crisis was one in the US housing market and would remain largely confined to that. It would eventually go away, and would not affect the greater US economy, let alone the international economy. Consequently, their overriding public posture was one of reassurance ('t Hart and Tindall 2009a).

• Acceptance of events as a *critical threat* to society and the public interest. This posture is likely to lead to a defence from criticism of incumbent office-holders, policies and organizational practices. After the collapse of Lehman Brothers, an acute breakdown of trust occurred within the financial markets, creating a psycho-financial firestorm of mistrust, indecision and breakdown that threatened to engulf not only the major financial institutions but entire national economies (the seemingly ultra-prosperous Icelandic economy went bankrupt), and indeed the very core of the international capitalist system. Political and financial authorities around the world felt compelled to take swift, drastic, unprecedented and highly risky actions to avert a catastrophe that would have dwarfed the impact of the 1929 Wall Street crash.

- Recognition of a *critical opportunity* to expose deficiencies in the status quo *ex ante*. When particular events or conditions become widely viewed as a crisis, advocates of reform and change will attack what they can now claim to be clearly dysfunctional policies, organizations and office-holders. On the wings of public fear and outrage, they can marshal support for radical alternatives to the established order. If there was any big surprise in the wake of the 2008–09 global economic breakdown, it was the relatively muted nature of the blame game that followed, and the dearth of a concerted, successful advocacy for a radical redesign of the international economic order. Still, the crisis did offer governments the possibility of clipping the wings of once untouchable bankers and financiers. There were moves to cap or tax corporate bonuses, and bailout operations enabled a stronger state involvement in corporate governance – both would have been completely repugnant, even unthinkable, prior to the crisis.

With this in mind, it becomes easy to see that there are two strategically significant layers of perception and argumentation in the interpretation of any given set of unanticipated events (Boin *et al.* 2009). The first centres on their *significance*: are they inside or outside a policy-maker's 'zone of indifference' and standard coping routines? Are they 'big as well as bad' for the communities affected (the UN panel of scientists' view of climate change); 'bad but not really big' (the view of the nuclear industry on incidents at nuclear power plants); 'big but not really all that bad' (the 2006 Stern Review's report on the economics of climate change), or neither (the espoused view of many US banks and financial institutions in the early stages of the 2007–08 wave of mortgage defaults)?

As interpretations of unscheduled events differ, policy-makers may engage in a framing contest about their significance with other interests such as opposition parties, the media, and victims and their families. At stake in this contest is the agenda status of the unscheduled events: will they be seen as top priority opportunities or threats (positions 2 and 3), or can they safely be ignored, downplayed and dealt with through existing programmes and routines (position 1)?

When denial is infeasible, the main emphasis in the construction of crisis centres on *causality*: who or what is the driving force behind the course of events? At stake here are two matters of great concern to leaders: the accountability and future careers of senior office-holders, as well as the future for beleaguered policies, programmes and organizations (see Box 6.1, and the political and policy stances of the three positions in Figure 6.1).

BOX 6.1 An institutional crisis in law enforcement

On 7 December 1993, the mayor, chief prosecutor and police commissioner of Amsterdam publicly announced the dissolution of an interregional criminal investigation team (IRT). The IRT – one of several such teams in the Netherlands – had been established in 1989 to fight organized crime. The main reason for the decision had been the use of 'inappropriate' investigation methods (such as the use of civilian informers, and the 'controlled' import and distribution of illicit drugs), but this information was not revealed at the time. Shortly afterwards, the police commissioner of the Utrecht police force, a force that had participated in this IRT, alleged that the true reason for the dissolution had been corruption within the Amsterdam force. He claimed that top-secret information about the criminal gangs under investigation had been leaked from Amsterdam to the very targets of the investigation.

Following the highly publicized clash between two of the Netherlands' largest police forces, the ministers of Justice and Home Affairs established a national commission of inquiry. The commission refuted the corruption charge but signalled a chronic lack of coooperation between the police forces involved. However, it did not end with this blue-ribbon report. These initial events were followed by a two-year sequence of investigations, press leaks, political infighting, the resignation of two ministers, a full-scale parliamentary inquiry with live television coverage of interviews, culminating in a damning conviction of the state of criminal investigation policy in the Netherlands. The parliamentary commission finally concluded that crime-fighting in the Netherlands was beset by a threefold crisis:

- a crisis of norms concerning appropriate police methods and tactics in major criminal investigations;
- an organizational crisis of overlapping tasks and responsibilities and a lack of co-ordination and collaboration; and
- a crisis of authority, to the extent that the public prosecutors had in effect lost their grip on the criminal investigation activities of the policies they were supposed to supervise and control.

The parliamentary commission's findings and recommendations triggered an often painful process of identifying the culprits, public discussions around sanctioning the responsible administrators, and efforts to develop a consensus about a set of legal and organizational changes set out by the commission. The recommendations were aimed at restoring the effectiveness and legitimacy of the officials and institutions responsible for the formulation and implementation of criminal investigation policy. The report heralded a wave of reforms that both constrained and transformed Dutch crime-fighting institutions and policies (for further reading, see Bovens *et al.* 1999).

Challenges of crisis leadership

Quite independently of these varieties of perception and resolve on the part of leaders, citizens whose lives and well-being are threatened expect governments and public agencies to do their utmost to keep them from harm. They expect officials in charge to make critical decisions and provide direction even in the most difficult circumstances. So do the journalists who produce the stories that help to shape the crisis in the minds of the public. And so do members of legislatures, interest groups, institutional watchdogs, non-governmental organizations and other voices on the political stage. No matter how misplaced, unfair or illusory these expectations may be, they are real in their political consequences.

In contemporary Western societies, a crisis sets in motion extensive follow-up reporting, investigations by political forums, and civil and criminal juridical proceedings. It is not uncommon for public officials and agencies to be singled out as the responsible actors for prevention, preparedness and response failures. Public leaders must routinely defend themselves against seemingly incontrovertible evidence of their incompetence, ignorance or insensitivity. Force majeure and misfortune are no longer accepted as legitimate accounts of why crises occur; something or someone needs to be blamed (Douglas 1992; Bovens and 't Hart 1996).

At the strategic level of senior public office-holders, crisis management therefore amounts to more than harnessing the coping capacity of governments and public organizations; it boils down to the intensely political and sometimes deeply controversial activity of confronting the de-legitimation of the status quo that institutionalized crises produce ('t Hart 1993). Table 6.2 contrasts the standard view of emergency management as a dominantly operational, technocratic, consensual, collective problem-solving activity with the less often voiced, but no less pertinent politico-strategic perspective on crisis leadership that we adopt in this chapter.

Research suggests that once a perception of crisis has taken hold in a particular community or organization, a number of strategic leadership challenges present themselves (Boin *et al.* 2005; 't Hart and Tindall 2009a). Meeting them is an essential requirement for effective crisis management, but there is no rulebook for doing so. Nor is it always clear that each of these challenges is to be met by one or a small set of 'top dogs' high up in the food chain. Each will be discussed in greater detail below.

Sense-making: diagnostic leadership

With the exception of swift and devastating events such as tsunamis, nuclear explosions and terrorist bombings, a crisis does not announce

TABLE 6.2   *Coping with situational versus institutional crises: management versus leadership*

Situational crises: 'emergency management'	Institutional crises: 'crisis leadership'
Crises occur in the physical world: signals, shocks, systems	Crises occur in the political world: perceptions, passions, players, positions
Citizens as passive victims	Citizens as active advocates
Media report events	Media frame interpretations
Key arenas: 'on-site', line agencies, co-ordination centres	Key arenas: media, parliament, inquiries, inner circles
Key stakes: physical damage control, community recovery	Key stakes: political damage control, policy/organizational consequences

its arrival. The attack on the World Trade Center took the USA completely by surprise that morning of 11 September 2001. In the hours and days following the first ghastly television images, officials at all levels of government scrambled to understand what exactly had happened, and why and how. They worried what would be next and what could be done to prevent it. In hindsight, it is clear what happened that day. But for those who lived through it, 11 September was the day that nothing 'made sense'. The world as they knew it had changed for ever.

Disturbances, especially in the very early stages, produce vague, ambivalent, and often conflicting signals, which policy-makers must interpret and recognize as 'crises' rather than routine problems that can be dealt with using standard procedures and techniques. For example, is an explosion at an electricity generating plant an isolated incident, or is it the beginning of a cascading sequence of breakdowns? And is the cause is the explosion a technological malfunction or a deliberate attack? First responders and policy-makers alike must 'make sense' of events as they unfold (Weick 1993). Leaders need to determine the likely level of threat, who or what will be affected, the scope for operational and strategic interventions, and how the crisis is likely to develop. Signals come from many sources: some loud, some soft, some accurate, some merely rumour and speculation, and some bearing no relation to reality. How can crisis policy-makers judge which is which? How can they extract coherent and credible signals from the noise of crisis?

The bewildering pace, ambiguity and complexity of a crisis can easily overwhelm normal modes of situation assessment. Stress may further impair sense-making abilities. The organizations in which crisis managers typically function can produce additional cultural and political barriers to crisis appreciation. In fact, research shows that many organizations are unable to detect even the most simple incubation processes with only a few factors at work, standard interactions and long lead-in times (Turner and Pidgeon 1997).

Some types of people are known for their capacity to remain calm and collected under conditions of stress and uncertainty. They have developed a mode of information processing that enables competent performance under crisis conditions (Flin 1996; Klein 1999). Veteran military officers, journalists, and fire and police commanders generally possess such well-developed capacities. Senior politicians and bureaucrats are also likely to be veterans of many political and bureaucratic conflicts during their years of ascending their respective ladders. Those who reach the top in political and bureaucratic arenas tend to have a strong capacity to cope with stress, though even that provides no guarantees that they will get it right every time (see Box 6.2).

Some organizations have developed a proactive culture of 'looking for problems' in their environment. These so-called high reliability organizations, often in high-risk professions or industries such as air traffic control systems, nuclear and chemical industries, fire-fighting teams and medical emergency rooms, have somehow developed a capacity for thorough yet fast-paced information processing and updating their responses to emerging problems under stressful conditions (see Box 6.3). The unresolved question is whether any organization can feed these features into their existing operational cultures.

Meaning-making: performative leadership

In the run-up to the invasion of Iraq in the spring of 2003, the British government prepared the ground by releasing intelligence reports suggesting that Saddam Hussein possessed 'weapons of mass destruction' (WMDs) that could reach the UK within minutes. The BBC soon reported that the underlying intelligence was 'sexed up' to make the claim. The British government denied the charge and demanded an apology from the BBC, which stood by its claim. When pressured, the BBC finally revealed its source: Dr Kelly, an arms expert, who was subsequently found dead and had apparently committed suicide. The BBC entered a deep institutional crisis, which resulted in the ousting of its chairman. But at the same time, British prime minister Tony Blair was facing a growing credibility gap when his strident performances in the House of Commons and the media arguing the case for intervention on the grounds of the WMD risk Saddam posed were not borne out by any material findings after the invasion took place.

In times of crisis, there are high expectation on leaders to quell uncertainty and produce an authoritative account of what is happen-

BOX 6.2   A failure of sense-making in crisis: hurricane Katrina and the White House

Why did the US response to hurricane Katrina, fail so badly? One key factor was that president George W. Bush acquired and maintained a deeply flawed, over-optimistic picture of the damage done by Katrina and the extent to which its impact far outstripped the local and state response capacities. As a result, Bush was one, if not several, steps behind events and emotions 'on the ground' right from the start, and never really caught up. This affected the performance of the two other crisis leadership tasks. Few strategic White House decisions were required during the first week of Katrina, but the pivotal one – the release of massive federal military and other resources – became a case of 'too little, too late'. Moreover, and largely for the same reason, the depth of the meaning-making challenges facing Bush was severely underestimated. For several days, Bush was advised to continue in 'business as usual' mode, which made him look out of touch, if not outright indifferent. A downward credibility spiral was set in motion: when he did employ some of the same meaning-making techniques that were so successful in enhancing his communicative performance in the wake of the 9/11 terrorist attacks (photo-ops during fly-overs, site visits, speeches), they backfired completely given the graphic discrepancy between his gestures of reassurance and the frightening reality of abandoned victims that was on display for all to see.

The Select Committee of the House of Representatives (2006) framed the bungled response to Katrina in terms of a 'failure of initiative' and lack of clear leadership. Bush's leadership during Katrina suffered mainly because neither he nor his inner circle, nor the vital gatekeepers of information about the hurricane's impact that was flowing to the White House, really had the imagination to grasp that the worst-case scenario that had been talked about for such a long time – and that Bush *et al.* had been briefed on just days before Katrina's landfall – had actually materialized. With the sense-making foundation upon which crisis leadership inevitably rests being so misguided and disorganized, Bush and his inner circle were set up to fall short in those first few days of the Katrina catastrophe (see also Committee on Homeland Security and Governmental Affairs 2006). In contrast to 9/11, when the president needed no persuasion to be engaged instantly and enduringly, throughout Katrina Bush was lulled into maintaining an essentially reactive posture, thus depriving the advisory configuration around him of a key animating force that had prompted it to perform so well four years earlier (for further reading, see 't Hart *et al.*, 2009).

ing, what caused it to happen and what action needs to be taken. Once they have made sense of events, appraised the situation and made strategic policy choices, leaders must gain acceptance for this account

BOX 6.3   Maintaining performance in the face of high risk and high pressure

High-reliability organizations practice a form of organizing that reduces the pain created by unexpected events, helps to contain them, and speeds recovery. They have forged a modus operandi and a 'cultural DNA' that enables them to absorb 'un-ness' (unexpected, unwanted, uncertain, unpleasant contingencies) without succumbing to it.

Their operating principles include:

1. Continual tracking of deviations and small failures.
2. Resisting oversimplification of tasks and routines.
3. Top-to-bottom sensitivity to operational realities and requirements.
4. Resisting efficiency pressures in order to maintain capabilities for resilience.
5. Taking advantage of shifting locations of expertise.

High reliability organization (HRO) skills include the ability to recognize weak signals of trouble ahead, to apply novel approaches to problem resolution, to maintain respectful communication under duress, and having a deep knowledge of how operating systems actually function. HROs are unconventional in that they *expect* people to make mistakes and systems to fail in unimagined ways. Continuous updating of this risk awareness in a mindful way minimizes the likelihood of large failure, speeds recovery through intelligent improvisation, and protects the capacity for organizational learning from being subverted by post-incident finger-pointing and buck-passing (for further reading, see Weick and Sutcliffe, 2007).

from others. They must give 'meaning' to the unfolding crisis in order to gain legitimacy for their crisis management efforts. If they fail to do so, or when their account is challenged or undermined by revelations or allegations made by others (as in the case example above), their policies will neither be understood nor respected.

Two problems often recur. First, government or agency leaders do not have a monopoly on framing the crisis. Their messages are often countered by the news media, political opponents and others, who advocate alternative frames of the causes of the crisis, its consequences and the specific action that is needed. Censoring such voices is politically and logistically unviable in a plural democracy which enables mass communications through the internet, mobile phones, Facebook and YouTube and so on – as evidenced by the failure of the US strategy of 'embedded journalism' in shaping (that is, constraining) the images of the Iraq War. Al Jazeera and the World Wide Web provided plenty of rude corrections to the US-led coalition's propaganda machine, as exemplified by the revelations of torture in the Abu Ghraib prison. Even years later, Chelsea Manning and WikiLeaks were to drive home the message further.

Second, authorities often struggle to cope with masses of raw data (second-hand reports, rumours, speculation, pictures) that quickly accumulate in the midst of extraordinary events. Translating and rationalizing these to produce a coherent picture is a significant challenge. A major public relations effort is then needed to impart accurate, accessible information, which can be used as the basis for appropriate action. Such efforts may be hindered because they need to reach an anxious, and even fearful, audience. Stress and arousal can easily lead to the messages of leaders being misinterpreted and distorted – especially among those parts of the audience who do not see government as their ally. Pre-existing opposition and distrust in government do not simply disappear just because a crisis has arrived on the scene.

Moreover, public perceptions of a crisis are often shaped in contests between competing 'frames' (definitions of the situation) put forward by actors who seek to contain or exploit crises (see, for example, Alink *et al.* 2001; Boin *et al.* 2009). Crises invite four types of framing efforts, concerning their nature and severity, their causes, the responsibility for their occurrence or escalation, and their policy implications. Actors both inside and outside government will strive to have their particular interpretations of the crisis accepted in the media and by the public as the authoritative account ('t Hart 1993; Tarrow 1994; Brändström and Kuipers 2003; De Vries 2004; Kaplan 2008). In other words, they seek to 'exploit' the disruption of 'governance as usual' that emergencies and disturbances entail: to defend and strengthen their positions and authority, to attract or deflect public attention, to get rid of old policies and sow the seeds of new ones (Keeler 1993). When a particular 'crisis narrative' takes hold, it can be an important force for non-incremental changes in policy fields that are normally stabilized by the forces of path dependence, inheritance and veto-playing (Hay 2002; Kay 2006; Kuipers 2006).

The more severe a current crisis is perceived to be, and the more it appears to be caused by foreseeable and avoidable problems in the design or implementation of the policy itself, the bigger is the opportunity space for critical reconsideration of current policies and the successful advancement of (radical) reform proposals (Keeler 1993; Birkland 2006; Klein 2007). Hence the now clichéd maxim: 'Never waste a good crisis'. By their very occurrence (provided they are widely felt and labelled as such), crises tend to benefit critics of the status quo: experts, ideologues and advocacy groups already on record as challenging established but now compromised policies. They also present particular opportunities to newly incumbent office-holders, who cannot be blamed for present 'messes' but who can use these messes to highlight the need for policy changes that they might have been seeking to pursue in any case.

Decision-making: decisive leadership

Responding to crises confronts governments and public agencies with pressing choices. The classic example of crisis decision-making is the Cuban Missile Crisis (1962), discussed earlier, during which US president John F. Kennedy was presented with pictures of Soviet missile installations under construction in Cuba. The photographs conveyed a geostrategic reality in the making that Kennedy considered unacceptable, and it was up to him to decide what to do about it. Whatever his choice from the options presented to him by his advisers – an air strike, an invasion of Cuba, a naval blockade – and however hard it was to predict the exact consequences, one thing seemed certain: his decision would have a momentous impact on Soviet–American relations and world peace.

The threats and demands generated by crises may be so huge that scarce resources available will need to be prioritized. In some senses this is little different from routine political choices, except that under conditions of crisis, the gap between the demand for and supply of public resources is typically much bigger. Crises also test governments and leaders beyond the stresses and strains of routine politics and bureaucracy; for example, concerning the strategic deployment of military resources, the use of lethal force against another nation, or the radical curtailing of civil liberties. Critical decisions surrounding such issues must be made under conditions of uncertainty and volatility, with little time to consult and gain acceptance from colleagues, advisers and others who would normally be engaged in decision-making processes.

Crisis decision-making is about taking tough decisions amid conflicting values and major political risks (Janis 1989; Brecher 1993): about backing down or stepping up, helping or by-standing, doing deals or acting on principle, speaking out or keeping silent, denying or accepting responsibility, and so on. In the heat of a crisis, those choices can be highly consequential, not least for the decision-makers themselves. Research into small-group decision-making has shown the impact that crisis conditions – stress, pressure and uncertainty – can have on the quality of the decision-making process. While the myth of the strong crisis leader will have us believe that individual brilliance can overcome these hurdles, research shows that getting good advice up to the top and managing ad hoc, small-group crisis response teams to produce balanced judgements are crucial but delicate and failure-prone leadership challenges (Janis 1982; Tetlock *et al.* 1992; 't Hart 1994; 't Hart *et al.* 2009; Schafer and Crichlow 2010)

However, many pivotal crisis decisions are *not* taken by individual leaders or by small informal groups of senior policy-makers. They can also emerge from various alternative, decentralized loci of decision-making and co-ordination ('t Hart *et al.* 1993). In fact, the crisis response in modern society is best characterized in terms of a network. This is not necessarily counterproductive. The delegation of decision-making authority down the line can enhance resilience rather than detract from it, particularly when the delegations go to well-trained, experienced, sensible officials in the field.

Co-ordination: facilitative leadership

In a crisis the question 'who is in charge where, when and for what?' can arouse great passions and produce many different answers. A well-documented disaster phenomenon, as witnessed in the 2004 Asian tsunami, is the 'battle of the Samaritans', where different aid organizations and agencies struggle to co-ordinate among their different priorities, technologies and communication systems. Moreover, a crisis does not make organizations suddenly 'forget' long-standing sensitivities, conflicts and even rivalries. As discussed earlier, after hurricane Katrina broke through the levees and flooded New Orleans, the response to this natural disaster just seemed to fall apart. Survivors spent days on highways, in the Superdome and the Convention Center, without food, water or ice. A wide variety of organizations – national and international, public and private – descended on the Crescent City, but logistical chains did not reach the survivors for weeks. Local, state and federal government agencies were operating at cross-purposes.

An effective response to a large-scale crisis or disaster requires inter-agency and intergovernmental co-ordination (Hillyard 2000). After all, each decision must be implemented by a set of organizations; only when these organizations work together is there a chance that effective implementation will happen. Such co-operation cannot be mandated. Leaders may call upon organizations to be flexible and improvise, but this requires a sea change that many public organizations cannot muster. After all, these organizations were originally designed to conduct their core business in accordance with such values as fairness, lawfulness and efficiency. The required behaviour in times of crisis runs against deeply institutionalized bureaucratic instincts.

For crisis leaders to be effective co-ordinators, they must understand that a truly effective crisis response is to a large extent the result of intensive pre-crisis joint training, naturally evolving collaboration processes, and decentralized networks. A crisis cannot be managed in a linear, step-by-step and comprehensive fashion from a single crisis centre, even if it is full of top decision-makers and has access to state-of-the-art technology. There are simply too many hurdles that separate a strategic decision from its timely execution in the field. Effective crisis leaders facilitate – rather than direct – collaboration between network agencies. They do so by information sharing, resource allocation, problem solving and by publicly giving credit where credit is due.

Consolidation: boundary-setting leadership

When the financial turbulence of 2008 spiralled out of control and governments found themselves into the business of bailing out banks and other corporations threatened with collapse, key judgements were to be made regarding the scoping of crisis responses. Which corporations were deemed to be 'too big to fail', and on what grounds? Why give emergency aid to banks or car manufacturers and not to retailers or aircraft manufacturers? What if corporations receiving support kept coming back for more? Such questions generated robust public debate as well as significant disagreement among policy-makers within and across different countries. In the post-acute stage of the global meltdown, other scoping issues became poignant. After the financial sector stabilized somewhat and stock markets were buoyant again, many sectors of the 'real economy' continued to struggle and unemployment figures remained high in many countries. This raised a strategic question for economic policy-makers: would they accept as given that a recession of this depth inevitably leaves residues of hundreds of thousands, if not more, people who will not make it back from the dole to a job? Or would they see merit in continuing to define this 'fallout' as part and parcel of the crisis, implying that they would continue to commit vast sums of public resources to bring all the socio-economic indicators down to pre-crisis levels? When would they release their hold on 'market forces' to do their work of creative destruction in the usual fashion? How, in other words, does one determine when a crisis is over? When does one say so? (Remember president George W. Bush's premature 'mission accomplished' speech after the 2003 invasion of Iraq). And when does one adjust one's distribution of attention and effort accordingly?

Highly similar discussions arise during disaster relief and recovery when there can be tough judgement calls regarding the distribution of scarce emergency aid, relief workers, and reconstruction resources. In any disaster, urgent and legitimate demand for collective resources and special benefits almost always exceeds supply. Moreover, in the heat of emergencies it can be very difficult to discern legitimate from opportunistic, and even criminal, demand.

The pressure on responsible policy-makers to show solidarity and generosity in the face of emergencies can be immense. They can be lured into making promises to groups or regions that they cannot actually keep. A classic example occurred in the wake of the sinking of the MS *Estonia* ferry between Talinn and Stockholm. Many hundreds of Swedes perished in the disaster. Moved to distraction, the Swedish prime minister publicly promised the bereaved that the government would bring the bodies of their loved ones back on shore, so that each could have a proper funeral. The problem was that doing so would be extremely difficult, time-consuming and indeed highly risky for the navy divers involved. The promise – understandable, but hastily made and ill advised – later had to be retracted.

Accountability: cathartic leadership

Crisis leadership is also about 'ending' the crisis at the appropriate time – both operationally and strategically. Doing so requires a scaling down and eventually a cessation of crisis operations. It also requires, at the political-strategic level, the provision of a coherent and credible account of what has happened and persuading others to accept it. These two aspects of crisis termination are conceptually distinct, but in practice are often closely interconnected. The system of governance – its rules and conventions, institutions, power hierarchies and networks – has to be (re-)stabilized. There must be a restoration of sufficient legitimacy to govern and perform the routine functions of government. Leaders cannot do so by unilateral decree, even if they possess authoritative legal or policy powers to terminate a crisis; for example, by ending a state of emergency or revoking martial law.

Formal termination attempts may be out of touch with the mood among citizens and communities. Premature closure may even rebound, bringing with it allegations of an underestimation of the threats or a cover-up of difficult issues. For example, after a tsunami struck Indonesia, Thailand and Sri Lanka, and with thousands of their citizens dead, bereaved, homeless or unaccounted for, the governments of Sweden and Norway were taken by surprise and reacted very slowly and not very effectively in sending aid. The Norwegian government accepted blame and apologized for its inadequate crisis response, but the Swedish cabinet, in contrast, remained steadfast in its denial of wrongdoing, and proceeded to attempt to shift any blame towards the public service. For the Swedish nation that had lost many hundreds of its citizens, this satisfied no one. A prolonged political crisis ensued, which shattered public trust in the government. An extremely critical inquiry report followed a year later, opening up the wounds and raising renewed calls for the government to accept responsibility. The government was ousted decisively in the 2006 elections.

The political and legal dynamics of accountability processes play a significant role in determining which crisis actors emerge unscathed and which end up with reputations and careers damaged (Brändström and Kuipers 2003). Policy-makers can be competent and conscientious, but that alone says little about how their performance will be evaluated when the crisis is over. If they 'manage' the political game of crisis-induced accountability well, they may prevent losses to their reputation, autonomy and resources (Hearit 2006; Boin *et al.* 2008).

The burden of proof in public discussions lies typically with the leaders. They must demonstrate with conviction that they cannot be held responsible for the cause of the crisis or any subsequent escalation. Such accountability debates are often little more than 'blame games' focused on identifying and punishing culprits rather than deliberating and reflecting seriously on crisis causes and consequences (Hood 2011). A key challenge for leaders is coping with the politics of crisis accountability without the use of unseemly and potentially self-defeating tactics of blame avoidance or 'finger pointing' that only serve to prolong the crisis and heighten political tensions.

Learning: self-reflective leadership

The extent to which lessons are learnt after crises (if they are learnt at all) is one of the most under-researched aspects of crisis management (Lagadec 1997; Dekker and Hansén 2004; Birkland 2006; Deverell 2009). A crisis or disaster carries considerable potential for lessons to be drawn about the institutional production or amplification of risk, risk regulation regimes, contingency planning and training, and components of community vulnerability and resilience. In an ideal world, we might expect all relevant players to study these lessons carefully and apply them in order to reform organizational practices, policies and laws. In reality, there are many barriers to lesson-drawing.

Organizations and governments are not the best of learners, and certainly not in the aftermath of crises, especially when their own performance is called into serious question in the media and political arenas. One crucial barrier is the lack of authoritative and widely accepted explanations of the causes of a crisis or disaster. Potential factors encompass individual, organizational, technological and societal shortcomings, all of which can be subject to many different interpretations and assumptions about their significance. Such interpretation struggles are usually central to official inquiry processes, and continue in a hidden fashion long after investigation reports have been published and their recommendations symbolically 'accepted' by top leaders. Yet even if explanations could attract common agreement, many endemic features of political and organizational incentive structures – such as an excessive focus on 'core goals' or short-term pressures at the expense of proactive, non-heroic 'looking for trouble' can act as barriers to preventing future crises and improving coping capacities in the event that they do occur. Most public service organizations, for example, are focused strongly on delivering front-line public services, rather than on scenario planning and crisis training. Worst-case thinking is rarely high on institutional agendas (Clarke 2005).

In addition to cognitive and institutional influences on learning lessons after crisis, political and social aspects of a crisis can also be crucial. A dominant political depiction of a crisis as the product of failures of prevention or lack of foresight in contingency planning, can set the agenda for rethinking about policies, processes and organizational rules. However, other players in the lesson-drawing game might attempt to use the political reform rhetoric to advocate very different types of reforms from those put forward by the leaders. Therefore the stakes are high for leaders in terms of their capacity to steer lesson-drawing processes. The key challenge is to ensure that, in the wake of crisis, they have a dominant influence on the feedback stream, and that existing policy networks and public organizations follow the leader's desired pathway.

Despite complex barriers to post-crisis learning, there remains a strong belief in the academic literature, as well as in conventional wisdom, that crises also present learning opportunities (Boin and 't Hart 2003; Boin *et al.* 2009). A crisis can create windows of opportunity for policy reform, institutional overhaul and even leadership revival. The 2001 foot-and-mouth disease crisis in the UK, during which many thousands of animals were slaughtered, led to the abolition of an insular and backward-looking agricultural department. Barack Obama's victory in the 2008 US presidential elections was helped by a perception that he was better placed than his rival, John McCain, to lead the country's economic revival. His chief of staff Rahm Emanuel's quip that 'one should never let a good crisis go to waste' summed it all up: while the financial breakdown in the USA further discredited Republican claims to authority, it provided a whole new set of political possibilities and policy agendas for the Democratic candidate, untainted by any air of responsibility for the crisis of the moment.

Still, even leaders presented with an opportunity to take firm, unconventional action in response to a crisis may face the risk of changing policy on a whim instead of it being grounded in appropriate reflection. 'Knee jerk' reactions that are high on symbolic value undermine crisis leadership because they create an impression of swift and decisive reform, but are not properly road-tested. It was, for example, one thing for government leaders to announce unprecedented stimulus packages to boost domestic demand at the depth of the global financial crisis, but actually delivering stimulus measures in timely, effective and measured fashion turned out to be much more cumbersome. Sweeping reforms and the rapid replacement of key officials in response to a crisis or a critical inquiry report may help to create the impression that a leader is 'in charge'. However, such action may severely limit the capacity for genuine lesson-drawing, and may in fact create new vulnerabilities or reinforce old ones.

Dealing with the inevitable

Crisis leadership has become an integral feature of life at the top in both government and the public sector. The language and rituals of crisis have pervaded media reporting of current affairs. Nature is set to become harsher in many parts of the world, and more likely to produce major catastrophes. Economies and societies have become more tightly interconnected, meaning that economic, technological and socio-political disturbances in one country or system produce stronger and faster ripple effects across others. They have also become more complex, meaning that for our day-to-day lives we rely on systems that have an in-built capacity to surprise and defy the coping capacities of operators, managers and regulators, and provide opportunities to those bent on causing chaos and destruction. And, perhaps pivotally, in contemporary societies, citizens have been raising the bar on governments, corporations, charities and international organizations. The public expect more from them, see more of how they actually operate, and are less inclined to forgive them for mishaps and failures to deliver than any preceding generation.

All this means that both situational and institutional crises will become more rather than less frequent, and probably more rather than less severe in magnitude. Trying to prevent crises from occurring remains pivotally important, and sometimes is the only palatable alternative (for example, in preventing nuclear meltdowns). But enhancing their own as well as organizational and community resilience in the face of critical conditions has become a pivotal challenge for political, administrative, corporate and non-governmental organization (NGO) leaders alike. Doing so effectively means dedicating considerable attention and resources to contingency planning, training and practice. Getting and keeping these activities under way used to be an uphill struggle, and it was always possible to gamble that 'it won't happen here'. That has become an increasingly self-defeating posture. Facing the prospect of critical contingencies and mobilizing collective capacity to deal with them is an integral and pivotal part of public leadership today.

Chapter 7

Evaluating Public Leadership

From hero to villain, and back

We shall begin this chapter on evaluating leadership by pondering the careers of Rudy Giuliani and Christine Nixon a little further. We met both of them earlier in this book, in different roles on distant continents, brought into the text separately to illustrate particular parts of the argument. But now we put the two of them together: two public officials, one elected, the other appointed, who have both scaled the heights and depths of life in the public and political spotlight, where the assessment of an individual's performance can go up and down nearly as fast as the value of stocks. Both have written a book about their experiences (Giuliani 2002; Nixon and Chandler 2012).

Was Rudy Giuliani a successful leader of New York City's metropolitan government? His commercial success as a 'leadership guru' certainly seems to suggest this: his book, simply entitled *Leadership* and containing 10 key principles he said he had discovered and lived by throughout his long public career, sold millions of copies. Most people buying his book probably did so because Giuliani was widely credited with responding calmly, energetically, empathically and with dignity to the horrors of the 9/11 attack on the Twin Towers. But had that attack not happened as it did, at the tail end of his two terms as mayor of New York, would we still be turning to Giuliani's advice on how to lead in such numbers? Would he have been a credible Republican Party contender for the presidential nomination in 2008? The answer to both these questions is probably a resounding 'no'. Giuliani's star had been sinking deeply prior to 9/11. He was embroiled in personal scandal, and public respect for his considerable achievements in restoring law and order in the city of his public prosecutor and early days as mayor had long been replaced by disenchantment with his authoritarian style, and with his lack of effectiveness in addressing the city's nagging infrastructural, educational and social problems. Moreover, when he was stepping up his presidential nomination bid, the firefighters' union of New York had become one of his most strident opponents. It released a documentary video blaming Giuliani for the lack of investment in their communications equipment after the 1993 Al-Qaeda attack on the World Trade Center had demonstrated that the existing equipment was deficient. The video claimed that hundreds of firefighters died needlessly on 9/11 because the order to evacuate the towers before their collapse never got through to them, following Giuliani's unwillingness to invest in the upgrade.

Christine Nixon was the first-ever female police chief in Australia. Transferring from the New South Wales police into the job as Chief Commissioner of Victoria in 2001, she inherited a force marred by internal in-fighting and high levels of community dissatisfaction and mistrust. When she resigned eight years later to become head of the Bushfire Recovery Authority set up in the wake of devastating bush-fires that killed almost 200 people and ravaged entire townships on the outskirts of Melbourne, she had become an icon of the state of Victoria, and was widely credited with 'turning around' the culture of the police organization, dramatically enhancing its effectiveness (crime rates such as burglaries and car theft dropped consistently and dramat-ically during her tenure, as did the road death tolls), especially in long-neglected yet pivotal areas such as the management of domestic violence. She transformed the standing the police enjoyed in the community. Under her leadership the force was also able to put an end to a bloody gang war that had taken to the streets and endangered public safety. A people-oriented innovator by nature, her participative leadership was widely lauded; at the same time, her toughness in taking on rogue elements within the force and driving them out was (text to follow). On her departure in March 2009, the tributes flowed in from all sides. In a special issue of the *Journal of Women and Policing* her 'brilliant career' was universally applauded. One year later, however, public perceptions of her leadership changed dramati-cally when it was revealed during the public hearings of a Royal Commission set up to investigate the February 2009 bushfires that Nixon, the state's designated emergency response co-ordinator, had not been present in the operations centre when the fires hit the townships and began to kill large numbers of people. She had gone home, to a hairdresser's appointment and later on had a meal in a pub with friends instead. Her impassioned defence that she had made appropri-ate delegations for command and control arrangements during the day and that she had been on stand-by via her mobile phone all afternoon and evening was to no avail: the court of public opinion had given its verdict, bringing her public service career to a premature end.

As one does over long public lives, Giuliani and Nixon both left office with mixed track records. Both had at times faced bursts of intense media criticism, and negative reactions from within their own organizations, trade unions and some segments of the community. However, they had also enjoyed high profile successes and produced positive performance statistics in many pivotal areas of their responsi-bility. Both had also left much 'unfinished business' and even some awkward 'skeletons in the closet' when they moved on. In all of this, they epitomized drastically highly different leadership styles: Giuliani was essentially a bully with charm, while Nixon was fundamentally a nurturing visionary. And to make it more complex, the appreciation of their styles and their effectiveness as leaders has been shifting over time. Those shifts did not stop after they left office, and are likely to continue in the future.

We see the same for many public office-holders. For example, many former US presidents (apart from the most iconic and or most vilified) move up and down the rankings of the 'historical greatness' polls regularly conducted among both academic experts and the general community. These shifts are obviously not caused by any changes in these leaders' own performances – they are, after all, retrospective judgements. In a limited number of cases the shifts are caused by new information about their performances becoming public: the appreciation of Dwight D. Eisenhower, written off for decades as a hands-off, do-nothing president changed markedly when newly available archival materials revealed that behind the scenes Eisenhower had been much more switched on and had steered the ship of state actively and cleverly. Now dubbed 'the hidden-hand president' (Greenstein 1987), he shot up the rankings. For Christine Nixon, things went the other way once the story about the hairdresser and the pub meal had come to light.

But the most important cause of shifts in the assessment of leaders is caused by changes in the kinds of criteria employed in assessing them. The underlying shifts are a product of the passing of time, which bring changes in values, cultures and dominant coalitions. One man's and one era's hero leader is another's mere trier, and yet another's wrecker.

Talking about success and failure of leadership is therefore a complex and tricky business. It is subject to all the vagaries of evaluation: multiple, conflicting, ambiguous, shifting criteria, applied often by largely uninterested assessors who form judgements in the face of partially incomplete, contradictory and contested information (see, for example, Bovens *et al.* 2006). At the very least, we should be clear about the kinds of criteria we apply, how we gather evidence to assess performance against them, and what 'don't knows' and counterfactuals we absorb into the assessment. So it goes for evaluating public policy in general (Fischer 2003), and so it ought to apply to the assessment of public leadership. We should heed this principle when assessing the careers of public leaders, or the outcomes of one or several historical episodes in which leadership was exercised (or called for).

Engaging in such assessments should logically precede any effort to prescribe to others how best to lead (and what to avoid). In practice, this is hardly the case. There are more than 15,000 leadership books and many more journal and magazine articles scattered across a wide range of social science disciplines and covering a wide range of social spheres. It is fair to say that a significant majority of these publications aims to teach readers how they can become better leaders. But remarkably few examine the question that precedes these 'how to' prescriptions: how do we define and assess leadership success (Lord 2001; Kellerman 2004; Nye 2008; Tilley 2010)? We cannot simply equate successful leadership with successful political, policy or organizational outcomes; that would entail as massive risk of attribution error. The corporate literature suggests that it is difficult to demonstrate unequivocally that CEO performance affects business performance: there are simply too many intervening factors to make straightforward and strong causal connections plausible. The same can be said of political and administrative leaders: certainly, who leaders matters for some issues some of the time, but is extremely unlikely to be decisive on all the issues governments deal with all of the time. Contextual and institutional factors loom large in contemporary assessments of governance success and failure (Feit 1978; Blondel 1987; Hargove and Owens 2003). Moreover, in a world in which public leadership roles are widely dispersed, institutional outcomes have many (co-)authors. Leaders may work at cross-purposes, or actively complement one another. All this makes the question of leadership assessment a vexing one, which is perhaps precisely why so many leadership studies have shied away from posing it in the first place.

While this may be understandable, it is a grave omission. Without a proper normative grounding and systematic evaluation processes, all forms of leadership prescription lack an Archimedean point. They are prescriptions without diagnosis. In this chapter I will address both sides of the assessment coin: assessing outcomes and ways of achieving desired outcomes. First, I examine how we might evaluate the performance of public leaders and, more generally, the exercise of public leadership. Thinkers, researchers and practitioners have addressed it over the centuries, and there is no simple answer to this question. Public leadership is a multi-faceted phenomenon, which cannot be captured in a single and straightforward criteria set. Moreover, our expectations of leaders and leadership are embedded in our underlying ideas about good government. To do justice to this normative complexity, I propose a multidimensional assessment framework. This framework does not remove the inevitable trade-offs, but it helps us to bring them out into the open and forces us to acknowledge that even the most impressive feats of leadership tend to come at a price, and that few leaders fail completely and utterly in every relevant respect.

Then I turn to the million-dollar question: how can we bring about good public leadership, or at least avoid seriously 'bad' leadership from taking hold in our public domains? Book after book after book have been filled with exhortations and admonitions designed to help would-be leaders to flourish. Most of these focus on the personal traits, skills and behaviour of individual office-holders, whether they be CEOs in business, heads of government, senior public servants or heads of non-profit agencies. Some of this advice rests on contingency approaches where the core trick is to encourage leaders to match their cognitive and behavioural styles to the kinds of context, issue or constituents they might be dealing with in different roles or at different times. Some of this 'how to' work rests on painstaking experimental work in the laboratory. Some is grounded in large-N comparative case research. However, a large proportion of 'how to' books are grounded in the personal, idiosyncratic experiences of veteran leadership practitioners and the pet models of senior consultants. They have great stories to illustrate their points, but much of their advice lacks robust empirical corroboration. This makes the prescriptive component of leadership studies an essentially non-cumulative knowledge enterprise, with the airplay enjoyed by leading texts being more dependent on the celebrity and writing prowess of the author than on the independently assessable quality of the research underpinning the muscular prose in which these books specialize. Importantly for our present purposes, virtually none of these studies seriously addresses the specific context and challenges of *public* leadership, which is why I shall make precisely that central to the argument presented below.

The public leadership assessment triangle

Where to begin? There are so many different routes to arriving at criteria for evaluating public leaders and leadership. Why not keep it simple and focus the effort on what happens to the office-holders themselves as a result of the way they do their jobs? We could look at the extent to which leaders are able to consolidate their positions through (re)election and (re)appointment, based on the idea that good leaders thrive and bad leaders fail. Length of tenure, and formal judgements passed by elective, promotion and professional bodies then become pivotal to assessing leaders, as does the reputation for influence that they develop. We could also adopt a follower-centric perspective and focus on the extent to which leaders are perceived to satisfy their followers' needs and wants, as reflected in constituents' assessments of their values, character and above all their performance in the job. Or we could adopt an institutional perspective, where good leadership is indicated by the legitimacy, performance and continuity of public organizations (Boin and Christensen 2008). The list of possibilities is long, but what is lacking is a common denominator that can be applied meaningfully to all the forms of public leadership (political, administrative and civic) covered in this book. To develop such a generic model, I draw upon some of my prior work as well as that of others who assess public leadership within a broader perspective on effective, democratic governance and public management (Moore 1995; Bovens and 't Hart 1996; Bovens *et al.* 2001; Wren 2007; Bovens *et al.* 2008; Kane *et al.* 2009). I propose that we should assess public leadership by taking into account three families of core criteria, relating to:

- *Prudence*: the value of the community and/or organizational outcomes that can be attributed to their postures and actions.
- *Support*: the responses leaders evoke in both their operating (that is, colleagues, subordinates) and their authorizing (that is superiors, boards, legislatures, the general public) environment.
- *Trustworthiness*: the degree to which leaders can be said to respect the responsibilities attached to their roles, including observing the institutional limitations placed on their exercise of these roles.

The criteria complement one another, but also harbour potential trade-offs. They can be thought of as points in a triangle, with the sides of the triangle constituting the balancing act that public leaders have to engage in continuously when trying to reconcile conflicting imperatives in how they operate (see Figure 7.1).

Prudence: smart leadership

In the first perspective, the preoccupation is with what philosophers since Plato have grappled: the need to make sure that the people at the top are people who will govern wisely – not just courageously but smartly, realistically and with a sense of proportion and reflection. A modern version of the prudence perspective can be found in Lindblom (1965), who sang the praises of the ostensibly 'messy' and opportunistic democratic form of government. Lindblom, contrary to conventional defences of democracy centring on it being a safeguard against tyranny, highlighted 'the intelligence of democracy': its capacity to produce clever solutions to complex predicaments and adapt to changing circumstances. Public leadership structures and processes should facilitate this key aim, which is to be achieved by maintaining and strengthening their learning capacity (Van den Berg 1999: 40; Aucoin and Heintzman 2000: 52–4). This hinges on the extent to which public leaders are willing to consider evidence in the way they conduct their business, including the all-important generating of feedback regarding their own personal and organizational performance (Deutsch 1963; Luhmann 1966).

In this perspective, awareness that they inhabit a world in which not just they themselves but many others play crucial public leadership roles should be foremost in prudent leaders' minds. They know they need to produce and consider public feedback about their own performance (Behn 2001) – in short, to truly communicate with stake-

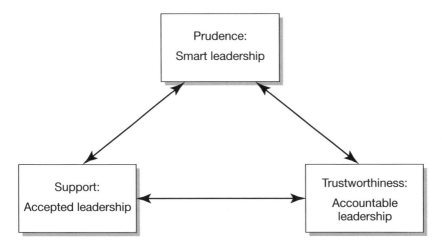

FIGURE 7.1 *The public leadership assessment triangle*

Source: 't Hart (2011b).

holders and other parties – to stay in the picture and 'on top'. The possibility of sanctions from clients and other stakeholders in their environment in the event of errors and shortcomings motivates leaders to search for more intelligent ways of organizing their businesses. Moreover, the public nature of the dialogue between overlapping and competing leaders teaches them all what is expected of them, what works and what does not. In the prudence perspective, leadership is ultimately about wisdom: an intricate mix of judgement, discernment, intuition and comprehension. The wisdom needed to exercise leadership prudently does not come about through any single public office-holder monopolizing the policy-making process, however gifted and experienced he or she might be. Wisdom cannot exist in such a vacuum. It comes from critical reflection, from dialogue and dialectics, and presupposes leaders who accept, manage and negotiate difference – who organize diversity 'in' rather than 'out' of the policy-making process (Korac-Kakabadse *et al.* 2001).

Support: accepted leadership

The criterion of support, rooted in the work of scholars such as Jean-Jacques Rousseau and Max Weber, holds that the core animating principle of contemporary democratic government is popular sovereignty: the idea that the people should rule. Naturally, those in senior leadership positions inevitably exercise far more public authority than the ordinary citizens who technically are their ultimate authorizers. From this perspective, a permanent tension between the leader and the sovereign people that engenders the kind of suspicion of leadership which has generated centuries of efforts to curb public power by fragmenting it and surrounding governments with institutional watchdogs to which they owe various forms of accountability. The fact that this key tension is, in principle, irresolvable gives public leadership its special character, explaining both its remarkable strengths and acknowledged weaknesses. Democratic public leadership is challenging because it must be most carefully exercised under conditions of institutional constraint and perennial public wariness.

Popular sovereignty in practice takes the form of a chain of delegation, which can run all the way from citizens to legislatures to political executives to administrative agencies to private (non-profit and for-profit) public service providers, thus creating a complex and multifaceted authorizing environment for the average senior public office holder (Moore 1995). This idea has been refined in the principal–agent model, according to which a modern representative democracy can be described as a concatenation of principal–agent relationships (Strøm 2000, 2003; Lupia 2003). The people, who are the primary principals in a democracy, have transferred their sovereignty to popular representatives, who, in turn, have transferred the drafting and enforcement of laws and policy to the government. Ministers subsequently entrust policy implementation to their ministries, who proceed to delegate parts of these tasks to more-or-less independent bodies and institutions. Public servants at the end of this chain of delegation end up spending billions in taxpayers' money, using their discretionary powers to, among many other things, furnish licences and subsidies, distribute benefits, impose fines, prosecute people, and keep them locked up.

Each set of principals in the chain of delegation seeks to monitor the execution of the delegated public tasks by calling the agent-leaders to account. At the end of the chain are the citizens, who pass judgement on the conduct of those leaders and who indicate their displeasure by voting for others. Hence citizens and their most directly elected representatives should be able to assess and express their support (or lack of it) for how the full range of public office-holders exercise political and administrative leadership (Przeworski *et al.* 1999). Good leaders in this perspective are those whom the public and other key parts of the authorizing environment support and are prepared to tolerate into the future.

Trustworthiness: accountable leadership

The final mode of thought about public leadership in our triangle is found in the liberal tradition of John Locke, Baron de Montesquieu and the American Federalists (O'Donnell 1998). The main concern underlying this perspective is that of preventing tyranny by absolute rulers, presumptuous elected leaders, or an expansive and 'privatized' executive power. This perspective answers the central question of leadership ethics – whether the distinctive features of leadership justify rule-breaking behaviour (Price 2008: 34) – in the negative. More precisely, it claims that the judgement of whether that rule-breaking is warranted at any given time ought to be made not only by leaders themselves, but primarily by constitutionally and/or democratically empowered 'legitimate value judges' that are able to hold office-holders accountable for the way in which they exercise leadership (Dror 1986). The remedy against overbearing or improper government leaders is the organization of institutional countervailing powers. Other public institutions, such as an independent judicial power or a court of audit, are to act as such, complementary to the voter, Parliament and political watchdogs. They are to be given the power to keep leaders in check. Good leadership requires that public office-holders respect and honour these accountability obligations.

So, from the trustworthiness perspective, good governance arises from a dynamic equilibrium between the various powers (legislative, executive and judicial) within – and increasingly beyond – the state (Witteveen 1991; Braithwaite 1997; Fisher 2004: 506–7). It proposes that a polycentric polity in all its messiness is to be preferred over a monocentric one. This bias may be pitted against other ideas; these include the aristocratic idea that democracies amount to letting mediocrity reign. They also include the 'novo-Platonic' (Dror 1986 2001) notion that we have created utterly fragmented, inchoate, paralytic systems of governance prone to 'disjointed incrementalism', even in the face of complex challenges and urgent threats that require coherent and decisive collective action. Some of the latter preoccupations can be found in the many critical accounts of the growing size, prominence and complexity of the transparency and accountability 'industry' (Bovens *et al.* 2008; Meijer *et al.* 2014). They argue that in many democracies there are so many watchdogs trying to keep public leaders in check that the system as a whole has gone 'M.A.D.' – suffering from 'Multiple Accountabilities Disorder' (see Koppell 2005). It can also be found within the US literature on the presidency, where proponents of strong presidential leadership routinely deplore the high and increasing institutional fragmentation of the American political system (Shapiro *et al.* 2000; Ellis and Nelson 2010), though this view also has many detractors, who are more concerned by the undue concentration of power and authority in an 'imperial presidency' (Schlesinger 1973; Edwards and Howell 2009).

In sum, when each of the three perspectives assesses leadership, it applies distinctive yardsticks. Each yardstick also implies a set of distinctive preferences for particular ways of organizing leadership into the fabric of public institutions. Table 7.1 develops the leadership assessment triangle further into an operational criteria map.

TABLE 7.1   *Evaluating public leadership: criteria*

	Prudence	*Support*	*Trustworthiness*
Key criteria	Leaders demonstrate good judgement in agenda-setting, decision-making and communicating	Leaders are perceived to honour the social contract with their constituents as well as other authorizing institutions	Leaders comply with institutional norms relevant to their positions and roles; their performance is checked by public accountability forums
Operational indicators	*Process:* Soliciting a wide variety of sources of information and advice Tolerance for cognitive and value complexity Effective management of self Political and managerial skills	*Process:* Level and quality of engagement with authorizing actors, assemblies and bodies Public communication proficiency	*Process:* Observance of institutional role requirements in exercise of the office Mode of handling role conflicts and/or ethical dilemmas Engagement with transparency rules and accountability bodies
	Outcomes: Impact on public and policy agendas Rate of successful 'big calls' (strategic decisions) Efficient use of resources Overall policy legacy	*Outcomes:* Depth, width, duration of authorizing environment's willingness to sustain the leader or leadership team	*Outcomes:* Absence of scandal and 'cover up' Reputation for public integrity

Applying the assessment triangle

Applying the map is less straightforward than it might seem at first sight. There are important questions of scope and method to be faced, the answers to which greatly influence the rigour and relevance of the entire exercise. These include the following.

Generic or tailor-made criteria?

The first question is whether one size fits all. Can we apply these three families of generic public leadership performance regardless of person, role and situation? This has the great virtue of parsimony. But how relevant would it be, given the breadth and diversity of 'public leadership' as defined in this book? We are more likely to need some form of 'horses for courses': more specific and contingent operationalizations of the criteria for political, administrative and civic leadership, given the specific tasks associated with each, as explained in Chapter 2 (see, in particular, Table 2.1)? What, for example, does 'prudence' mean in leading a civil rights protest movement? How, in this regard would Martin Luther King and Malcolm X compare, for example? Both addressed the same issue – racial inequality in the USA of the 1960s – but took different strategic and tactical positions on how to go about it. King chose to operate inside the established network of mainly Christian civil rights organizations and was firmly wedded to a Gandhi-inspired strategy of peaceful civil disobedience. In contrast, Malcolm X embraced Islam, toyed with black supremacist ideas, and did not shy away from advocating more militant forms of attacking white racism. It will take a careful operationalization of 'good judgement' and significant in-depth knowledge of how both leaders arrived at and justified their stances to pass a plausible comparative judgement (see, for example, Waldtschmidt-Nelson 2012). Likewise, does one need to adapt the criteria of prudence and trustworthiness when assessing the leadership of a human rights NGO in a democratic as opposed to an authoritarian or failed-state environment? How to interpret and weigh the (process and outcome) indicators of the criterion of support when assessing the public authorization to act of a government minister, a head of a government department, an elected mayor, a police chief, a whistleblower such as Edward Snowden, or a radical transparency social activist such as Julian Assange?

In general, one might say that one size is quite unlikely to fit all in a way that can still be considered substantively meaningful. Though all play roles of intense political significance, it is infeasible that we can apply the same set of generic criteria meaningfully to a minister, a senior public official or a civic leader. One should take into account the fundamentally different types of tasks each is expected to perform; and each individual task arguably entails a different weighting of prudence, trustworthiness and support considerations (see again Table 2.1). Think of the roles of holding governments to account and providing public services which many not-for-profit organizations seek to combine: these are different worlds, with different leadership challenges and thus performance tests. Moreover, the looser the institutional footing of their leadership, the more of a judgement call by the evaluator on the selection and interpretation of the criteria in the triangle map is required.

Leader, leaders, leadership?

Do we apply the criteria to an individual holding some senior position, such as a prime minister, an agency head or the CEO of a charitable organization? Do we instead focus on a designated entity or group of senior office-holders, such as an executive team or a cabinet? Or do we examine the actions and impact of whoever are seen to have been 'event-shaping' or 'game-changing' people in a particular group or government, which may cause the focus to switch to or at least include the role of informal, lower-ranking or non-office-holding leaders as well as of people who are technically 'only' advisers? In the latter vein, Rod Rhodes (2013), for example, has argued that we should not study the leadership of a prime minister, but of the entire 'court' that surrounds him or her, comprising, among others, political confidantes, personal staffers and senior public officials; others have argued that to assess presidential leadership one should look at both the structure and process of the advisory systems that presidents put in place around them (George and Stern 2002; 't Hart *et al.* 2009).

Career, role, domain, episode?

Suppose we want to evaluate the leadership of German politician and Nobel Peace Prize winner, Willy Brandt (1913–92)? What is it about him that we include in the assessment? In his long political career, Brandt held numerous political offices at party, local, national and international levels, covering both executive and advocacy roles: he was the mayor of West Berlin, opposition leader and Social Democratic chancellor candidate at several elections, foreign minister and deputy chancellor, chancellor, party chairman, president of the Socialist International, and chairman of the Independent Commission for international Development Issues. Each of these roles harboured different challenges and put Brandt into different institutional structures with distinctive rules of the game. Each, moreover, placed him in different historical circumstances and political constellations. Can we in some way arrive at a synthetic judgement about his overall prudence, support and trustworthiness, or should we evaluate his performance in his various discrete roles?

Suppose, further, that we narrow it down to his chancellorship of West Germany, which lasted from 1969 until 1974. Then we still face scoping issues. Like any head of government, Brandt had a massive array of matters to attend to: domestic and foreign policy issues; managing the cabinet, coalition and party; policy-making and crisis management; behind-the-scenes bargaining and public debating; governing and campaigning; his public and his private lives. Which of these are we going to factor in, and which out of the assessment? Moreover, Brandt operated with markedly different parliamentary majorities in his first (ultra-narrow) and second term (much expanded). His domestic standing was often at variance with his international reputation. He gained more political capital than he lost over the course of his five years in office, receiving a ringing popular endorsement in his 1972 re-election campaign, yet he stepped down prematurely just two years later under a cloud of scandal (his personal assistant had been exposed as an East German spy). Arguably, judgements about the quality of his leadership performance will vary as a result of the scoping decisions we make in all of these matters. *Ceteris paribus*, the more one focuses on specific episodes or tasks, the great the potential precision and robustness of the assessment, but also the more limited its potential relevance. There is no right or wrong choice in here, but rather a call to analysts to be very clear about their evaluation's purposes and scope them accordingly.

Apple, apples with apples, apples with oranges?

Can we reasonably evaluate each public leader in their own right, or are we not always at least implicitly comparing them to relevant others? If this is so, is it not better to be explicit about it, and construct relevant pair-wise or cohort comparison? The question then becomes who are relevant comparators. To assess Willy Brandt's chancellorship, the most obvious candidates are the seven other individuals who have held the position in the post-war democratic (West) German republic. In this vein, one could pair Brandt with his immediate predecessor (Kurt Georg Kiesinger, with whom he reluctantly joined a 'grand coalition' between Brandt's social democrats and Kiesinger's Christian Democrats, which lasted from 1966 to 1969, and who he defeated by a very thin margin at the 1969 federal elections); or his immediate successor (his ambitious deputy Helmut Schmidt, with whom he formed two-thirds of a complex but powerful political triumvirate (which also included party veteran Herbert Wehner) which controlled the course of the German Social Democrats throughout the 1960s and much of the 1970s), and assess each in terms of criteria derived from the triangle.

To prove a broader comparative perspective, one could look at the entire cohort of office-holders up to its present holder, Angela Merkel. This is a common method in so-called expert rankings of heads of government, in which historians and other knowledgeable observers of a country's government are surveyed and asked to put in rank order heads of government against the expert's own understanding of 'historical greatness' and/or against a range of explicit performance criteria provided by those running the study. In our case, we could use the criteria from the assessment triangle as the basis of an expert survey concerning the eight chancellors of modern Germany, or indeed any other of the European heads of government, presidents of the European Commission, or the secretaries-general of the United Nations). One could even evaluate non-governmental leaders in this way; for example, leaders of major trade unions (where experts in labour history and social-economic policy would be the focus of the data-gathering effort). When such exercises are repeated over time, one can gain a sense of the dynamics of leaders' reputations. These expert rankings are deeply institutionalized in the USA and have made inroads into most other Anglo political systems, but are still to gain momentum in other polities (Strangio *et al.* 2013; 't Hart and Schelfout 2014)?

There is, however, also a different way of thinking about what makes a useful comparison. Perhaps, as Steven Skowronek (1993, 2008) has argued, we should look more carefully at the kinds of political contexts and leadership challenges that different office-holders faced (see Chapter 5). Would it not make at least as much sense to compare Brandt to some of his contemporaries in the Western world, particularly in terms of how each dealt with common predicaments, such as the youth and protest culture of the late 1960s and early 1970s; the rise of terrorism (it was the era of plane hijacks and other mass hostage-takings); the Cold War and the move towards détente between the West and the Warsaw Pact nations; and perhaps most important, the oil crisis of 1973–4 and the economic conditions of stagflation and government budget crises this helped to trigger around much of the OECD world? So, instead of looking at Brandt in comparison with Konrad Adenauer, Kiesinger, Schmidt, Kohl and others, one would be comparing him to the likes of Olof Palme (Sweden), Edward Heath (UK), Georges Pompidou (France) and Pierre Trudeau (Canada).

The pros and cons of these two ways of constructing a cohort are the mirror image of each other. Going for a group of holders of a similar office allows the evaluator to hold many institutional variables constant: though the rules of the game surrounding the German chancellorship have changed somewhat over the years, and the level of the staff support the chancellor receives has ballooned in recent decades, there is much continuity. At the same time, in terms of the broader policy and political contexts, the game Adenauer (founding chancellor, 1949–63) faced was quite different from the one that Willy Brandt inherited in 1969. The post-unification chancellors, Gerhard Schröder and Angela Merkel arguably operated in a transformed domestic and international political context compared to their six predecessors (Helmut Kohl, the 1982–8 chancellor who engineered the unification after the fall of Communism in the East German Democratic Republic in late 1989, was a transitional figure who to some extent governed in two structurally different chancellorships prior to and following unification), and from a contextual perspective it makes more sense to evaluate their performances in a pair-wise comparison rather than to those of the pre-1990 West German chancellors.

In short, as in any form of comparative analysis, there are many ways to cut the leadership evaluation pie. In the case of the German chancellorship, plausible cases can be made for a whole range of constructed comparisons: Social Democratic versus Christian Democratic chancellors; the one female versus the seven male chancellors; one-term versus long-serving chancellors; those who were adults during the Second World War versus those who were children or not even born; or those presiding over economic booms versus those having to manage economic woes.

How to deal with conflicting imperatives?

Despite their different normative preoccupations, all three criteria realize that one cannot have 'too little' leadership. All of them seem to harbour a curvilinear view instead, in which there can also be 'too much' leadership: too elitist and too uniform; too opportunistic and populist; too isolated and unbridled (see also Kellerman 2004). This becomes even clearer when we examine the built-in trade-offs between the three criteria families. First, there is what we might call the *Machiavellian trade-off between smart (prudent) versus accountable (trustworthy) leadership*. It presents office-holders with the classic trade-off between ends and means: how defensible is it to cut procedural and ethical corners in trying to achieve laudable objectives (Price 2008)? Is it, for example, acceptable leadership practice for a minister seeking to attract a new, job-creating petrochemical plant to an economically depressed region to rely on backroom dealings, and to manipulate public consultation processes to make sure that opponents of the new development will not be able to put up time-consuming and potentially deal-breaking planning and legal hurdles? Conversely, how to assess a minister who is so concerned about going by the book and remaining squeaky clean that he or she is reluctant to take any decision at all that risks a legal challenge? What to make of a senior public servant so concerned with bringing down the number of complaints to the Ombudsman about his/her unit's decisions to repeal asylum claims that he/she instructs his/her staff to switch from a 'no, unless...' to a 'yes, provided...' posture, and apply it even to citizens from regions where current levels of human rights risk are widely deemed to be significantly decreased? He or she is evidently discounting the risk of unwittingly sending a signal of encouragement that might jeopardize the larger policy settings of the government – but how, and when, are we to judge the wisdom of that judgement call?

Second, there is the equally classic political *trade-off between accepted (supported) versus smart leadership*. This tension is palpable in times of austerity and international pressure, for example. Take a country such as debt-ridden Greece. For many years, the few Greek leaders who prudently advocated major cutbacks in public expenditure in order to reduce the stranglehold of escalating repayments and degenerating credit ratings risked political marginalization and popular revolt (quite literally). The need to retain office overcame the need to implement tough measures until the urgent risk of sovereign debt default changed the equation. Is this a leadership failure? Should, and could, the advocates of fiscal austerity have pushed much harder, much earlier? It is easy to say so in hindsight. But could this not have been a case where the forces inducing leaders to be responsive to their domestic authorizing environment were simply overwhelming, crowding out the voice of reason and prudence?

Finally, the governance *trade-off between accepted and accountable leadership* is one that is well known to leaders of strongly client-centred public and non-profit organizations. The strong identification with the social mission of the agency, the psychological identification with the client base, or the (perceived) need to retain its co-operation and support at all costs may crowd out the salience of due process considerations. The leadership dilemma is what to do when pressures arise around condoning co-optation by a rent-seeking clientele and the informal practices of 'flexible' rule application and service delivery to which it may have given rise. Is it defensible to protect these informal arrangements from external scrutiny and resist pressure for change? Or does sound leadership require the agency executive to risk antagonizing the client base as well as its own front-line workers, and introduce an ethos of transparency, procedural propriety and more vigorous 'nay-saying'?

Conclusion: from producing rankings to generating reflection

Given its complexities and the many choices analysts have to make, it would be amiss to see the production of 'rankings' or 'score sheets' as the added value of leadership assessment. I would argue that these are potentially useful but always contestable products. They are neither necessary nor sufficient conditions to make leadership assessment fruitful. Thinking about applying the triangle and grappling with the normative and methodological complexities helps to generate what I think are essential questions to ask when assessing public leadership performance. But it does not provide the answers automatically. Such answers cannot be given in the abstract. They need to be developed and debated. The framework alerts us to the multifaceted, inherently conflicted nature of public leadership roles and predicaments. Leaders in the private and public sectors alike inevitably operate in a world of competing values (Quinn *et al.* 2006). Judging how well such leadership is performed is thus always going to be 'messy'. But doing so along the lines suggested here challenges assessors to think carefully about and debate publicly what it is that a community values in office-holders and other public leaders, and what trade-off choices communities are making in effect when they are labelling some as 'heroes' and others as 'failures'.

So where does this leave us? Taking these principles to heart, and acknowledging the considerations and complexities presented in the latter part of this chapter, I end with a proposal for a 6-step public leadership evaluation strategy.

Step 1: Determine the objectives of the evaluation. What should the evaluation enable or bring about? Should it primarily allow the evaluator to say something about the degree of success of the individuals and groups targeted in the exercise? Or should it (also) allow the evaluator to generate a discussion about the nature, design and implications evaluating a particular form of public leadership?

Step 2: Determine the scope of the evaluation Given your objectives, who or what can be the most useful focus of the exercise? What, if any, types of comparisons can be usefully constructed by selecting more than individuals or team by taking into account particular offices/roles, episodes and time frames, leadership tasks, and institutional and cultural contexts?

Step 3: Determine who is doing the evaluating. Is all the assessment going to be performed by the evaluators themselves; in other words, are they the ones gathering and weighing the relevant evidence against a particular criteria set? Or is the assessment based around a strategy of intersubjectivity, where the evaluator gets groups of others to engage in the assessment work – through, for example, expert panels, stakeholder consultation or public surveys – and focusing on aggregating their products and interpreting the degree of agreement and difference among the assessors and assessment methods used?

Step 4: Determine the use and operationalization of the evaluation criteria. Is a deductive, criteria-led application of the assessment triangle map feasible? Or should one adopt a more inductive criteria-seeking form of evaluation where assessors are asked to articulate and explain their own criteria that are most suitable and feasible given the objectives and scope of the evaluation? In the case of a criteria-led leadership assessment, it becomes pivotal to develop tailor-made operationalizations and possibly weightings of (selected) criteria in the assessment triangle map depicted in Figure 7.1. In the case of an inductive design it becomes important to encourage assessors to document (the evolution of) their thinking about which criteria they are applying to the leaders and/or events combinations they have been asked to assess. Only then can the evaluator start to compare their assessments meaningfully, and develop an insight into the kinds of criteria that different assessors have been using.

Step 5: Gather the data needed to apply the evaluation design that has emerged from going through Steps 1–4. Depending on the design chosen and the appetite and resources of the evaluator, data-gathering may thus involve a wide variety of activities. Just as in any other form of evaluation study, these can range from running an expert survey and focus group discussions to mining opinion polls, social surveys and organizational performance data, to content analysis of speeches, interviews, newspaper coverage, social media traffic, or even of primary documents unearthed in archives.

Step 6: Articulate and implement an analytical strategy that allows the evaluator to construct a cogent feedback loop to the original objectives of the exercise. Some evaluators will 'simply' want to assess a particular leader's actions and impacts in a particular domain or time interval against a set of assessment criteria (for example, did this police chief contribute to a lowering of the crime rate in his/her jurisdiction?). Others will want to produce a focused (for example, how did this police chief's impact on crime statistics compare to his/her last two predecessors, or to his/her current peers in two similar-sized and socio-economically similar cities?) or a population-wide (for example, to what extent did all police chiefs in this jurisdiction since the end of the Second World War have a discernible impact on the incidence and social costs of crime?) comparative designs. Yet others want to get a sense of what different stakeholders, constituents or indeed followers expect of leaders, how this translates in the way that they evaluate leaders' performances, and whether this varies over time, space and social categories. What is essential is that at the end of the day they have been able to put themselves in a position where they are actually able to deliver on these objectives. This implies thinking in advance about how they are going to make sense of the data once it starts coming in, and how in this sense-making process they can remain 'in tune' with the questions about leadership that drove them to this point in the first place. The way this sense-making then finds its way into the products of the evaluation – the publication of a ranking, the articulation of a summative historical judgement about a leader or leadership team, the conduct of a dialogue about community expectations of leadership – and finds its way into a coherent account that is transparent about the assumptions and choices upon which it is built, is what determines the final utility of the project.

Leadership will always be hard to assess in a way that meets with universal recognition and stands the test of time. It is too complex for that; it is no doubt one of those 'essentially contested concepts' that social scientists like to go on about. I have no illusion that the procedure for leadership evaluation developed in this chapter is going to do anything to diminish that. But I hope it will provide its users with a script they can follow which they find helpful in going about the challenge in a way that encourages them to be systematic, rigorous and reflective.

Chapter 8

Memo to an Agent of Change

And now for something completely different...

This chapter will be quite different from those preceding it. So far, I have been in diagnostic mode. I have presented you with questions, concepts, models and research insights that each illuminates different aspects of public leadership:

- The distinctive challenges ('work') it entails, and the tools leaders have at their disposal to perform that work (Chapter 2).
- The nature and variability of the 'licence to operate' that leaders receive from followers and constituents (Chapter 3).
- The often overlooked reality that the work of public leadership in a particular setting is seldom performed exclusively by a single person ('the' leader) but generally by different authority figures or otherwise influential actors aligning their actions with those of their respective constituents (Chapter 4).
- The importance of context – ideational, situational, historical, temporal, and the ways in which leaders discern and relate to contexts – to understand leadership processes and outcomes (Chapter 5).
- The distinctive challenges and opportunities which 'crises' – in particular threatening, emotive and often urgent developments that prompt public calls for non-routine, often drastic forms of intervention – present for public leaders, agencies, and their critics and opponents (Chapter 6).
- The vexed issue of how one can evaluate the quality of public leaders and/or leadership (Chapter 7).

Taken together, these chapters were designed to provide the reader with an analytical toolkit for – as the book's title suggests – 'understanding' (that is, describing, interpreting and evaluating) the exercise of leadership in politics, government, public organizations and public issue networks.

So far, so good, I hope. But this chapter has a more practical, hands on, even prescriptive content. It entails a little thought experiment that goes like this: if we follow John Kotter's (1996) argument that the essence of the work of leadership (as opposed to that of management)

167

is coping with change; and if we also follow his claim that very often this 'coping with change' boils down to the challenge of purposively chang*ing* an organization or system that finds itself needing to adapt to changing circumstances, then what is it that a student of public leadership would actually have to say to people taking on the task of becoming an agent of change? (Certainly, in the concluding Chapter 9 I will pour some cold water on the common inference that bringing about planned change is the primary purpose of leadership, but for now we shall assume that a particular leader to whom I am an adviser wants to drive change.)

So the tone of the argument will shift from diagnostic exploration to hands-on advice. In doing so, I attempt to show that, while leadership studies may be a complex, messy, empirically patchy academic enterprise, it can nevertheless be drawn upon to ask smart questions, provide cautionary tales and suggest viable strategic and tactical pathways to leaders as they embark on a path of crafting and delivering change to public policies and institutions. What follows therefore is not quite the 'solid science' I have attempted to produce in Chapters 2–7 and will advocate again in Chapter 9. We move from pure 'science' to the art of practical advice giving. This inevitably means cutting conventional academic corners, and letting intuition fill the gaps in our knowledge of 'what works' and what doesn't that inconclusive empirical research sometimes leaves empty. Some of the best (and oldest – think of Machiavelli's *The Prince* or Sun Tzu's *The Art of War*, for example) leadership writing I know is in the self-consciously adopted format of advice to 'rulers' (see also Lord 2001; Keohane 2005). It is a genre that does not provide leaders with ready-made scripts, but is designed to make them pause, think and reflect systematically before they act. It does not presume that it can tell them what to do, but it presumes that it has things to say that they can ill afford to ignore. In this chapter I do so for the archetype of leaders as agents of change, but there are many other types of leaders and leadership situations for which one could write such advisory treatises. I hope this chapter paves the way for readers to take up that task.

I have split it into four parts, each tackling what I consider to be a pivotal area of the change process (see also Cels *et al.* 2012). First, there is advice on how a leader needs to look at, interpret and frame the context in which their intended change is going to take place – I assume cavalierly that the agent of change already knows in some way what changes they want the organization or system to embark upon. From that context, the rationale of the change presumably emanates, but in that context the changes leaders want to bring about (as of now I shall call these 'reforms' to denote their purposive and planned character, to distinguish them from the exogenous and emergent changes that leaders find it necessary to pre-empt or respond to) will also have to 'land' and become not only accepted but also enacted by stakeholders. Second, whatever their private motives and calculations, reforming leaders will need to make a public case for change. Third, reforming leaders will need to 'play the political game' that goes on inside every social system in such a way as to get meaningful changes officially adopted in the system's governance structures and processes (policies, regulations, budgets, standard operating procedures, mission statements, professional codes and so on). Finally, reforming leaders must ensure that any changes made are hard to reverse at a time when they themselves are no longer 'on the case' or may even have left the stage completely. Systems have a way of 'normalizing' and neutralizing change that allows them to keep doing what they have always been doing, and so the final challenge of reform leadership is to prevent them from doing precisely that.

Here we go. Four challenges, which require leaders to master four different games. As of now I am talking to you as if you are one of those leaders and not just any reader.

Game 1: Reading the context of reform

No pain, no gain

Getting people to actively and seriously question 'the way things get done around here' is one of the hardest things to do in leadership. Without that, nothing happens: do not expect to gain traction on reforms when most people feel the status quo is not bad at all. Latent unease and constituent discontent with existing norms, choices and practices need to be articulated and amplified. When you are the only one trying to do so, the perceived costs of your reform ambitions – uncertainty, adjustment, enforcement – can all too easily be construed by your opponents as not being worth the potential gains. Shattering complacency comes before everything else. Raise the public salience of change by demonstrating how intolerable present arrangements and practices really are. And make sure you are not alone. Give ample voice to those who feel the pain of the present and to those who can communicate authoritatively what future pain will result in the absence of reforms.

Sometimes 'events' provide you with opportunities to dramatize the case for change. When a major, unexpected 'shock to the system' – a major incident, a damning set of numbers, a media feeding frenzy, a geopolitical surprise – presents itself on your watch, avoid the temptation to deal only with its impact and with helping people to cope with that. History rewards those who have the capability to understand and interpret the crisis of the day to underpin hitherto infeasible attitude and policy changes. Be prepared to err on the side of risk of exaggeration in (re-)framing nagging problems and recent incidents – if the strategic opportunities for breaking existing policy deadlocks they present are worth it. Never forget that 'turning up the heat' is a *sine qua non* of reformist leadership. Unscheduled adversity provides a rare opportunity to do so without exhausting one's political capital. Don't be precious: never let a 'good crisis go to waste'. In fact, don't shy away from framing problems as crises in the first place.

Have your bottom drawer well stocked

'Shit happens', as they say. And when it does, it presents change agents with opportunities. When a discourse of crisis takes hold in a community, that in itself helps to discredit the legitimacy of the status quo and the actors and institutions that uphold it. Only then do stakeholders become hungry for new ideas that hold the promise of moving them towards a better future. You need to invest in an ongoing brains trust doing regular 'what if' exercises, scenario development and strategic contingency planning. This helps you provide the intellectual leadership when the time is ripe. Having a few concrete, symbolically significant and readily implementable designs for programmes and projects does not hurt either. Crises concentrate the mind, free up money and reduce procedural barriers – and you had better be ready for them when they occur.

Game 2: Arguing the case for reform

Use the R-word judiciously

History tends to look most kindly on reforming leaders – those who are credited with the transformation of old orders into new ones. The growing awareness of this reality has led to every government and every minister compulsively talking up their reformist credentials. Reform has become, in other words, a political must for leaders. No self-respecting new CEO can afford not to announce grand plans for reorganization; no self-respecting government can avoid employing the rhetoric of reform. The risk is that even the most timid, technical and trivial policy changes are talked up as 'reforms'. This gives reform a bad name.

The term 'reform' ought to be reserved for methodical attempts to achieve far-reaching changes in key beliefs and behaviour within a community and the governance structures underpinning them. Marginal adjustment of existing practices – however defensible – is not reform; it is public policy as usual. To oversell it as reform sets you up as an emperor who has no clothes.

When you feel that the time for needed reform is simply not ripe in your sector or organization (for example, because the power of the status quo players arguing that things 'ain't broken' is too entrenched at the time), content yourself with trying to create that ripeness by trying to make people face the reality of the problems they (ought to) be facing rather than prematurely selling them ready-made 'reforms' as solutions for those problems. Whatever you do, concentrate your rhetoric of reform on a limited number of areas where you feel not just the objective need but also the subjective sense of urgency for significant change are most palpable.

Be prepared to be unloved

Reforms that have only winners all the time are few and far between. If things were that easy, they would have been adopted long ago. True reforms have redistributive effects. They shake up the status quo. They will therefore be opposed by those who benefit from that status quo, as well as by people who are fooled into thinking *they* benefit from it. You do not have to go as far as to fully embrace Machiavelli's assertion that it is better for a ruler to be feared than loved. But you still need to be prepared for pushback – anticipate it, not take it personally, tolerate it gracefully but resolutely, and most of all find ways to keep talking meaningfully to reform opponents.

Zeal and courage alone won't hack it

Never forget that the burden of proof is always on the reformer; you need to be able and willing to articulate the implicit theory of behavioural change that underpins your reform vision (and encourage it to be tested as much as possible before it is put into wholesale practice). If you do not have an unassailable argument, do not expect to be able to persuade anyone. And if you do not have the power to persuade, do not expect to make reform happen by its brutal imposition in any except the direst circumstances (for example, in cases of war and violent conflict, acute fiscal crisis, systemic breakdowns, popular revolts and so on). Crucial to the power to persuade are impeccable analysis and compelling narratives. Let us look at each of these in turn.

Truly understand the system you are trying to tackle

Too often reformers focus their mental energy on bolstering their preferred interventions in one particular area instead of working methodically through how they stem from and will impact on the larger system in which they are embedded. This gets you nowhere.

Developing truly 'killing' reform arguments requires an investment in holistic analysis – and, in particular, in systems thinking. One needs to know the system that it is proposed to reform inside and out – all of it, not just a particular part of it. Water reform cannot succeed without a systemic analysis of natural resources management. Traffic congestion cannot be tackled without a systemic analysis of urbanization. Hospital reform cannot succeed without a systemic analysis of public health.

Also, one should never forget that key knowledge of the intricacies of any system does not reside exclusively at the top or within government. The task of underpinning reforms cannot be left to government economists, lawyers and technical specialists just because the public service happens to be full of them. The reformer's role is to make sure that the expertise of multiple professions, government insiders and outsiders, and strategic thinkers is brought to bear in a rigorous fashion – to bridge the gap between the 'life world' of those who operate and negotiate the system at its operational end on a day-to-day basis, and the 'system world' of those who prepare and make policy decisions about the architecture and future of the system at its strategic apex.

Game 3: Getting reform adopted

Every reform needs a compelling narrative

Unassailable arguments require more than just a sound diagnosis of past, present and future. They also require an investment in public communication of those diagnoses and of the policy implications that are desired to be drawn from that diagnosis. The principal tool of that communication is you, the reformer (at least until you have gathered a coalition of fellow change agents around you): your language, your timing and your performances. A compelling narrative is essential in 'selling' the reform to the mainstream of uncommitted 'wait-and-see' public servants and stakeholders out there to have a guiding narrative to help them to 'make sense' of what is going on. This is not about spin; it is about building a public case designed to make people face the need for major change, and gaining those critical first followers.

Enthusiastic reformers can get caught up in arcane policy detail and thus forget that the ultimate source of authority and momentum lies with their constituents, clienteles and citizens, and not with the narrow community of technocrat-insiders. In the absence of a compelling narrative, a reform effort misses the chance of making a significant discursive impact; it will not change the language in which we think and talk about ourselves and about the challenges we face. That is a missed opportunity, as discursive interventions cost little yet can have great effects.

Most important, a coherent narrative delivered in a compelling fashion can give people reasons to *believe* in the process and the changes they are expected to make in their thinking, rules and practice. Successful change agents win most of their reform battles because they are able to muster a wide spectrum of persuasive skills and are prepared to experiment with a range of persuasive formats that go well beyond merely releasing White Papers and whipping up party support. As American political sociologist V. O. Key once remarked: the ordinary voter is no fool. So when the public comprehensively rejects reform plans that the elites espousing them see as self-evidently benign and irresistible – the Irish, French and Dutch referendums on the proposed 'European Constitution' in the mid-2000s come to mind – one has to assume those elites simply have not done the work of giving the people reasons to believe them. And the same applies to those public managers who are annoyed that support for their cherished new 'restructure' in the staff survey is much more limited than they had hoped or presumed. If that happens to you, it is your problem, not that of the non-appreciative targets of your reform efforts.

Leading from the front is not your only option

The neo-liberal economic reforms in New Zealand in the mid-1980s, led by the NZ Labour Party prime minister David Lange and Treasurer Roger Douglas, are a textbook example of a 'heroic' reform style, the public policy equivalent of the kind of stalwart, top-down approach to change management we encounter so often in the management literature. Lange and Douglas went out there in the context of stagflation and looming national bankruptcy, argued the case, got the numbers and took the plunge. Though appealing to romantic ideals of 'great-man leadership', this style works only when the number of decisional forums and the number of veto players in each of them are comparatively small. When that number is larger – as tends to be the case in most contemporary democracies and in most complex professional organizations – barging in through the front door just does not work, but patient coalition building does. Some change agents excel at it, and reap its rewards. Though Lange and Douglas's Australian contemporaries Bob Hawke and Paul Keating also entertained *Über*-romantic visions of themselves as strong leaders, they were smart enough to realize that the kind of economic transformation they envisaged for Australia would not work without co-opting organized labour and, to some extent the 'big end of town', into co-determining the pace and shape of the Australian neo-liberal reform process. Lange and Douglas had their moment in history, one big wave of 'shock therapy', but the tandem and its momentum did not last for very long. Hawke, Keating and the broad social, political and bureaucratic coalition they built, managed to sustain and institutionalize reforms over a long period of time.

In working towards that ideal, backstage diplomacy is as vital – and often even more vital – in building support for reforms as front-stage dramaturgy. To use a military analogy: policy wars to reduce smoking, improve road safety or legalize same-sex marriages are generally not won by public-sector equivalents of the charismatic general of the Montgomery and Patton kinds. More often than not they are won by persistent coalition building in the general Eisenhower and Marshall – of 'Marshall plan' fame – mould. One step beyond that lies the option of actually empowering – or provoking – constituents and stakeholders to do the hard yards of reform work themselves instead of thinking that it has to be you and you alone that has to assume responsibility for the design and delivery of reforms. As Grint (2000: 6) observes: 'While we traditionally look for leaders to solve our problems, it would seem that leaders are most likely to be successful when they reflect the problems straight back to where they have to be solved – at the feet of the followers.' Ronald Heifetz's theory of adaptive leadership is built entirely on that premise, and has by now been cast into a concrete, usable (if by its very nature irreducibly risky) script for change agents to 'turn up the heat' among their constituents to own up to the need to address the disparity between the values they hold and the realities they face (Heifetz 1994; Heifetz and Linsky 2002; Heifetz *et al.* 2009).

Grand plans are not the only way to package reform

Grand ambitions do not necessarily require a 'crash through' approach aimed at achieving all targets in one fell swoop. In fact, this can create such levels of uncertainty, fear and resistance that it can lead to its own undoing. Even fearless reformers such as Ronald Reagan and Margaret Thatcher often used 'salami tactics' (a mix of alliances and threats: 'divide and rule') and patience to work through sticky points during lengthy deliberations. Grand designs are always high on lofty but abstract promises yet low on specifics and are therefore prone to peter out in implementation. Those grand reforms that are more concrete – such as the Al Gore-led 'reinventing government' operations in the US federal bureaucracy under Bill Clinton, or Obama's health insurance reform plan – also invite big opposition. Obama fought his way through and got at least a watered-down version of his plan across the line in Congress, but more often than not, political sponsors are jittery when it comes to spending political capital on grand reforms that run into headwinds. They need it more badly on the big-ticket substantive policy struggles of the day. Or they simply lose interest when they realize that there are no votes for the reforms that are on the table.

When political backing is sporadic and inconsistent, a piecemeal reform approach is not such a bad choice. It allows for proceeding much more unobtrusively and therefore less controversially. Political economist Charles Lindblom was fundamentally right that small, mutually reinforcing changes, when maintained and accumulated over a period can take one a long way from the status quo (Lindblom 1979). His ploy to achieve change – 'smuggling in' successive incremental changes rather than going for a single 'big bang' of the five-year plan ilk – fits the reality of public policy-making in democratic systems as well as in complex public organizations. At the very least, consider it a serious alternative to the raw energy of grand visions and best-made plans, which entices reformers to try too much too soon.

Engage widely early on

Reformers always face the temptation of keeping the circle of those in the know as small as possible. This temptation should be resisted. Do not succumb to the groupthink that might well result from talking only to fellow reform proponents. It sets you up for unpleasant surprises: badly vetted ideas, unexpected opposition, and implementation problems. Widening the circle and broadening the substance of the conversation are generally good ideas; in case of doubt, err on the side of inclusiveness. It is simply foolish not to bring to the design table the groups whose position and behaviour are to change as a result of the reform.

It is equally foolish not to benefit from the practical experience of those who will be implementing the reforms, both inside and outside your own organizations and networks. You should, moreover, bring those actors to the table at a time and in a manner that can still have a significant impact on the framing of key reform parameters. Expecting them to turn up to essentially swallow proposals pre-cooked by a tightly held inner circle is politically naive and most probably counterproductive.

Yes, of course, engaging widely even at the early stage of reform design will increase the transaction costs of the design process. And certainly, getting increasingly diverse stakeholders to the table and nudging them towards agreement can be time-consuming and energy sapping. These discussions are not love-ins. They can be tough and painful as well as creative and empowering. But all these costs of collaborative design are a good price to pay for what is achieved when it is done well: smarter, more robust reform proposals and the all-important buy-in from those whose collaboration is essential in making and consolidating change.

Craft creative deals

It is astounding how often zealous reformers forget the basic principles of negotiation and bargaining. One such principle is that of enlarging the pie. Research in this area finds time and again that people will fight to the death over individual issues but are more often than not able to reach agreement over creatively designed broader reform packages (bundling up a range of issues and areas) or bandwagons (where short-term costs for actors are offset by the certainty of longer-term gains on subsequent reform moves in the same area). This is especially so when they have been able to take part in the very scoping and framing of those packages and bandwagons.

Whatever one might think of the EU's recent constitutional imbroglio and subsequent euro malaise, viewed historically it has been an astounding saga of cascading institutional reform against all odds. In just a few decades, its architects and entrepreneurs have been able to extend its depth (the degree of delegation of state sovereignty granted to EU-level institutions), scope (the range of policy areas covered) and membership. Creating bandwagons and packages to overcome impasse and circumvent veto power has been vital to this success every step of the way. They are the best possible ways of sharing the gains as well as splitting and trading the pains of reform.

Game 4: Making reforms stick

A minimal winning coalition is not good enough

Few, if any, contemporary democracies are constitutionally wired in the way that Lange and Douglas's New Zealand was. In contrast, the name of the game in most public-policy arenas is dispersed power, not executive dominance. Reformers who think they can simply impose big changes once they are adopted in cabinets or legislatures will find themselves forced into humiliating back-downs and U-turns. Reformers who rely on the smallest of possible coalitions and ignore the remaining 49 per cent set themselves up for relentless rearguard battles during implementation and quite possibly for outright policy reversals once they lose the power to impose their will.

The long-term viability of reforms is greatly enhanced when the coalition that is carrying it is 'oversized'. If this can be achieved only at the price of some of the ideological purity of the original reform philosophy, then so be it. You will need the broad support base to withstand the forces of reaction that will seek to undermine the reform process. You will need to embed the reform momentum as widely as possible within the government bureaucracy – pivotally including the central agencies – so as to make its memory, diligence and, paradoxically, its inertia work *for* rather than *against* the integrity and continuity of already enacted reforms.

Just because they are big achievements does not mean reforms succeed

Therefore, winning the battle to have them designed and adopted is a necessary but not a sufficient step to make reforms work and make them last. Reforms are wars, not battles. When you do not attend to their implementation and long-term maintenance, do not expect them to deliver the goods – as Barack Obama was finding to his considerable cost when 'Obamacare' finally reached the stage of implementation and became bogged down in IT and administrative system failures, which gave its opponents another shot at reversing it. When the implementation is ill-designed and under-managed, the negative unintended consequences ultimately dwarf those that were targeted and planned for. Well-intentioned reforms can easily end up looking like 'fatal remedies' (Gillon 2000; Sieber 1981). Reform opponents seize their chance to fight back, and to sabotage and twist the process of putting intentions into action.

It is not hard to find reforms that are reversed as soon as the political tide has turned, and there are plenty of reforms that suffer from what Patashnik (2008) calls 'death by a thousand cuts': while nominally still in force, their force and integrity are undermined by lobbying from special interests, resulting in watered-down implementation or legislative emasculation. What goes for public policy in general applies even more so to high-stakes reforms; as a proponent, one cannot rest on one's laurels once the bill has become law. One has to be in it for the long haul, and needs to be as attentive, inventive and tenacious in the implementation and consolidation phases as in the design and adoption processes. If this is not the case, one's reforms risk falling over before they have well and truly begun, or the life of one's successors is unnecessarily complicated by them.

Incorporate mechanisms that make reforms self-sustaining

It is important to think about why citizens and stakeholders change their behaviour as a result of the implementation of a reform. You need to understand that basic 'carrots and sticks' buy only opportunistic compliance that is costly to keep bankrolling and policing. Sometimes there is no other way – for example, in industrial relations and health and safety, where employers will always be tempted to engage in races to the bottom, given the relentless pressures on them to raise productivity (by reducing costs).

Yet the most robust reforms change people's norms and values. Once new standards of appropriateness have been internalized and disseminated widely, compliance costs tumble, and so does the risk of reform erosion or reversal. Child labour is now considered to be simply unacceptable in Western countries. Smoking is now firmly socially stigmatized (though, pivotally, not made illegal) in most. Drink driving is getting there, though there is a considerable way to go in some countries.

These ideational changes have not happened by accident. As Patashnik (2008) shows, they are the product of clever reform designs that have managed to create behavioural incentives which get into people's heads and hearts. If one is serious about protecting the long-term integrity of reforms, this is the way to go. It is about cleverly combining the logic of economics with the logic of behavioural research in psychology, sociology and communication studies (teaching us to consider the subconscious and social drivers of human perception, identity, judgement and preference formation). Thaler and Sunstein's *Nudge* (2008) is a good place to start if one is serious about this ambition (Sunstein was subsequently appointed Barack Obama's regulation tsar, so do not think it is just two eggheads talking).

The case for prudence

This 'memo' has summed up what I think our current knowledge about leading change allows us to convey to public leaders who want to make a difference on issues they care about, and who have concluded that the way to do so is to embark on a path of bringing change to a system. It is up to them to explore how they can make some, or ideally all, of these lessons work for them. This will no doubt include exploring the potential tensions between these various imperatives. After all, the craft of reformist leadership is an art, not a science. The rules of experience provided above do not make a recipe book, nor could such a book ever be written. In most cases, there are multiple potentially passable pathways to reform. There will always remain a need for situation-specific judgements and intuitions about the 'what, when and how' of going down one road or another – and when to reassess that choice.

And it is best to tread carefully, because the price of trying and failing is probably at least as high as that of failing to try. It is good to heed Gardner's (1990: 8) sobering observation that 'leaders suffer from the mistakes of predecessors and leave some of their own misjudgments as time bombs for successors' – ill-conceived and badly executed reforms and restructures are at the top of the list of costly leadership mistakes. Unless the status quo is truly bad, hopeless or definitely getting irreversibly worse (John Kotter's 'melting iceberg'), err on the side of gradualism in one's approach to advocating, designing and delivering change. More reforms – and leadership careers – have ended in tears because of excessive ambition and hubris than because of excessive caution and timidity. The future does not belong to the faint-hearted, as Ronald Reagan powerfully observed in his 1986 post-Challenger disaster speech to the nation, but neither does it necessarily belong to the brave (as he argued). It belongs to the prudent (Kane and Patapan 2014). It was Aristotle who imparted that timeless truth to us, a mere 23 centuries before contemporary leadership scholars rediscovered it.

Chapter 9

Retrofitting Public Leadership

Looking ahead

This book has been about 'understanding' public leadership. One of its take-home lessons is that the challenges, shape and style of public leadership will vary as a function of (changes in) the contexts in which it operates. In the final chapter I get into a helicopter, and take a bird's-eye view of the changing context in which contemporary public leadership is unfolding. With these contextual changes in mind, I also survey the landscape of public leadership discourse and offer both a critical account of where we stand today and where we should be heading tomorrow.

In many ways, the 'public leadership' described in the literature and talked about in the earlier chapters of this book is of a thoroughly nineteenth-/twentieth-century kind. It is embedded in constitutional arrangements, nation states, and electoral and party systems. It is a product of modernity, and thus grounded in rules, hierarchy, specialization, professionalism, and tailored for industrial-era large-scale organizations and communities. Much of this has persisted into at least the early part of the twenty-first century. At the same time, since around the mid-1990s there have also been marked, and indeed profound, technological, demographic, socio-cultural and institutional changes within and beyond nations that have severely tested their existing leadership arrangements and practices.

Let us therefore take a look at what I believe are robust and important changes in the social contexts in which public leaders will have to operate. These changes affect the kinds of issues communities face, what constituents and colleagues expect of leaders, and how institutional rules and cultures empower and constrain various leadership styles. In Table 9.1, I signal seven such social trends. Taken together, they constitute an agenda for public leadership today and tomorrow. This agenda, and the challenges it implies, affects the practice of public leadership – how it is imagined, designed, performed, legitimated and checked in the public realm. It should also challenge those of us who do indeed seek to 'understand' public leadership professionally to adapt the ways in which we conceptualize, observe, explain and evaluate it.

The trends described in Table 9.1 are largely well-documented in studies such as the *World Values Survey* and comparative studies of public governance (see, for example, Dror 2001; Inglehart and Norris

180

2004, 2009; Inglehart and Welzel 2005; Frederickson *et al.* 2012; Levi-Faur 2012) though some – such as Bauman's liquid modernity thesis – await empirical corroboration. Among their chief drivers are economic development, individualization, democratization, secularization, advances in information technology and mass transportation, and the uptake of evolving ideologies of government, governance and management, though there are significant regional and cross-national differences in some of these. When we let these trends and their implications sink in, it becomes clear that, like the societies from which they emanate, the institutions of political, administrative and civic leadership we developed and learned to live with in the twentieth century are themselves facing major adaptive challenges – for which there are indeed 'no easy answers' (Heifetz 1994). To highlight this, I have phrased them in terms of balancing ambiguous imperatives. I represent them in Figure 9.1.

Perhaps the meta-tension overlaying all of these is that in twenty-first-century public governance, wise and authoritative leadership is at more necessary and at the same increasingly hard to find. It is more necessary because the challenges and opportunities that communities and organizations face have become more complex: fast evolving, complexly intertwined, transnational in their origins, locally variable in their manifestations, and transgenerational in their implications (think of ageing populations, energy security, water management, food supply, climate change and biogenetic engineering). Moreover, citizens have become more demanding and less dependable authorizers of public office-holders, whose performances they are now much more able to closely scrutinize and feel much more empowered to repudiate if they don't like what they are seeing. To be effective and remain 'authentic' at the same time is not easy in such an operating environment (see, for example, Sinclair 2007; Grube 2013; Gaffney 2014).

The relative salience and specific manifestations of these challenges obviously vary across jurisdictions, organizations and leadership structures. The search for appropriate ways of balancing these imperatives will be a work in progress for decades to come. The trial and error we shall see in this regard will be influenced by locally contingent leadership traditions, cultural proclivities and power relationships. Think, for example, of the rise of women leaders we are seeing in many spheres of public life around the world. There is great variation in the numbers and percentages that express this trend in quantitative terms across sectors and countries (Foley 2013: 218–24). But in qualitative terms, the picture is even more complex and contingent, as attitudes of, and towards, women in senior leadership positions and the relative merits of (ideal typical) masculine and feminine leadership styles are being renegotiated at different speeds and to different extents. As a result, the

TABLE 9.1   *Social trends and public leadership challenges*

Trend	Characteristics	Leadership implications
1. The age of *networks* Key source: Castells (1996)	Rise of complex interdependencies, distributed authority and resources, and public demand for integrated policies, programmes and public service delivery	Need to balance the reality of specialization, hierarchy and 'turf'-based 'top-down' leadership with a need for collaborative leadership in shared-power settings.
2. The age of *empowerment* Key source: Ryde (2013)	Reduction of the 'power distance' between authorities and constituents. Decline of 'automatic' public deference towards authority figures and established public institutions.	Need to balance a post-paternalistic, more interactive way of leaders–community/group engagement with need for authoritative leadership that remains capable of making hard calls.
3. The age of *transparency* Key source: Mulgan (2014)	Increased public access to information about how public institutions and organizations operate, and when they fail. Rapid growth of the proportion of citizens and social groupings who want to (and think they) 'know' how they are being governed.	Need to balance maximum openness about conduct of public office-holders and performance of public organizations with the confidentiality and reflective space required to handle sensitive issues and craft delicate multi-actor compromises
4. The age of *immediacy* Key source: Gleick (2000)	Information technology and increased mobility have created time–space compression in economic, cultural and political life. Rise of tightly inter-connected, speeded-up, interactive forms of collective deliberation and feedback.	Need to balance speed, responsiveness and a sense of urgency with prudence, patience and the ability to take a long-term view. ➡

boundaries between a leader's gender and his/her style are no longer as clear-cut (Campus 2013: 115–25; Sykes 2013, 2014), and at the same time it would be woefully inaccurate to say that male and female public leaders are now operating on a level playing field – for example, when it comes to media portrayals of character, style and competence – as some female leaders such as French party leader and presidential contender Ségolène Royal and Australian prime minister Julia Gillard have found to their considerable cost (Gaffney 2010: 179–90; Walter 2014; see also Rhode 2003; Keohane 2010: 121–54).

TABLE 9.1   *Continued*

Trend	Characteristics	Leadership implications
5. The age of *accountability* Key source: Bovens *et al.* (2014)	Continued growth of formal and informal mechanisms of oversight, evaluation, quality control and comparative assessment ('rankings'). Legitimacy of public authorities and institutions is now much more contingent on (perceptions of) their 'past performance'.	Need to balance production of believable, confidence-inspiring 'performances' in a high-scrutiny marketplace for public trust with the transaction costs and unintended effects of 'managing' multifaceted accountability regimes.
6. The age of *fluidity* Key source: Bauman (2006)	Decline of the socializing power of traditional identities, institutions and social ties. Growing eclecticism and ephemerality and thus declining predictability and dependability of people's values, preferences, fears and life styles.	Need to balance a form of leadership that is credible through clarity, consistency and tenacity in values and purposes with a form of leadership that is responsive and adaptive to more changeable public moods, priorities and loyalties.
7. The age of *glocalisation* Key source: Blij (2009)	Increased salience of transnational problems and development of a deepening field of transnational governance arenas. At the same time, a growing anti-cosmopolitan cultural backlash driven by fear of losing locally based identities, values and institutions.	Need to balance institutionalizing post-national leadership capacities with keeping public leadership grounded in the national and local communities from which it emanates and which it affects.

The challenge is at least threefold. For individual leaders, positioning oneself in an operating environment characterized by these features requires the leaders themselves to re-calibrate their skills sets, styles and behavioural repertoires, to increase the agility with which they manage their complex dependencies, temporal ambidexterity, and multiple accountabilities. Second, the leader selection and support systems that operate in politics, public administration and the not-for-profit sector should come to terms with the new imperatives of public leadership by rethinking how they spot, recruit, equip, advise, evaluate

Segmented, top-down ....Shared, collaborative

Engaged, interactive..............................Autonomous, authoritative

Transparent...Discrete

Fast, near-sighted ....Prudent, far-sighted

Accountable, performative.....................Lean, purposive

Value-driven, consistent, principled ....Goal-seeking, adaptable, opportunistic

Post-national ....Locally grounded

FIGURE 9.1   *Reinventing public leadership: a balancing act*

and remove political, administrative and civic office-holders. Lastly, at the systemic level there is a need to rethink the leadership rhetoric that shapes community understandings of who can and should lead, what leadership is for, and how it is to be exercised. This has produced a corresponding need to recalibrate the way that leadership is organized into the fabric of public governance and organizational design: more collegiate, more shared, and endowed with mandates and resources that provide office-holders with a fighting chance to persuade more autonomous, sceptical and unforgiving constituents and watchdogs to give them the benefit of the doubt.

There is no self-evident single best way forward in all of this. Retrofitting public leadership for the twenty-first century is an unfolding process for which there is no rulebook. But we do know a little about what *not* to do. There are some unhelpful assumptions and action reflexes that should be avoided, because they are demonstrably ineffective in a shared-power, fast-based, liquid, borderless, high-scrutiny world. Some of these are lurking in the very leadership industry – which is in effect what it has become, both inside and outside academia – itself. It is with a reflection on that industry, and its pitfalls in addressing the emerging public leadership challenges, that I will conclude this book.

Retrofitting the leadership industry

Calls for 'more', 'better', 'genuine', 'transformational' or 'authentic' leadership are often heard from those in politics and government. But what do these callers really want? How realistic are their expectations? Who should heed them? What can we learn from these pleas? Tough talk on leadership fits the times. The leadership industry provides us with plenty of persuasive stories about successful leaders, ranging from the heroic to the humble. In mainstream leadership thought, dominated as it has been by US-/Anglo-based or oriented voices, a particular master narrative has long reigned in which 'leadership' is exercised by extraordinarily driven and resourceful (dynamic, wise, persistent, proactive and the entrepreneurial) people who, often by defying conventional wisdoms and battling sticky, conservative institutions, transform dysfunctional or stagnant communities and ineffective, wasteful or unethical organizations into success stories. This late modernity version of the 'great man' theory finds its starkest articulations in many a leader's autobiography. It runs like this:

- When I took over, things were messy.
- Nobody wanted to face up to how bad things were.
- Then I challenged the complacency and the despair.
- I repudiated the past and articulated a new vision.
- That vision formed the basis for the fundamental reforms I instigated.
- 'They' did not like that.
- It was a real struggle.
- But I persevered and built a coalition that drove change against the odds.
- Now things are great.
- I am in control.
- I am in tune with my authorizers and constituents.
- The people love me, or at least respect me.
- All this is because I am very, very competent.

(*And, left unsaid*: If only there were more leaders like me...)

This might strike you as an exaggeration, but let me assure you, despite decades of academic repudiation, the heroic leadership narrative is alive and well, not just in corporate but also in political and civic leadership discourse (Allison and Goethals 2013). A whole industry of publishing, training and consulting has been built up around it (Kellerman 2012). As with any success story, however, one needs to question whether the heroic narrative is accurate and how well it travels beyond the individuals concerned. Yes, there are kernels of truth in many of these stories, in the corporate, academic and public sector worlds alike. When Lee Iacocca, Bill Gates or Steve Jobs talked about their leadership experiences, they were not fabricating – ample evidence to demonstrate their success as leaders exists on the public record. Or when Goleman *et al.* (2002) find that a high level of emotional intelligence correlates with certain forms of leadership success, they are on to something. When respectable observers of public sector leadership such as the *Public Administration Review* or

The Guardian's Public Leaders Network publish profiles of high-performing public service leaders, or when serious students of social movements write about their most notable leaders they tend to argue that these individuals have really made a difference in producing public value (see, for example, Williams 1996; Cels *et al.* 2012; Moore 2012).

On the other hand, the more sweeping claims of much contemporary leadership talk are debatable. What, then, are some of its problems? First, as noted in Chapter 1, much modern leadership-speak talks down 'management' as dull and unimaginative store-minding. While deeming it good enough for less dynamic times, this notion oddly dismisses the 1950s, 1960s, 1970s and 1980s as periods of stability, when management rather than 'leadership' was the buzzword, and managers were hot property in professionalizing governance. Many leadership 'gurus' and leadership programmes direct aspiring leaders to look first at themselves, to improve their skills and competencies, to assert themselves, and then to make a difference by visioning and delivering 'change'. Through their personal artistry, real leaders innovate and reform, we are told.

In the public sector context, with its solid institutions, its democratic constraints on heroic leadership, and its pivotal need for order, continuity and predictability in the way public services are delivered, both parts of that message can prove problematic. As for the obsession with 'change', Christopher Pollitt (2008) tells the tragi-comic tale of the permanent 'redisorganization' of the British National Health Service brought about by a succession of reform-focused leaders. Pollitt documents how the relentless waves of reform – new ones being announced before their predecessors had run their course – resulted in organizational introversion, loss of institutional memory, plummeting staff morale, and precious little improvement in service delivery to customers. That tale strikes a familiar chord with many working in and observing major public organizations. We are in danger of reorganizing ourselves to death, and in no small measure because many people in charge of these organizations are conditioned – by their socialization and incentive structures as 'leaders' – to think that this is the reason why they are there.

To counterbalance the field's long-standing obsession of leadership with delivery of change, I suggest we pay equally serious attention to alternative voices, which conceptualize public leadership as 'conservatorship' (Terry 1995) – stewardship of core regime values that transcend the issue of the moment and are worth protecting against short-sighted and often self-serving efforts to undermine them– or as 'gardening' (Frederickson with Matkin 2007), with effective leadership boiling down to the patient nurturing of self-organizing and adaptive capacities of people and organizations, have long been crowded out but are now gradually getting more of a hearing.

As for the focus on the personal qualities of leaders, let me be clear: of course I believe that the public interest is best served by having people in key roles within politics, the public service and civil society who are skilful, wise, reflective, courageous, entrepreneurial, humble, inspiring and empathic. And of course I believe in the importance of trying to nurture such generic professional qualities in people training to be the public leaders of the future. However, I wonder about the utility of the countless courses and seminars on leadership where the suggestion is that it is *all* about 'you' – your drive, your skills, your attitudes, your self-confidence, your communication, your aura, your humility. Public problem-solving must also have a resilient institutional fabric, which fosters an intelligent interplay between holders of various public offices, and between those running government and those scrutinizing them on behalf of the community. Good governance must maximize opportunities for interaction, debate, reflection and reconsideration (Torfing *et al.* 2012). To achieve this, key public offices embedded within those institutions should be made (and kept) 'idiot-proof' and 'tyrant-resistant', by keeping those offices and their holders in a web of checks and balances that is tangible and if need be consequential, but at the same time does not paralyse them. Even a cursory glance at the history of politics and public administration shows that open, resilient, democratic public institutions are far more important to the quality of government than any effort to groom and select an elite of wise individuals to lead the country (Keane 2009; Kane and Patapan 2012).

Furthermore, focusing so strongly on the creative power of leaders risks implicitly promoting a Platonic view of leadership where wisdom and drive should come from the top. As we have just seen in a twenty-first-century context, such a view is at best incomplete and at worst outright counterproductive. And indeed, other classic philosophers and political theorists have much to offer to counterbalance the Platonic view (Keohane 2010; Ladkin 2010). A key challenge for today's and tomorrow's politicians, public managers and civic leaders is not simply how to lead their governments, agencies and organizations, but also to figure out how each of these institutions can even remain relevant when open borders, critical and discerning citizens, empowered women and minority groups, complex dependencies and self-conscious professionals continuously challenge these institutions' adaptive capacities (Dror 2001). Contemporary public leadership theory and practice should thus focus more on understanding and improving the dynamics of leadership in shared power settings – that is, understanding how senior public office-holders can persuade their colleagues and organizations to be more effective collaborators, partners and negotiators, and less on persevering with the tired narrative of top-down, visionary, transformational leadership (Van Wart 2013).

In a similar vein, we can question the empirical foundations of much of the 'how to' leadership prescriptions that have been flooding the corporate and now also the public leadership markets. I never cease to be amazed by the audacity with which people advocate their preferred normative conception of good leadership. Entrepreneurial leadership, transformational leadership, coaching leadership, servant leadership, empowerment leadership and charismatic leadership: these catchphrases abound in the titles of the books that pack the shelves of airport and railway station bookstores. It seems that every time you look, another author has coined a new leadership adjective, along with its own philosophy, model, success stories, proverbs, lessons and 'how to' tips. But how firmly grounded are these insights at the end of the day?

Good science is cumulative; its students today possess a common language, a set of shared assumptions, and above all a widely accepted body of robust empirical knowledge produced by their predecessors. Not so in the world of leadership studies, where people cannot even agree on basic definitional issues, let alone on theory and methods (Banks 2008). Such a field is essentially footloose. Semantic seductiveness is a more effective way to sales, impact and professional advancement than systematic articulation, testing and retesting of refutable propositions. The gulf between guru-style confessional and prescriptive self-help books and empirically thorough academic leadership studies is vast. Those who have been at the vanguard of leadership studies for decades – scholars including James McGregor Burns, Robert House, Erwin Hargrove, Manfred Kets de Vries, Fred Greenstein and Margaret Hermann – refrain from offering us proverbs. As scholars who have spent lifetimes in the trenches of empirical research on political, administrative, civic and corporate leaders, their great contribution has been to make their readers aware of the contingencies, predicaments, traps and constraints of leadership. They know better than to simply tell aspiring leaders what to do when they know that the knowledge to back up those prescriptions is contestable.

In the fields of public policy, public management and political science, we need a self-consciously *public* leadership discourse that is driven by careful reasoning and allows itself to be informed by sound evidence rather than the slogans and maxims of leadership gurus whose expertise is mainly rooted in and aimed at the business sector. The kind of public leadership discourse I advocate must pertain not only to the personal, but also on the institutional and contextual dimensions of public leadership. Consideration of electoral politics, the politics–administration distinction, the rule of law, ubiquitous accountability requirements, and the growing limits to the power of centralized government must be part of the public leadership story.

I particularly want the public leaders of the future to be acutely aware that powerful leaders can destroy as much as they create.

Leaders of the future should be socialized in a manner that encourages a self-reflective rather than a 'can-do' attitude, one that recognizes the value of dissent as much as that of the deft wielding of hard, soft and smart power (Banks 2008). We need leaders who eschew change for change's sake, and recognize that their desire to deliver change always needs to be balanced against the need to exercise stewardship of key public values and institutions. We need a public leadership discourse that does not presume that all wisdom resides at the top, and does not tell aspiring leaders they should possess unrealistic competency profiles. We need leadership training that balances attention to personal development with an acute appreciation of community, culture, context, contingency and collaboration.

More and stronger transformational leadership in the traditional, heroic and individualistic mode will not remedy the current crisis of governance in many Western countries. Today, as much as in any other era, we need prudent leaders *and* strong institutions harnessing and checking their powers of creation and destruction.

Appendix: Ten 'Must Reads' on (Public) Leadership

During or after class, students sometimes ask me for suggestions on what to read if they want to deepen their knowledge of the subject. Now that is an impossible request if ever there was one. The leadership literature is a behemoth, or rather an ever-expanding universe of behemoths, many of which are not talking to one another. But here – in alphabetical order – are my 10 current favourites in the more academic, analytical genre of writing specifically devoted to various forms of *public* leadership (biographies, ethnographies or self-help books would make for quite a different list, which would be topped by Michael Ignatieff's impressive memoir of his period as Canadian opposition leader cum poignant analysis of contemporary politics, *Fire and Ashes* (Cambridge, MA: Harvard University Press 2013)):

- Frederick Bailey, *Treasons, Stratagems, and Spoils: How Leaders Make Practical Use of Beliefs and Values*, Boulder, CO: Westview Press, 2001.
- Barbara Crosby and John Bryson, *Leadership for the Common Good: Tackling Public Problems in a Shared Power World*, San Francisco: Jossey-Bass, 2005.
- Alex Haslam, Steve Reicher and Michael Platow, *The New Psychology of Leadership*, New York: Psychology Press, 2010.
- Ronald Heifetz, *Leadership Without Easy Answers*, Cambridge, MA: Harvard University Press, 1994.
- John Kane and Haig Patapan, *The Democratic Leader: How Democracy Defines, Empowers and Limits Its Leaders,* Oxford: Oxford University Press, 2012.
- Nannerl Keohane, *Thinking About Leadership*, Princeton, NJ: Princeton University Press, 2010.
- Joseph K. Nye, *The Powers to Lead: Soft, Hard, and Smart*, Oxford: Oxford University Press, 2008.
- Amanda Sinclair, *Leadership for the Disillusioned: Moving beyond Myths and Heroes to a Leadership that Liberates*, Sydney: Allen & Unwin, 2007.
- Steven Skowronek, *The Politics Presidents Make: Leadership from John Adams to George Bush*, New Haven, CT: Yale University Press, 1993.
- Larry D. Terry, *Leadership of Public Bureaucracies: The Administrator as Conservator*, London: Sage, 1995.

Bibliography

Aarts, K., Blais, A. and Schmitt, H. (eds) (2011) *Political Leaders and Democratic Elections*, Oxford: Oxford University Press.

Aberbach, J., Putnam, R. and Rockman, B. (1981) *Bureaucrats and Politicians in Western Democracies*, Cambridge, MA: Harvard University Press

Adam, B. (1990) *Time and Social Theory*, Cambridge: Polity Press.

Adizes, I. (1999) *Managing Corporate Life Cycles*, Englewood Cliffs, NJ: Prentice- Hall

Agranoff, R. (2007) *Managing Within Networks*, Washington, DC: Georgetown University Press.

Agranoff, R. and McGuire, M. (2003) *Collaborative Public Management: New Strategies for Local Governments*, Washington, DC: Georgetown University Press.

Aldrich, J.H. and Shepsle, K.A. (2000) 'Explaining institutional change: soaking, poking, and modeling in the U.S. Congress', in H. Bianco (ed.), *Congress on Display, Congress at Work*, Ann Arbor, MI: University of Michigan Press, pp. 23–45.

Alesina, A. and Roubini, N., with Cohen, G.D. (1997) *Political Cycles and the Macroeconomy: Theory and Evidence*, Cambridge, MA: MIT Press.

Alford, J. (2008) 'The limits to traditional public administration: Rescuing public value from misrepresentation', *Australian Journal of Public Administration*, 67(3): 357–66.

Alink, F., Boin, A. and 't Hart, P. (2001) 'Institutional crisis and reforms in policy sectors: The case of asylum policy in Europe', *Journal of European Public Policy,* 8(2): 286–306.

Allison, S.T. and Goethals, G.R. (2013) *Heroic Leadership: An Influence Taxonomy of 100 Exceptional Individuals*, New York: Routledge.

Alvarez, J.L. and Svejenova, S. (2005) *Sharing Executive Power: Roles and Relationships at the Top*, Cambridge: Cambridge University Press.

Anonymous (1996) *Primary Colors: A Novel of Politics*, New York: Random House.

Ansell, C.K. and Fish, M.S. (1999) 'The art of being indispensable: Noncharismatic personalism in contemporary political parties', *Comparative Political Studies*, 32(3): 283–312.

Ansell, C. and Gash, A. (2007) 'Collaborative governance in theory and practice', *Journal of Public Administration Research and Theory*, 18(4): 543–71.

Archer, D. and Cameron, A. (2013) *Collaborative Leadership*, London: Routledge.

Aucoin, P. and Heintzman, R. (2000) 'The dialectics of accountability for performance in public management reform', *International Review of Administrative Sciences*, 66(1); 45–56.

Avolio, B.J., and Yammarino, F. J. (eds) (2013) *Transformational and Charismatic Leadership: The Road Ahead*, Monographs in Leadership and Management, Vol. 2, Bingley: JAI/Elsevier.

Badie, D. (2010) 'Groupthink, Iraq and the war on terror: Explaining the policy shift toward Iraq', *Foreign Policy Analysis*, 6(3): 277–96.

Bailey, F. (2001) *Treasons, Stratagems, and Spoils: How Leaders Make Practical Use of Beliefs and Values*, Boulder, CO: Westview Press.

Bakvis, H. (1997) 'Advising the executive: Think tanks, consultants, political staff and kitchen cabinets', in P. Weller, H. Bakvis and R.A.W. Rhodes (eds), *The Hollow Crown: Countervailing Trends in Core Executives*, London: Macmillan.

Banks, S.P. (2008) 'The troubles with leadership', in S.P. Banks (ed.) *Dissent and the Failure of Leadership*, Cheltenham: Edward Elgar, pp. 1–21.

Baraket, J. (2008) *Strategic Issues for the Non-Profit Sector*, Sydney: UNSW Press.

Barber, J.D. (1972) *The Presidential Character*, Englewood Cliffs, NJ: Prentice- Hall.

Barker, C., Johnson, A. and Lavalette, M. (eds) (2001) *Leadership in Social Movements*, Manchester: Manchester University Press.

Baron, R. S. (2005) 'So right it's wrong: Groupthink and the ubiquitous nature of polarized group decision making', *Advances in Experimental Social Psychology*, 37(2): 219–53.

Bass, B. (1998) *Transformational Leadership*, Mahwah, NJ: Lawrence Erlbaum.

Bass, B. (1999) 'Two decades of research and development in transformational leadership', *European Journal of Work and Organizational Psychology*, 12: 47–59.

Bauman, Z. (2006) *Liquid Times: Living in an Age of Uncertainty*, Cambridge: Polity Press.

Bauman, Z. (2007) *Consuming Life*, Cambridge: Polity Press.

Baumgartner, F., and Jones, B.D. (2009) *Agendas and Instability in American Politics*, 2nd edn, Chicago, IL: Chicago University Press.

Baylis, T. (1989) *Governing by Committee*, Albany, NY: SUNY Press.

Behn, R. (2001) *Rethinking Democratic Accountability*, Washington, DC: Brookings Institution.

Bell, S. and Hindmoor, A. (2009) *Rethinking Governance*, Cambridge: Cambridge University Press.

Bendor, J.W. (1985) *Parallel Systems: Redundancy in Government*, Berkeley, CA: University of California Press.

Benington, J. and Moore, J. (eds) (2011) *Public Value: Theory and Practice*, Basingstoke: Palgrave Macmillan.

Bennis, W.G. (1989) *On Becoming a Leader*, Reading, MA: Addison-Wesley.

Bennister, M. (2012) *Prime Ministers in Power*, Basingstoke: Palgrave Macmillan.

Bennister, M., 't Hart, P. and Worthy, B. (2014) 'Leadership capital: Measuring the dynamics of leadership', Paper presented at ECPR Joint Sessions, Granada, Spain, 14–19 April.

Bevir, M. and Rhodes, R.A.W. (2003) *Interpreting British Governance*, London: Routledge.

Bevir, M. and Rhodes, R.A.W. (2010) *The State as Cultural Practice*, Oxford: Oxford University Press.

Bezes, P. (2001) 'Defensive versus offensive approaches to administrative reform in France (1988–1997): The leadership dilemmas of French prime ministers', *Governance*, 14(1): 99–132.

Bingham, L.B. and O'Leary, R. (eds) (2008) *Big Ideas in Collaborative Public Management*, Armonk, NY: M.E. Sharpe.

Bion, W.R. (1961) *Experiences in Groups*, London: Tavistock.

Birkland, T.A. (2006). *Lessons of Disaster: Policy Change after Catastrophic Events*, Washington, DC: Georgetown University Press.

Blij, H. de (2009) *The Power of Place*, Oxford: Oxford University Press.

Blondel, J. (1987) *Political Leadership: A General Analysis*, London: Sage.

Blondel, J. and Muller-Rommel, F. (eds) (1993) *Governing Together*, London: Macmillan.

Boekhout van Solinge, T. (1999) 'Dutch drug policy in a European context', *Journal of Drug Issues*, 29: 511–28.

Boin, A. (2001) *Crafting Public Institutions: Leadership in Two Prison Systems*, Boulder, CO: Lynne Rienner.

Boin, A. and Christensen, T. (2008) 'The development of public institutions: Reconsidering the role of leadership', *Administration and Society*, 40(3): 271–97.

Boin, A.L. and Goodin, R.E. (2007) 'Institutionalizing upstarts: the demons of domestication and the benefits of recalcitrance', *Acta Politica*, 42(1): 40–57.

Boin, A. and 't Hart, P. (2003) 'Public leadership in times of crisis: Mission impossible?', *Public Administration Review*, 63(5), 544–53.

Boin, A. and 't Hart, P. (2010) 'Organizing for effective crisis management: Lessons from research', *Australian Journal of Public Administration*, 69(4): 357–71.

Boin, A., 't Hart, P. and McConnell, A. (2009) 'Towards a theory of crisis exploitation: Political and policy impacts of framing contests and blame games', *Journal of European Public Policy*, 16(1): 81–106.

Boin, A., 't Hart, P., Stern, E. and Sundelius, B. (2005) *The Politics of Crisis Management: Public Leadership Under Pressure*, Cambridge: Cambridge University Press.

Boin, A., McConnell, A. and 't Hart, P. (eds) (2008) *Governing After Crisis: The Politics of Investigation, Accountability and Learning*, Cambridge: Cambridge University Press.

Bolden, R. and Gosling, J. (2006) 'Leadership competencies: Time to change the tune?', *Leadership*, 2(2): 147–63.

Bouckaert, G. and Pollitt, C. (2000) *Public Management Reform: A Comparative Analysis*, Oxford: Oxford University Press.

Bovens, M. (1998) *The Quest for Responsibility*, Cambridge: Cambridge University Press.

Bovens, M., Goodin, R.E. and Schillemans, T. (eds) (2014) *Oxford Handbook of Public Accountability*, Oxford: Oxford University Press.

Bovens, M., Schillemans, T. and 't Hart, P. (2008) 'Does public accountability work? An assessment tool', *Public Administration*, 86(2): 225–42.

Bovens, M. and 't Hart, P. (1996) *Understanding Policy Fiascoes*, New Brunswick, NJ: Transaction.

Bovens, M. P. 't Hart, and Peters, B.G. (eds) (2001) *Success and Failure in Public Governance: A Comparative Analysis*, Cheltenham: Edward Elgar.

Bovens, M., P. 't Hart and Kuipers, S. (2006) 'The politics of policy evaluation', in: R. Goodin, M. Moran and M. Rein (eds), *Oxford Handbook of Public Policy*, Oxford: Oxford University Press, pp. 317–33.

Bovens, M., 't Hart, P., Dekker, S. and Verheuvel, G. (1999) 'The politics of blame avoidance: Defensive tactics in a Dutch crime-fighting fiasco', in H. Anheier (ed.), *When Things Go Wrong: Organizational Failures and Breakdowns*, London: Sage, pp.123–47.

Braithwaite, J. (1997) 'On speaking softly and carrying big sticks: Neglected dimensions of a republication separation of powers', *University of Toronto Law Journal*, 47(3): 305–61.

Brändström, A. and Kuipers, S. (2003) 'From "normal incidents" to political crises: Understanding the selective politicization of policy failures', *Government and Opposition*, 38(3): 279–305.

Brändström, A., Bynander, F. and 't Hart, P. (2004) 'Governing by looking back: Historical analogies and contemporary crisis management', *Public Administration*, 82(1): 191–210.

Brecher, M. (1993) *Crises in World Politics: Theory and Reality*, Oxford: Pergamon Press.

Breslauer, G.W. (2002) *Gorbachev and Yeltsin as Leaders*, New York: Cambridge University Press.

Brett, J. (2007) 'Exit right: The unravelling of John Howard', *Quarterly Essay*, no. 28.

Brett, J. (2009) 'Graham Little's theory of political leadership', *International Journal of Applied Psychoanalytic Studies* 6(2): 103–10.

Brooker, P. (2005) *Leadership in Democracy: From Adaptive Response to Entrepreneurial Initiative*, Basingstoke: Palgrave Macmillan.

Brown, A. (2014) *The Myth of the Strong Leader: Political Leadership in the Modern Age*, New York: Vintage.

Brown, J.M. (1991) *Gandhi: Prisoner of Hope*, New Haven, CT: Yale University Press.

Bryman, A. (1992) *Charisma and Leadership in Organisations*, London: Sage.

Bryson, J., Crosby, B. and Stone, M. (2006) 'The design and implementation of cross-sector collaborations: propositions from the literature, *Public Administration Review*, 66(s1): 44-55

Bulpitt, J. (1986) 'The discipline of the new democracy: Mrs Thatcher's domestic statecraft', *Political Studies*, 34(1): 19–39.

Burke, J.P. and Greenstein, F. (1989) *How Presidents Test Reality*, New York: Russell Sage.

Burns, J.M. (1978) *Leadership*, New York: Harper & Row.

Burns, J.M. (2003) *Transforming Leadership*, New York: Atlantic Monthly.

Bytzek, E. (2008) 'Flood response and political survival: Gerhard Schroeder and the 2002 Elbe Flood in Germany', in A. Boin, P. 't Hart and A. McConnell (eds), *Governing After Crisis*, Cambridge: Cambridge University Press, pp. 85–113.

Cameron, K.S., Sutton, R.I. and Whetten, D.A. (eds) (1988) *Readings in Organizational Decline: Frameworks, Research, and Prescriptions*. Boston, MA: Ballinger Publishing Company.

Campbell, C. and Wyszomirski, M.J. (eds) (1991) *Executive Leadership in Anglo-American Systems*, Pittsburgh, PA: Pittsburgh University Press.

Campus, D. (2013) *Women Political Leaders and the Media*, Basingstoke: Palgrave Macmillan.

Caro, R. (1974) *The Power Broker*, New York: Knopf.

Caro, R. (2012) *The Years of Lyndon Johnson: Passage to Power*, New York: Knopf.

Castells, M. (1996) *The Network Society*, Oxford: Basil Blackwell.

Cels, S., De Jong, J. and Nauta, F. (2012) *Agents of Change*, Washington, DC: Brookings Institution.

Chaleff, I. (2009) *The Courageous Follower: Standing up to and for Our Leaders*, San Francisco: Bennett-Koehler.

Chapman, J. (2002) *System Failure*, London: Demos.

Checkland, P. (1981) *Systems Thinking, Systems Practice*, New York: Wiley.

Chrislip, D. and Larson, C. (1994) *Collaborative Leadership*, San Francisco: Jossey-Bass.

Christensen, T. and Lægreid, P. (2004) 'Coping with complex leadership roles', *Public Administration*, 81(4): 803–31.

Clarke, L. (2005) *Worst Cases: Terror and Catastrophe in the Popular Imagination*, Chicago: University of Chicago Press.

Committee on Homeland Security and Governmental Affairs (2006) *Hurricane Katrina: A Nation Still Unprepared*, Washington, DC: Government Printing Office.

Conger, J. and Kanungo, R. (1987) 'Toward a behavioral theory of charismatic leadership in organizational settings', *Academy of Management Review*, 12(4): 637–47.

Conger, J. and Kanungo , R.(1998) *Charismatic Leadership in Organizations*, Thousands Oaks, CA: Sage.

Cook, B.J. (1998) 'Politics, political leadership and public management', *Public Administration Review*, 58(3): 225–30.

Cooper, A. (2008) *Celebrity Diplomacy*, London: Paradigm.

Cooper, J. and Brady, D.W. (1981) 'Institutional context and leadership style: The House from Cannon to Rayburn', *American Political Science Review*, 75(3): 411–25.

Coser, L. (1956) *The Functions of Social Conflict*, New York: Free Press

Courpassion, D. and Thoenig, J.-C. (2010) *When Managers Rebel*, Basingstoke: Palgrave Macmillan.

Cronin, T. (2008) '"All the world's a stage…": Acting and the art of political leadership', *The Leadership Quarterly*, 19(3): 459–68.

Crosby, B. and Bryson, J.W. (1992) *Leadership for the Common Good*, San Francisco, CA: Jossey-Bass.

Cross, W. and Blais, A. (2011) 'Holding party leaders to account: The Westminster cases', in 't Hart, P. and Uhr, J. (eds) *How Power Changes Hands*, Basingstoke: Palgrave Macmillan, pp.133–56.

Cross, W. and Blais, A. (2012) *Politics at the Centre: The Selection and Removal of Party Leaders in the Anglo Parliamentary Democracies*, Oxford: Oxford University Press.

Daalder, I. and Destler, I. (2011) *In the Shadow of the Oval Office*, New York: Simon & Schuster.

Daleus, P. (2012) *Politisk Ledarskapstil*, Stockholm: Stockholm Studies in Politics.

Dallek, R. (2007) *Nixon and Kissinger: Partners in Power*, New York: Penguin.

Davis, K.M. and Gardner, W.L. (2012) 'Charisma under crisis revisited: Presidential leadership, perceived leader effectiveness, and contextual influences', *The Leadership Quarterly*, 23(6): 918–33.

Davis, K. M. and Seymour, E. (2010) 'Generating forms of media capital inside and outside a field: The strange case of David Cameron in the UK political field', *Media, Culture and Society*, 32(5): 739–59.

DeVries, M. (2004) 'Framing crises', *Administration and Society*, 36(5): 594–614.

Dekker, S. and Hansén, D. (2004) 'Learning under pressure: The effects of politicization on organizational learning in public bureaucracies', *Journal of Public Administration Research and Theory*, 14(2): 211–30.

Deutsch, K.W. (1963) *The Nerves of Government*, New York: Free Press.

Deverell, E. (2009) *Crisis-Induced Learning in Swedish Public Sector Organizations*, Stockholm: CRISMART.

Dobel, J.P. (1998) 'Political prudence and the ethics of leadership', *Public Administration Review*, 58(1): 74–81.

Docters van Leeuwen, A. (1990) 'Het mangen van crises', in P. 't Hart and U. Rosenthal (eds), *Kritieke Momenten*, Arnhem: Gouda Quint: 198–212.

Douglas, M. (1992) *Risk and Blame*, London: Routledge.

Dowding, K. (2013) 'Power in prime-ministerial performance: Institutional and personal factors', in P. Strangio, P. 't Hart and J. Walter (eds), *Understanding Prime-Ministerial Performance*, Oxford: Oxford University Press.

Dowding, K. and Dumont, P. (2009) *The Selection of Ministers in Europe: Hiring and Firing*, London: Routledge.

Dror, Y. (1986) *Policymaking Under Adversity*, New Brunswick, NJ: Transaction.

Dror, Y. (2001) *The Capacity to Govern: A Report to the Club of Rome*, London: Frank Cass.

Dyson, K. (2009) 'The evolving timescapes of European economic governance: Contesting and using time', *Journal of European Public Policy*, 16(2): 286–306.

Dyson, S.B. and 't Hart, P. (2013) 'Crisis management', in L. Huddy, D.O. Sears and J. Levy (eds), *Oxford Handbook of Political Psychology*, Oxford: Oxford University Press.

Edwards, G., and Howell, W.G. (eds) (2009) *The Oxford Handbook of the American Presidency*, Oxford: Oxford University Press.

Eichbaum, C. and Shaw, R. (2014) 'Prime ministers and their advisers in parliamentary democracies', in R.A.W. Rhodes and P. 't Hart (eds), *Oxford Handbook of Political Leadership*, Oxford: Oxford University Press, in press.

Ekengren, M. (2002) *The Time of European Governance*, Manchester: Manchester University Press.

Elcock, H. (2001) *Political Leadership*, Cheltenham: Edward Elgar.

Elgie, R. (1995) *Political Leadership in Western Democracies*, London: Macmillan.

Elkington, J. and Hartigan, P. (2008) *The Power of Unreasonable People*, Cambridge: Harvard Business Review Press.

Ellis, R.J. and Nelson, M.J. (eds) (2010) *Debating the Presidency: Conflicting Perspectives on the American Executive*, Washington, DC: CQ Press.

Erikson, E.H. (1958) *Young Man Luther: A Study in Psychoanalysis and Power*, New York: W.W. Norton.

Errington, W. and Van Onselen, P. (2007) *John Winston Howard: The Biography*, Carlton, Victoria: Melbourne University Press.

Fairholm, M. (2004) 'Different perspectives on the practice of leadership', *Public Administration Review*, 64(5): 577–90.

Feit, E. (ed.) (1978) *Governments and Leaders: An Approach to Comparative Politics*, Boston, MA: Houghton Mifflin.

Ferguson, M.R. and Barth, J. (2002) 'Governors in the legislative arena: The importance of personality in shaping success', *Political Psychology*, 23(4): 787–808.

Fiedler, F. (1967) *A Theory of Leadership Effectiveness*, New York: McGraw-Hill.

Finer, S. E. (1970) *Comparative Government: An Introduction to the Study of Politics*, Harmondsworth: Penguin.

Fischer, F. (2003) *Reframing Public Policy*, Oxford: Oxford University Press.

Fisher, E.C. (2004) 'The European Union in the age of accountability', *Oxford Journal of Legal Studies*, 24(3): 495–515.

Fleming, J. (2008) 'Managing the diary: What does a police commissioner do?', *Public Administration*, 86(3), 679–98.

Flin, R. (1996) *Sitting in the Hot Seat: Leaders and Teams for Critical Incident Management*, New York: John Wiley.

Foley, M. (2013) *Political Leadership: Themes, Contexts and Critiques*, Oxford: Oxford University Press.

Frederickson, H.G., with Matkin, D.S.T. (2007) 'Public leadership as gardening', in R.S. Morse, T.F. Buss and C.M. Kinghorn (eds), *Transforming Public Leadership for the 21st Century*, Armonk, NY: M.E. Sharpe, pp. 34–46.

Frederickson, H.G., Smith, K.B., Larimer, C.W. and Licari, M.J. (2012) *The Public Administration Theory Primer*. Boulder, CO: Westview Press.

Gaffney, J. (2010) *Political Leadership in France: From Charles de Gaulle to Nicolas Sarkozy*, Basingstoke: Palgrave Macmillan.

Gaffney, J. (2014) 'Understanding leadership as performance', in R.A.W. Rhodes and P. 't Hart (eds), *Oxford Handbook of Political Leadership*, Oxford: Oxford University Press, in press.

Gardner, J.W. (1990) *On Leadership*, New York: Free Press.

Garretsen, H.F.L. (2003) 'The decline of Dutch drug policy?', *Journal of Substance Use*, 8: 2–4.

Garrison, J. (2007) 'Constructing the 'national interest' in US–China policy making: How foreign policy decision groups define and signal policy choices', *Foreign Policy Analysis,* 3(1): 105–26.

Garrison, J., Hoyt, P.D. and Wituski, D. (1997) 'Managing intragroup relations in foreign policy', *Cooperation and Conflict*, 32(3): 261–86.

Geer, L. (1996), *From Tea Leaves to Opinion Polls: A Theory of Democratic Leadership*, New York: Columbia University Press

Geertz, C. (1973) *The Interpretation of Cultures*, New York: Basic Books.

George, A.L. (1974) 'Adaptation to stress in political decision making: The individual, small group and organizational contexts', in G.V. Coelho, D.A.

Hamburg and J.E. Adams (eds), *Coping and Adaptation*, New York: Basic Books, pp. 176–245.

George, A.L. (1980) *Presidential Decisionmaking in Foreign Policy: The Effective Use of Information and Advice*, Boulder, CO: Westview Press.

George, A.L. and George, J.L. (1956) *Woodrow Wilson and Colonel House: A Personality Study*, New York: Day.

George, A.L. and Stern, E.K. (2002) 'Harnessing conflict in foreign policy making: From devil's to multiple advocacy, *Presidential Studies Quarterly*, 32(3): 484–508.

Gillon, S.M. (2000) *Reform and Its Unintended Consequences*, New York: W.W. Norton.

Giuliani, R. (2002) *Leadership*, Boston, MA: Little, Brown.

Gleick, J. (2000) *Faster: The Acceleration of Just About Everything*, London: Vintage.

Goetz, K.H. (2009) 'How does the EU tick? Five propositions on political time', *Journal of European Public Policy*, 16(2): 202–20.

Goetz, K. H. and Meyer-Sahling, J.H. (2009) 'Political time in the EU', *Journal of European Public Policy*, 16(2): 180–201.

Goldfinch, S. and 't Hart, P. (2003) 'Leadership and institutional reform: engineering macroeconomic policy change in Australia', *Governance*, 16(3): 235–70.

Goldhamer, H. (1978) *The Adviser*, New York: Elsevier.

Goldsmith, S. and Eggers, W.D. (2004) *Governing by Network: The New Shape of the Public Sector*, Washington, DC: Brookings Institution.

Goldsmith, S., Georges, G. and Burke, T.G. (2010) *The Power of Social Innovation: How Civic Entrepreneurs Ignite Community Networks for Good*, San Francisco: Jossey-Bass.

Goleman, D. (2013) *Focus: The Hidden Driver of Excellence*, New York: HarperCollins.

Goleman, D., Mackee, A. and Boyatzis, R.E. (2002) *Primal Leadership: Realizing the Power of Emotional Intelligence*, Cambridge, MA: Harvard Business Press.

Goodin, R. E. and Tilly, C. (eds) (2006) *The Oxford Handbook of Contextual Political Analysis*, Oxford: Oxford University Press.

Goodsell, C. (2011) *Mission Mystique: Belief Systems in Public Agencies*, Washington, DC: CQ Press.

Greenstein, F.I. (1969) *Personality and Politics: Problems of Evidence, Inference, and Conceptualization*, Chicago, IL: Markham.

Greenstein, F.I. (1987) *The Hidden-Hand Presidency*, Princeton, NJ: Princeton University Press.

Greenstein, F.I. (1992) 'Can personality and politics be studied systematically?', *Political Psychology*, 13(1): 105–28.

Greenstein, F.I. (2000) 'The Presidency of my mind's eye', *The Antioch Review*, 58 (Fall): 398–405.

Greenstein, F.I. (2002) 'The qualitative study of presidential personality', in L.O. Valenty and O. Feldman (eds), *Political Leadership for the New Century: Personality and Behavior Among American Leaders*, New York: Praeger.

Greenstein, F.I. (2009) *The Presidential Difference: Leadership Style from FDR to Barack Obama*, Princeton, NJ: Princeton University Press.

Grint, K. (2000) *The Arts of Leadership*, Oxford: Oxford University Press.

Grint, K. (2010) 'Leadership: An enemy of the people?', *International Journal of Leadership in Public Services*, 6(4): 22–5.

Groenleer, M.L.P. (2009) *The Autonomy of European Union Agencies: A Comparative Study of Institutional Development*, Delft, The Netherlands: Eburon.

Gronn, P. (1999) 'Substituting for leadership: The neglected role of the leadership couple', *Leadership Quarterly*, 10(1): 41–62.

Gronn, P. (2002) 'Distributed leadership as a unit of analysis', *Leadership Quarterly*, 13(4): 423–51.

Gronn, P. (2009) 'Leadership configurations', *Leadership*, 5(3): 1–13.

Grube, D. (2013) *Prime Ministers and Rhetorical Governance*, Basingstoke: Palgrave Macmillan.

Haggart, K. (n.d.) 'Civil society must get up to speed on cyber security, watchdog warns', International Development Research Centre (IDRC). Available at: http://www.idrc.ca/en/resources/publications/pages/articledetails.aspx?publicationid=14; accessed 27 February 2014.

Hajer, M. (1993) 'Discourse coalitions and the institutionalization of practice', in F. Fischer and J. Forester (eds), *The Argumentative Turn in Policy Analysis and Planning*, Durham, NC: Duke University Press, pp. 43–77.

Hajer, M. and Uitermark J. (2008) 'Performing authority: Discursive politics after the assassination of Theo van Gogh', *Public Administration*, 86(1): 1–15.

Hall, A.T., Blass, F.R., Ferris, G.R. and Massengale, R. (2004) 'Leader reputation and accountability in organisations: Implications for dysfunctional leader behaviour', *The Leadership Quarterly*, 15(4): 515–36.

Haney, P.J. (1997) *Organizing for Foreign Policy Crises*, Ann Arbor, MI: Michigan University Press.

Hargrove, E.C. (1994) *Prisoners of Myth: The Leadership of the Tennessee Valley Authority, 1933–1990*, Princeton, NJ: Princeton University Press.

Hargrove, E.C. (1998) *The President as Leader: Appealing to the Better Angels of Our Nature*, Lawrence, KS: University of Kansas Press.

Hargrove, E.C. and Glidewell, J. (eds) (1990) *Impossible Jobs in Public Management*, Lawrence, KS: University Press of Kansas.

Hargrove, E.C. and Owens, J.C. (eds) (2003) *Leadership in Context*, Lanham, MD: Rowman & Littlefield.

Harrison, S. and McDonald. R. (2008) *The Politics of Health Care in Britain*, London: Sage.

Hartley, J. and Manzie, S. (2014) 'Dual leadership: Perspectives of senior public managers working with elected politicians', *American Review of Public Administration*, forthcoming.

Haslam, S. A., and Reicher, S. D. (2007) 'Beyond the banality of evil: Three dynamics of an interactionist social psychology of tyranny', *Personality and Social Psychology Bulletin*, 33, 615-22.

Haslam, S.A., Reicher, S. and Platow, M. (2010) *The New Psychology of Leadership*, New York: Psychology Press.

Haslam, S.A., Platow, M.J., Turner, J.C., Reynolds, K.J., McCarty, C., Oakes, P.J., Johnson, S., Ryan, M.K. and Veenstra, K. (2001) 'Social identity and the romance of leadership: The importance of being seen to be "doing it for us"', *Group Processes and Intergroup Relations*, 4(3): 191–205.

Haus, M. and Sweeting, D. (2006) 'Local democracy and political leadership: drawing a map', *Political Studies*, 54(3): 267–88.

Hay, C. (2002) *Political Analysis*, Basingstoke: Palgrave Macmillan.

Head, B. and Alford, J. (2013) 'Wicked problems: implications for public policy and management', *Administration & Society*, 46.

Hearit, K. (2006) *Crisis Management by Apology*, New York: Erlbaum.

Heifetz, R.A. (1994) *Leadership without Easy Answers*, Cambridge, MA: Harvard University Press.

Heifetz, R., Grashow, A. and Lisnky, M. (2009) *The Practice of Adaptive Leadership*, Boston, MA: Harvard Business Review Press.

Heifetz, R.A. and Linsky, M. (2002) *Leadership on the Line*, Boston, MA: Harvard Business School Press.

Heineman, B.W., Jr. (2011) 'Crisis management failures in Japan's reactors and the BP spill', *Harvard Business Review Blog Network*. Available at: http://blogs.hbr.org/2011/03/crisis-management-failures-jap/; accessed 20 January 2014.

Helms, L. (2005) *Presidents, Prime Ministers and Chancellors: Executive Leadership in Western Democracies*, Basingstoke: Palgrave Macmillan.

Helms, L. (ed.) (2012) *Poor Leadership and Bad Governance*, Cheltenham: Edward Elgar.

Hendriks, F. and Karsten, N. (2014) 'Theory of democratic leadership in action', in R.A.W. Rhodes and P. 't Hart (eds), *Oxford Handbook of Political Leadership*, Oxford: Oxford University Press, in press.

Heppell, T. (2008) *Choosing the Tory Leader: Conservative Party Leadership Elections from Heath to Cameron*, London: Tauris.

Heppell, T. (2012) *Leaders of the Opposition: From Winston Churchill to David Cameron*, Basingstoke: Palgrave Macmillan.

Hermann, M. (ed.) (1986) *Political Psychology*, New York: Wiley.

Hermann. M.G. (2014) 'Political psychology', in R.A.W. Rhodes and P. 't Hart (eds), *Oxford Handbook of Political Leadership*, Oxford: Oxford University Press, in press.

Hess, S. and Pfiffner, J.P. (2002) *Organizing the Presidency*, Washington, DC: Brookings Institution.

Hesse, J.J., Hood, C. and Peters, B.G. (2003) *Paradoxes in Public Sector Reform: An International Comparison*, Berlin: Duncker & Humblot.

Hickson, D.J., Butler, R. J., Cray, D., Mallory, G.R. and Wilson, D.C. (1986) *Top Decisions: Strategic Decision-Making in Organizations*, Oxford: Basil Blackwell.

Hilsman, R. (1965) *To Move a Nation*, New York: Doubleday.

Hillyard, M. (2000) *Public Crisis Management: How and Why Organizations Work Together to Solve Society's Most Threatening Problems*, Bloomington, IN: Writers Club Press.

Hirschman, A.O. (1991) *The Rhetoric of Reaction: Perversity, Futility, Jeopardy*, Cambridge, MA: Harvard University Press.

Hofstede, G. (1997) *Cultures and Organizations: Softwares of the Mind*, New York: McGraw-Hill.

Hogg, M.A. (2005) 'Social identity and misuse of power: The dark side of leadership', *Brooklyn Law Review*, 70(4): 1239–57.

Hollander, E.P. (1979) 'Leadership and social exchange processes', in K.

Gergen, M. Greenberg and R. Willis (eds), *Social Exchange: Advances in Theory and Research*, New York: Winston/Wiley.

Hollander, E.P. (2008) *Inclusive Leadership: The Essential Leader–Follower Relationship*, New York: Routledge.

Hood, C. (2011) *The Blame Game*, Oxford: Oxford University Press.

Hood, C. and Lodge, M. (2004) *The Politics of Public Service Bargains*, Oxford: Oxford University Press.

Hook, S. (1943) *The Hero in History*, New York: John Day.

House, R.J. (1996) 'Path–goal theory of leadership: Lessons, legacy, and a reformulated theory', *Leadership Quarterly*, 7(3): 323–52.

House, R.J, Javidan, M. and Dorfman, P. (2001) 'Project GLOBE: An introduction', *Applied Psychology: An International Review*, 50(4), 489–505.

House, R.J., Hanges, P.J., Javidan, M., Dorfman, P.W. and Gupta, V. (2004) 'Culture, leadership, and organizations: The GLOBE study of 62 societies', *Journal of Cross-Cultural Psychology*, 36(5), 628–30.

Hoyt, P.D. and Garrison, J. (1997) 'Political manipulation in the small group: Foreign policy advisers in the Carter administration', in P. 't Hart, E.K. Stern and B. Sundelius (eds), *Beyond Groupthink: Political Group Dynamics in Foreign Policy*, Ann Arbor, MI: University of Michigan Press.

Hult, K.M. and Walcott, C.E. (2004) *Empowering the White House: Governance Under Nixon, Ford and Carter*, Lawrence, KS: University of Kansas Press.

Ignatieff, M. (2013) *Fire and Ashes: Success and Failure in Politics*, Cambridge: Harvard University Press.

Inglehart, R. and Norris, P. (2004) *Sacred and Secular: Religion and Politics Worldwide*, Cambridge, Cambridge University Press.

Inglehart, R. and Norris, P. (2009) *Cosmopolitan Communications: Cultural Diversity in a Globalised World*, Cambridge: Cambridge University Press.

Inglehart, R. and Welzel, C. (2005) *Modernization, Cultural Change and Democracy: The Human Development Sequence*, Cambridge: Cambridge University Press.

Jackall, R. (1988) *Moral Mazes: The World of Corporate Managers*, New York: Oxford University Press.

Janis, I.L. (1982) *Groupthink*, Boston, MA: Houghton Mifflin.

Janis, I.L. (1989) *Crucial Decisions*, New York: Free Press.

Javidan, M., Dorfman, P.W., de Luque, M.S. and House, R. J. (2006) 'In the eye of the beholder: Cross-cultural lessons in leadership from Project GLOBE', *The Academy of Management Perspectives*, 20(1): 67–90.

Jenkins, R. (2013) *Social Identity*, London: Routledge.

Johnson, R.T. (1974) *Managing the White House*, New York: Harper & Row.

Kaarbo, J. (1997) 'Prime minister leadership styles in foreign policy decision-making: A framework for research', *Political Psychology*, 18(3): 553–81.

Kaarbo, J. and Hermann, M.G. (1998) 'Leadership styles of prime ministers: How individual differences affect the foreign policymaking process', *Leadership Quarterly*, 9(3): 243–63.

Kane, J. (2001) *The Politics of Moral Capital*, Cambridge: Cambridge University Press.

Kane, J. and Patapan, H. (2012) *The Democratic Leader: How Democracy Defines, Empowers and Limits Its Leaders*, Oxford: Oxford University Press.

Kane, J. and Patapan, H. (eds) (2014) *Good Democratic Leadership*, Oxford: Oxford University Press.

Kane, J., Patapan, H. and 't Hart, P. (2009) *Dispersed Democratic Leadership*, Oxford: Oxford University Press.

Kane, J., Patapan, H. and Wong, B. (eds) (2008) *Dissident Democrats*, Basingstoke: Palgrave Macmillan.

Kaplan, S. (2008) 'Framing contests: strategy making under uncertainty', *Organization Science*, 19(5): 729–52.

Kavanagh, D. and Seldon, A. (1999) *The Powers Behind the Prime Minister: The Hidden Influence of Number Ten*, London: HarperCollins.

Kay, A. (2006) *The Dynamics of Public Policy*, Cheltenham: Edward Elgar.

Keane, J. (2009) *The Life and Death of Democracy*, New York: Simon & Schuster.

Keeler, J. (1993) 'Opening the window for reform: Mandates, crises and extraordinary policymaking', *Comparative Political Studies*, 25(3): 433–86.

Keller, J.W. (2005) 'Constraint respecters, constraint challengers, and crisis decision making in democracies', *Political Psychology*, 26(6), 835–67.

Kellerman, B. (2004) *Bad Leadership*, Boston, MA: Harvard Business School Press.

Kellerman, B. (2008) *Followership*, Boston, MA: Harvard Business School Press.

Kellerman, B. (2012) *The End of Leadership*, New York: HarperCollins.

Kelly, P. (2009) *The March of Patriots: The Struggle for Modern Australia*, Carlton, Victoria: Melbourne University Press.

Kelman, H.C. (2005) 'The policy context of torture: A social-psychological analysis', *International Review of the Red Cross*, 87: 123–34.

Kelman, H. and Hamilton, V.L. (1989) *Crimes of Obedience*, New Haven, CT: Yale University Press.

Keohane, N. (2005) 'On leadership', *Perspectives on Politics*, 3(4): 705–22.

Keohane, N.O. (2010) *Thinking about Leadership*, Princeton, NJ: Princeton University Press.

Kets de Vries, M. (1989) *Prisoners of Leadership*, New York: Wiley.

Kets de Vries, M. (2006) *Leaders on the Couch: A Clinical Approach to Changing People and Organizations*, New York: Wiley.

Kickert, W.J.M., Klijn, E.H. and Koppenjan, J.F.M. (eds) (1997) *Managing Complex Networks*, London: Sage.

Kille, K.J. and Scully, R.M. (2003) 'Executive heads and the role of intergovernmental organisations: Expansionist leadership in the United Nations and the European Union', *Political Psychology*, 24(1): 175–98.

Kingdon, J.W. (1984) *Agendas, Alternatives and Public Policies*, Boston, MA: Little, Brown.

Klein, G. (1999) *Sources of Power: How People Make Decisions*, Cambridge, MA: MIT Press.

Klein, N. (2007) *The Shock Doctrine: The Rise of Disaster Capitalism*, New York: Metropolitan Books.

Koppell, T. (2005) 'Multiple accountabilities disorder', *Public Administration Review*, 65(1): 94–108.

Korac-Kakabadse, N., Korac-Kakabadse, A. and Kouzmin, A. (2001) 'Leadership renewal: Towards the philosophy of wisdom', *International Review of Administrative Sciences*, 67(3): 207–27.

Kotter, J. (1996) *Leading Change*, Boston, MA: Harvard Business School Press.

Kouzes, J.M. and Posner, B.Z. (1987) *The Leadership Challenge: How to Get Extraordinary Things Done in Organizations*, San Francisco, CA: Jossey-Bass.

Kowert, P. (2002) *Groupthink or Deadlock: When Do Leaders Learn from Their Advisors?*, Albany, NY: State University of New York Press.

Kuipers, S. (2006) *The Crisis Imperative*, Amsterdam: Amsterdam University Press.

Kurzer, P. (2001) 'Cultural diversity in post-Maastricht Europe', *Journal of European Public Policy*, 8(2): 144–61.

Ladkin, D. (2010) *Rethinking Leadership: A New Look at Old Leadership Questions*, Cheltenham: Edward Elgar.

Lagadec, P. (1997) 'Learning processes for crisis management in complex organizations'. *Journal of Contingencies and Crisis Management*, 5(1): 24–31.

Laing, M. (2012) 'Towards a pragmatic Presidency? Exploring the waning of political time, *Polity*, 44(2): 234–59.

Laing, M. and McCaffrie, B. (2013) 'The politics prime ministers make: Political time and executive leadership in Westminster systems', in P. Strangio, P. 't Hart and J. Walter (eds), *Understanding Prime-Ministerial Performance*, Oxford: Oxford University Press.

Laing, M. and 't Hart, P. (2011) 'Seeking and keeping the hot seat', in P. 't Hart and J. Uhr (eds), *How Power Changes Hands*, Basingstoke: Palgrave Macmillan.

Landau, M. (1969) 'Redundancy, rationality and the problem of duplication and overlap', *Public Administration Review*, 29(4): 346–58.

Lauer, R.H. (1981) *Temporal Man: The Meaning and Uses of Social Time*, New York: Praeger.

Lebow, R.N. and Stein, J.G. (1994) *We All Lost the Cold War*, Princeton, NJ: Princeton University Press.

Levi-Faur, D. (ed.) (2012) *Oxford Handbook of Governance*, Oxford: Oxford University Press.

Lewis, E. (1980) *Public Entrepreneurship: Toward a Theory of Bureaucratic Power*, Bloomington, IN: Indiana University Press.

Lindblom, C.E. (1965) *The Intelligence of Democracy: Decision Making Through Mutual Adjustment*, New York: Free Press.

Lindblom, C.E. (1979) 'Still muddling, not yet through', *Public Administration Review*, 39: 517–26.

Linden, R. (2010) *Leading Across Boundaries: Creating Collaborative Agencies in a Networked World*, San Francisco: Jossey-Bass.

Lindquist, E.A., Vincent, S. and Wanna, J. (eds) (2011) *Delivering Policy Reform: Anchoring Significant Reforms in Turbulent Times*, Canberra: ANU Press, pp. 201–11.

Lipman-Blumen, J. (1996) *Connective Leadership*, San Francisco, CA: Jossey-Bass.

Lipman-Blumen, J. (2006) *The Allure of Toxic Leadership*, Oxford: Oxford University Press.

Little, G. (1985) *Political Ensembles: A Psychosocial Approach to Politics and Leadership*, Melbourne: Oxford University Press.

Little, G. (1988) *Strong Leadership: Thatcher, Reagan and an Eminent Person*, Melbourne: Oxford University Press.

Llanos, M. and Marheritis, A. (2006) 'Why do presidents fail? Political leadership and the Argentine crisis', *Studies in Comparative International Development*, 40(4): 77–103.

Lord, C. (2001) *The Modern Prince: What Leaders Need to Know Now*, New Haven, CT: Yale University Press.

Lowi, T. J. (1972) 'Four systems of policy, politics and choice', *Public Administration Review*, 33(4): 298–310.

Ludwig, A. (2002) *King of the Mountain: The Nature of Political Leadership*, Lexington, KY: University of Kentucky Press.

Luhmann, N. (1966) *Theorie der Verwaltungswissenschaft*, Cologne/Berlin: Grote.

Luhrmann, T. and Eberl, P. (2007) 'Leadership and identity construction', *Leadership*, 3(1): 115–27.

Lupia, A. (2003) 'Delegation and its perils', in B. Bergman, W. Müller and K. Strøm (eds) *Delegation and Accountability in West European Parliamentary Democracies*, Oxford: Oxford University Press, pp. 33–54.

Lynn, L.E. (1981) *Managing the Public's Business*, New York: Basic Books.

Machiavelli, N. (1993) *The Prince*, London: Wardsworth Classics (orig. edn 1513).

McCaffrie, B. (2012) 'Understanding the success of presidents and prime ministers: The role of opposition parties', *Australian Journal of Political Science*, 47(2): 257–71.

McDermott, R. (2008) *Presidential Leadership, Illness, and Decision Making*, Cambridge: Cambridge University Press.

Mahoney, J.P. and Thelen, K.D. (eds) (2010) *Explaining Institutional Change*, Cambridge: Cambridge University Press.

Maier, C.S. (1997) *Dissolution*, Princeton, NJ: Princeton University Press.

Mair, P. (1994) 'Party organizations: From civil society to the state', in R. Katz, and P. Mair (eds) *How Parties Organize*, London: Sage, pp. 1–22.

Mair, P. (2013) *Ruling the Void: The Hollowing of Western Democracy*, London: Verso.

March, J.G. and Olsen, J.P. (1989) *Rediscovering Institutions: The Organizational Basis of Politics*, New York: Free Press.

March, J.G. and Olsen, J.P. (1995) *Democratic Governance*, New York: Free Press.

March, J.G. and Weil, T. (2003) *On Leadership*, New York: Wiley.

Marsh, D., 't Hart, P. and Tindall, K. (2010) 'Celebrity politics: The politics of late modernity', *Political Studies Review*, 8(3): 322–40.

Masciulli, J., Molchanov, M.A. and Knight, W.A. (eds) (2009) *The Ashgate Research Companion to Political Leadership*, Aldershot: Ashgate.

Meeus, W. and Raaijmakers, Q. (1985) '*Gewoon Gehoorzaam*', PhD thesis, Utrecht, The Netherlands: Utrecht University.

Meijer, A.J., 't Hart, P. and Worthy, B. (2014) 'The transparency assessment toolkit', Unpublished MS.

Meltsner, A. (1988) *Rules for Rulers: The Politics of Advice*, Philadelphia, PA: Temple University Press.

Meyer, M.W. and Zucker, L.G. (1989) *Permanently Failing Organizations*, Newbury Park: Sage.

Meyer-Sahling, J.-H. and Goetz, K. (2009) 'The EU timescape: From notion to research agenda', *Journal of European Public Policy*, 16(2): 325–36.

Milgram, S. (1974) *Obedience to Authority*, New York: HarperCollins.

Mitchell, D. (2005) 'Centralizing advisory systems: Presidential influence and the U.S. foreign policy process', *Foreign Policy Analysis*, 2(2): 181–206.

Moon, J. (1995) 'Innovative leadership and policy change: Lessons from Thatcher', *Governance*, 8(1): 1–25.

Moore, C.W. (2003) *The Mediation Process*, San Francisco: Jossey-Bass.

Moore, M. (1995) *Creating Public Value*, Cambridge, MA: Harvard University Press.

Moore, M. (2013) *Recognizing Public Value*, Cambridge, MA: Harvard University Press.

Moran, M. (1999) *Governing the Health Care State: A Comparative Study of the United Kingdom, the United States and Germany*, Manchester: Manchester University Press.

Morgan, G. (1986) *Images of Organization*, Beverly Hills, CA: Sage.

Morrell, K. and Hartley, J. (2006) 'A model of political leadership', *Human Relations*, 59(4): 483–504.

Morse, R.S. and Stephens, J.B. (2012) 'Teaching collaborative governance: Phases, competencies, and case-based learning, *Journal of Public Affairs Education*, 18(3): 565–83.

Moskop, W.W. (1996) 'Prudence as a paradigm for political leaders', *Political Psychology*, 17(4): 619–31.

Mulgan, R. (2002) *Holding Power to Account*, Basingstoke: Palgrave Macmillan.

Mulgan, R. (2014) *Making Open Government Work*, Basingstoke: Palgrave Macmillan.

Nepstad, S. and Clifford, B. (2006) 'When do leaders matter? Hypotheses on leadership dynamics in social movements', *Mobilization*, 11(1): 21–42.

Neustadt, R. (1960) *Presidential Power*, New York: Macmillan.

Neustadt, R. and May, E.R. (1986) *Thinking in Time*, New York: Free Press.

Nixon, C. and Chandler, J. (2012) *Fair Cop*, Melbourne: Melbourne University Press.

Noordegraaf, M. (2000) *Attention!*, Delft, The Netherlands: Eburon.

Noordegraaf, M. (2014) *Public Management*, Basingstoke: Palgrave Macmillan.

Northouse, P.G. (2009) *Leadership: Theory and Practice*, London: Sage.

Nye, J.K., Jr. (2008) *The Powers to Lead: Soft, Hard, and Smart*, Oxford: Oxford University Press.

O'Connor, M.A. (2003) The Enron board: The perils of groupthink, *University of Cincinnati Law Review*, 71: 1233–78.

O'Donnell, G. (1998) 'Horizontal accountability in new democracies', *Journal of Democracy*, 9(3): 112–26.

O'Leary, R. and Blomgren-Bingham, L. (eds) (2009) *The Collaborative Public Manager: New Ideas for the Twenty-first Century*, Washington, DC: Georgetown University Press.

Olmeda, J. (2008) 'A reversal of fortune: Blame games and framing contests after the 3/11 attacks in Madrid', in A. Boin, P. 't Hart and A. McConnell (eds) *Governing after Crisis*, Cambridge: Cambridge University Press, pp. 62–84.

Osborn, R.N., Hunt, J.G. and Jauch, L.R. (2002) 'Toward a contextual theory of leadership', *The Leadership Quarterly*, 13(5): 797–837.

Owen, D. (2007) *The Hubris Syndrome: Bush, Blair and the Intoxication of Power*, London: Politico's.

Owen, D. (2008), *In Sickness and In Power*, London: Methuen.

Padilla, A., Hogan, R. and Kaiser, R. (2007) 'The toxic triangle: Destructive leaders, susceptible followers, and conducive environments', *The Leadership Quarterly*, 18(2): 176–94.

Patashnik, E.M. (2008) *Reforms at Risk: What Happens After Major Policy Changes Are Enacted*, Princeton, NJ: Princeton University Press.

Patterson, B. (2000) *The White House Staff: Inside the West Wing and Beyond*, Washington, DC: Brookings Institution.

Pearce, C.L. and Conger, J.A. (eds) (2003) *Shared Leadership: Reframing the Hows and Whys of Leadership*, Thousand Oaks, CA: Sage.

Perry, R.W. and Quarantelli, E. (eds) (2005) *What Is a Disaster? New Answers to Old Questions*, Newark, DE: International Research Committee on Disasters.

Peters, B.G. (1987) *The Politics of Bureaucracy*, London: Routledge.

Peters, B.G. (2005) *Institutional Theory in Political Science: The New Institutionalism*, London: Continuum.

Peters, B.G. and Pierre, J. (2001) *Governance, Politics and the State*, New York: Macmillan.

Peters, R. M. (1990) *The American Speakership: The Office in Historical Perspective*, Baltimore, MD: Johns Hopkins University Press.

Pfeffer, J. and Salancik, G. (2003) *The External Control of Organisations: A Resource Dependence Perspective*, Stanford, CA: Stanford University Press.

Pfiffner, J.P. (2005) 'Presidential decision making: Rationality, advisory systems, and personality', *Presidential Studies Quarterly*, 35(2), 217–28.

Pierson, P. (2004) *Politics in Time: History, Institutions, and Social Analysis*, Princeton, NJ: Princeton University Press.

Pious, R.M. (2002) 'Why do presidents fail?', *Presidential Studies Quarterly*, 32(4): 724–42.

Poguntke, T. and Webb, K. (eds) (2005) *The Presidentialization of Politics*, Oxford: Oxford University Press.

Pollitt, C. (2008) *Time, Policy, Management: Governing with the Past*, Oxford: Oxford University Press.

Post, J.M. (2004) *Leaders and Their Followers in a Dangerous World: The Psychology of Political Behavior*, Ithaca, NY: Cornell University Press.

Post, J.M. (2005) *The Psychological Assessment of Political Leaders*, Ann Arbor, MI: University of Michigan Press.

Post, J.M. (2013) 'Psychobiography: "The Child is Father of the Man"', in L. Huddy, D. Sears and J. Levy (eds) *Oxford Handbook of Political Psychology*, Oxford: Oxford University Press.

Preston, T. (2001) *The President and His Inner Circle*, New York: Columbia University Press.

Preston, T. and 't Hart, P. (1999) 'Understanding and evaluating bureaucratic politics: The nexus between political leaders and advisory systems', *Political Psychology*, 20(1): 49–99.

Price, T.L. (2008) *Leadership Ethics: An Introduction*, Cambridge: Cambridge University Press.

Pringle, H. (2004) *Celebrity Sells*, London: Wiley.

Przeworski, A., Stokes, S. and Manin, B. (eds) (1999) *Democracy, Accountability and Representation*, Cambridge: Cambridge University Press.

Putnam, R. (1975) *The Beliefs of Politicians*, New Haven, CT: Yale University Press.

Quarantelli, E. (ed.) (1998) *What Is a Disaster?*, New York: Routledge.

Quinn, R., Cameron, K., DeGraff, J. and Thakor, A. (2006) *Competing Values Leadership: Creating Value in Organizations*, Cheltenham: Edward Elgar.

Quinn, T. (2012) *Electing and Ejecting Party Leaders in Britain*, Basingstoke: Palgrave Macmillan.

Redd, S.B. (2005) 'The influence of advisers and decision strategies on foreign policy choices: President Clinton's decision to use force in Kosovo', *International Studies Perspectives*, 6(1): 129–50.

Reicher, S., Haslam, S.A. and Platow, M. (2014) 'The social psychological study of leadership', in R.A.W. Rhodes and P. 't Hart (eds), *Oxford Handbook of Political Leadership*, Oxford: Oxford University Press.

Rein, I., Kottler, P. and Stoller, M. (1987) *High Visibility*, New York: Dodd Mead.

Renshon, S. (2000) 'Political leadership as social capital: Governing in a divided national culture', *Political Psychology*, 21(1): 199–226.

Renshon, S. (2011) *Barack Obama and the Politics of Redemption*, New York: Routledge.

Renshon, S. and Larson, D.W. (eds) (2002) *Good Judgment in Foreign Policy: Theory and Research*, Lanham, MD: Rowman & Littlefield.

Rhode, D. L. (2003) *The Difference 'Difference' Makes: Women and Leadership*, Stanford, CA: Stanford University Press.

Rhodes, R.A.W. (1997) *Understanding Governance*, Buckingham: Open University Press.

Rhodes, R.A.W. (2011) *Everyday Life in British Government*, Oxford: Oxford University Press.

Rhodes, R.A.W. (2013) 'From prime ministerial leadership to court politics', in P. Strangio, P. 't Hart and J. Walter (eds) *Understanding Prime Ministerial Leadership*, Oxford: Oxford University Press pp. 318–33.

Rhodes, R.A.W. and 't Hart, P. (eds) (2014) *Oxford Handbook of Political Leadership*, Oxford: Oxford University Press.

Rhodes, R.A.W. and Tiernan, A. (2014), *Lessons in Governing: A Profile of Prime Minister's Cheifs of Staff*, Melbourne: Melbourne University Press.

Rhodes, R.A.W. and Wanna, J. (2007) 'The limits to public value, or rescuing responsible government from the Platonic guardians', *Australian Journal of Public Administration*, 66(4): 406–21.

Rhodes, R.A.W., Binder, S. and Rockman, B. (2006) *The Oxford Handbook of Political Institutions*, Oxford: Oxford University Press.

Rhodes, R.A.W., 't Hart, P. and Noordegraaf, M. (eds) (2007) *Observing Political Elites*, Basingstoke: Palgrave Macmillan.

Rhodes, R.A.W., Wanna, J. and Weller, P. (2009) *Comparing Westminster*, Oxford: Oxford University Press.

Riker, W. (1986) *The Art of Political Manipulation*, New Haven, CT: Yale University Press.

Rinehart, L. (1971) *The Dice Man*, New York: Harper & Row.

Rose, R. and Davies, J. (1994) *Inheritance in Public Policy*, Oxford: Oxford University Press.

Rosenthal, U., Charles, M.T.and 't Hart, P. (1989) 'Introduction', in U. Rosenthal, M.T. Charles and P. 't Hart (eds) *Coping with Crises: The Management of Disasters, Riots and Terrorism*, Springfield, IL: Charles C. Thomas, pp. 3–33.

Rowse, T. (2002) *Obliged to Be Difficult*, Cambridge: Cambridge University Press.

Rucht, D. (2012) 'Leadership in social and political movements: A comparative exploration', in L. Helms (ed.), *Comparative Political Leadership*, Basingstoke: Palgrave Macmillan, pp. 99–118.

Ruscio, K.W. (2004) *The Leadership Dilemma in Modern Democracy*, Cheltenham: Edward Elgar.

Ryde, R. (2013) *Never Mind the Bosses*, San Francisco, CA: Jossey-Bass.

Saunders, F.S. (2007) 'A dangerous liaison', *The Guardian*. Available at: http://www.theguardian.com/books/2007/aug/25/biography.history; accessed 20 January 2014.

Savoie, D. (1999) *Governing from the Centre*, Toronto: University of Toronto Press.

Savoie, D. (2003) *Breaking the Bargain: Public Servants, Ministers and Parliament*, Toronto: University of Toronto Press.

Schafer, M. and Crichlow, S. (2010) *Groupthink versus High Quality Decision Making in International Relations*, New York: Columbia University Press.

Scharmer, O. (2009) *Theory U: Leading from the Future as It Emerges*, San Francisco: Berrett-Koehler.

Scharpf, F. (1997) *Games Real Actors Play*, Boulder, CO: Westview Press.

Schier, S. (2009) *Panorama of a Presidency: How George W. Bush Acquired and Spent His Political Capital*. New York: M.E. Sharpe.

Schlesinger, A. (1973) *The Imperial Presidency*, Boston, MA: Houghton Mifflin.

Schmid, H. (2009) 'The contingencies of nonprofit leadership', in J. Kane, H. Patapan and P. 't Hart (eds), *Dispersed Democratic Leadership*. Oxford: Oxford University Press, pp. 193–210.

Schmitter, P. and Santiso, J. (1998) 'Three temporal dimensions to the consolidation of democracy', *International Political Science Review*, 19(1): 69–92.

Schon, D. (1971) *Beyond the Stable State*, New York: Norton.

Searing, D.D. (1995) 'The psychology of political authority: A causal mechanism of political learning through persuasion and manipulation', *Political Psychology*, 16(4): 677–96.

Select Committee of the House of Representatives (2006) *A Failure of Initiative: Final Report of the Select Bipartisan Committee to Investigate the Preparation for and Response to Hurricane Katrina*, Washington, DC: US Government Printing Office.

Selznick, P. (1957) *Leadership in Administration*, Evanston, IL: Row Peterson.

Shapiro, R.Y., Joynt Kumar, M. and Jacobs, L.R. (eds) (2000) *Presidential Power: Forging the Presidency for the Twenty-First Century*, New York: Columbia University Press.

Shergold, P. (2008) 'Governing through collaboration', in J. O'Flynn and J.

Wanna (eds) *Collaborative Governance: A New Era of Public Policy in Australia?* Canberra: ANU Press, pp. 13–20.

Shergold, P. (2009) 'Leadership at a time of crisis', *Contents*, 6: 5–10.

Shore, C. (2000) *Building Europe: The Cultural Politics of European Integration*, London: Routledge.

Sieber, S.D. (1981) *Fatal Remedies*, New York: Plenum Press.

Simonton, D.G. (1987) *Why Presidents Succeed,* New Haven, CT: Yale University Press.

Sinclair, A. (2007) *Leadership for the Disillusioned: Moving beyond Myths and Heroes to a Leadership that Liberates*, Sydney: Allen & Unwin.

Skowronek, S. (1993) *The Politics Presidents Make: Leadership from John Adams to George Bush*, Cambridge, MA: Belknap University Press.

Skowronek, S. (2008) *Presidential Leadership in Political Time: Reprise and Reappraisal*, Lawrence, KS: University Press of Kansas.

Smith, S. (1984) 'Groupthink and the hostage rescue mission', *British Journal of Political Science*, 15(4): 453–8.

Smith, S. and Lipsky, M. (1993) *Non-Profits for Hire: The Welfare State in the Age of Contracting*, Cambridge, MA: Harvard University Press.

Sørensen, E. and Torfing, J. (2003) Network politics, political capital and democracy, *International Journal of Public Administration*, 26(4): 609–34.

Strangio, P., 't Hart, P. and Walter, J. (eds) (2013) *Understanding Prime-Ministerial Performance*, Oxford: Oxford University Press.

Strangio, P., 't Hart, P. and Walter J. (2014) 'Leadership of reforming government: The role of political tandems', in J. Lewis and D. Alexander (eds), *Making Public Policy Decisions*, London: Routledge, forthcoming.

Strøm, K. (2000) 'Delegation and accountability in parliamentary democracies', *European Journal of Political Research* 37(3) 261–89.

Strøm, K. (2003) 'Parliamentary democracy and delegation', in K. Strøm, W.C. Müller and T. Bergman (eds), *Delegation and Accountability in Parliamentary Democracies*, Oxford: Oxford University Press, pp. 55–106.

Stutje, J.W. (ed.) (2012) *Charismatic Leadership and Social Movements*, Oxford: Berghahn.

Subasic, E. and Reynolds, K.J. (2011) 'Power consolidation in leadership change contexts: A social identity perspective', in P. 't Hart and J. Uhr (eds), *How Power Changes Hands: Transition and Succession in Government*, Basingstoke: Palgrave Macmillan, pp. 174–90.

Sullivan, T. (ed.) (2004) *The Nerve Center: Lessons in Governing from the White House Chiefs of Staff*, College Station, TX: Texas A&M University Press.

Sun Tzu, S. (2002), *The Art of War*, London: Courier Dover.

Svara, J.D. (2002) 'The myth of the dichotomy', *Public Administration Review*, 61 (2): 176–83.

Svara, J.D. (2007) 'Leadership by top administrators in a changing world: New challenges in political-administrative relations', in R. Morse, T. Buss and C. Kinghorn (eds), *Transforming Public Leadership for the 21st Century*, Armonk, NY: M.E. Sharpe, pp. 69–102.

Sykes, P.L. (2013) 'Gendering prime-ministerial power', in P. Strangio, P. 't Hart and J. Walter (eds), *Understanding Prime-Ministerial Performance*, Oxford: Oxford University Press, pp.102–24.

Sykes, P.L. (2014) 'Does gender matter?', in R.A.W. Rhodes and P. 't Hart (eds), *Oxford Handbook of Political Leadership*, Oxford: Oxford University Press, in press.

Tarrow, S. (1994) *Power in Movement*, Cambridge: Cambridge University Press.

Terry, L.D. (1995) *Leadership of Public Bureaucracies: The Administrator as Conservator*, London: Sage.

Terry, L.D. (1998) 'Administrative leadership, neo-managerialism and the public management movement', *Public Administration Review*, 58(3): 194–200.

Tetlock, P. E., McGuire, C., Peterson, R., Feld, P. and Chang, S. (1992) 'Assessing political group dynamics: A test of the groupthink model'. *Journal of Personality and Social Psychology*, 63(3): 402–23.

Thaler, K. and Sunstein, C. (2008) *Nudge*, New Haven, CT: Yale University Press.

't Hart, P. (1993) 'Symbols, rituals and power: The lost dimensions of crisis management', *Journal of Contingencies and Crisis Management*, 1(1): 36–50.

't Hart, P (1994), *Groupthink in Government*, Baltimore: Johns Hopkins University Press

't Hart, P. (2007) 'Spies at the crossroads: Observing change in the Dutch intelligence service', in R.A.W. Rhodes, P.'t Hart and M. Noordegraaf (eds) *Observing Government Elites: Up Close and Personal*, Basingstoke: Palgrave Macmillan, pp. 51–77.

't Hart, P. (2009) 'Public sector leadership: Moving beyond mythology', Occasional Paper 3, Victoria State Services Authority and the Australia New Zealand School of Government (ANZSOG), April.

't Hart, P. (2011a) 'Reading the signs of the times: Regime dynamics and leadership possibilities', *Journal of Political Philosophy*, 19(4): 419–39.

't Hart, P. (2011b) 'Evaluating public leadership: Towards an assessment framework', *Public Money and Management*, 31(5): 323–30.

't Hart, P. (2013) 'After Fukushima: Reflections on risk and institutional learning in an era of mega-crises', *Public Administration*, 91(1): 101–13.

't Hart, P. and Schelfhout, R. (2014) 'Assessing prime-ministerial performance in a multiparty democracy', Unpublished paper, under review.

't Hart, P. and Tindall, K. (eds) (2009a) *Framing the Global Meltdown: Crisis Rhetoric and the Politics of Recessions*, Canberra: ANU Press.

't Hart, P. and Tindall, K. (2009b) 'Leadership by the famous: Celebrity politics in democracy', in J. Kane, H. Patapan and P. 't Hart (eds), *Dispersed Democratic Leadership*, Oxford: Oxford University, pp. 255–78.

't Hart, P. and Uhr, J. (eds) (2008) *Public Leadership: Perspectives and Practices*, Canberra: ANU Press.

't Hart, P. and Uhr, J. (eds) (2011) *How Power Changes Hands*, Basingstoke: Palgrave Macmillan.

't Hart, P., Rosenthal, U. and Kouzmin, A. (1993). 'Crisis decision making: The centralization thesis revisited', *Administration & Society*, 25(1): 12–45.

't Hart, P., Stern, E.K. and Sundelius, B. (eds) (1997) *Beyond Groupthink: Political Group Dynamics and Foreign Policymaking*, Ann Arbor, MI: University of Michigan Press.

't Hart, P., Tindall, K. and Brown, C. (2009) 'Crisis leadership of the Bush presidency', *Presidential Studies Quarterly*, 39(3): 473–93.

Theakston, K. (2011) 'Gordon Brown as Prime Minister: Political skills and leadership style', *British Politics*, 6(1): 78–100.

Thompson, J.D. and Tuden, A. (1959) 'Strategies, Structures, and Processes of Organizational Decision', in J.D. Thompson, P.B. Hammond, R.W. Hawkes, B.H. Junker and A. Tuden (eds), *Comparative Studies in Administration*, Pittsburgh, PA: University of Pittsburgh Press, pp. 195–216.

Thompson, M., Ellis, R. and Wildavsky, A. (1990) *Cultural Theory*, Boulder, CO: Westview Press.

Thompson, P. (1998) *Persuading Aristotle: The Timeless Art of Persuasion in Business, Negotiation and the Media*, Sydney: Allen & Unwin.

Tiernan, A. (2007) *Power Without Responsibility? Ministerial Staffers In Australian Governments from Whitlam to Howard*, Sydney: UNSW Press.

Tilley, N. (2010) 'Can public leadership be evaluated?', in S. Brookes and K. Grint (eds), *The Public Leadership Challenge*, Basingstoke: Palgrave Macmillan.

Torfing, J., Pierre, J., Peters, B.G. and Sørensen, E. (2012) *Interactive Governance*, Oxford: Oxford University Press.

Tucker, R.C. (1981) *Politics as Leadership*, Columbia, MO: University of Missouri Press.

Turner, B.A. and Pidgeon, N. (1997) *Man-Made Disasters*, 2nd edn, London: Butterworth Heinemann.

Turner, J.C. and Haslam, S.A. (2001) 'Social identity, organizations, and leadership', in M.E. Turner (ed.), *Groups at Work: Theory and Research*, Mahwah, NJ: Erlbaum, pp. 25–64.

Turner, J.C., Reynolds, K.J. and Subasic, E. (2008) 'Identity confers power: The new view of leadership in social psychology', in J. Uhr and P. 't Hart (eds), *Public Leadership: Perspectives and Practices*, Canberra: ANU Press, pp. 57–72.

Turner, M.E. and Pratkanis, A.R. (eds) (1998) 'Special issue on 25 years of groupthink', *Journal of Organizational Decision Making and Human Decision Processes*, 73: 2–3.

Uhr, J. (2005) 'Professional ethics for politicians', *International Public Management Journal*, 8(2): 247–61.

Uhr, J. (2014) 'Rhetorical and performative analysis', in R.A.W. Rhodes and P. 't Hart (eds), *Oxford Handbook of Political Leadership*, Oxford: Oxford University Press, in press.

Van Assche, T. (2005) 'The impact of entrepreneurial leadership on EU high politics: A case study of Jacques Delors and the creation of EMU', *Leadership*, 1(3): 279–98.

Van den Berg, J. (1999) *Verantwoorden of Vertrekken: Een Essay over Politieke Verantwoordelijkheid*, The Hague: VNG Publishers.

Van Wart, M. (2013) 'Lessons from leadership theory and the contemporary challenges of leaders', *Public Administration Review*, 73(4): 553–65.

Van Wart, M. and Dicke, L.A. (eds) (2008) *Administrative Leadership in the Public Sector*, Armonk, NY: M.E. Sharpe.

Verbeek, B. (2003) *Decision-Making in Great Britain During the Suez Crisis: Small Groups and a Persistent Leader*, Aldershot: Ashgate.

Walcott, C.E. and Hult, K.M. (1995) *Governing the White House: From Hoover Through LBJ*, Lawrence, KA: University of Kansas Press.

Walcott, C.E. and Hult, K.M. (2005) 'White House structure and decision making: Elaborating the standard model', *Presidential Studies Quarterly*, 35 (2), 303–18.

Walcott, C.E., Warshaw, S.A. and Wayne, S.J. (2001) 'The Chief of Staff', *Presidential Studies Quarterly*, 31(3), pp. 464–89.

Waldtschmidt-Nelson, B. (2012) *Dreams and Nightmares: Martin Luther King Jr., Malcolm X, and the Struggle for Black Equality in America*, Tampa, FL: University of Florida Press.

Walter, J. (2014), '"No loans for ladies"': Julia Gillard and capital denied', Paper European Consortium of Political Research Joint Sessions of Workshops, Salamanca, Spain.

Wanna, J. (ed.) (2007) *Organisational Change and Project Management*, Canberra: ANU Press.

Weber, M. (1970) *From Max Weber: Essays in Sociology* (H.H. Gerth and C. Wright Mills, eds), London: Routledge & Kegan Paul.

Weick, K.E. (1993) 'The collapse of sensemaking in organizations: The Mann Gulch disaster', *Administrative Science Quarterly*, 38(4): 628–52.

Weick, K.E. and Sutcliffe, K.M. (2007) *Managing the Unexpected*, San Francisco: Jossey Bass.

Weller, P. (1983) 'The vulnerability of prime ministers: A comparative perspective', *Parliamentary Affairs*, 36(1): 96–117.

Weller, P. (1985) *First Among Equals: Prime Ministers in Westminster Systems*, Sydney: Allen & Unwin.

Weller, P. (2007) *Cabinet Government in Australia, 1901–2006*, Sydney: UNSW Press.

Wildavsky, A. (1979) *Speaking Truth to Power: The Art and Craft of Policy Analysis*, Boston, MA: Little, Brown.

Wildavsky, A. (1984) *The Nursing Father: Moses as a Political Leader*, Tuscaloosa, AL: University of Alabama Press.

Wildavsky, A. (1987) 'Choosing preferences by constructing institutions', *American Political Science Review*, 81(1): 3–21.

Wildavsky, A. (1989) 'A cultural theory of leadership', in B.D. Jones (ed.), *Leadership and Politics: New Perspectives in Political Science*, Lawrence, KS: University of Kansas Press.

Williams, D. (2005) *Real Leadership*, New York: Berrett-Koehler.

Williams, L.E. (1996) *Servants of the People: The 1960s Legacy of African American Leadership*, Basingstoke: Macmillan.

Williams, L.K. (2007) 'Endogenous election timing, election cycles and international conflict', Paper presented at the annual meeting of the American Political Science Association, Chicago, IL, 30 August. Available at: http://www.allacademic.com/meta/p_mla_apa_research_citation/2/1/1/2/1/p 211219_index.html.

Williams, P. (2012) *Collaboration in Public Policy and Practice*, Bristol: Policy Press.

Willner, A.R. (1984) *The Spellbinders*, New Haven, CT: Yale University Press.

Winter, D.G. (2002) 'Motivation and political leadership', in O. Feldmanand L.O. Valenty (eds), *Political Leadership for the New Century*, Westport, CT: Greenwood, pp. 25–47.

Witteveen, W.J. (1991) *Evenwicht van Machten*, Zwolle, The Netherlands: Tjeenk Willink.

Wood, B.D. (2007) *The Politics of Economic Leadership*, Princeton, NJ: Princeton University Press.

Wren, T.J. (ed.) (1995) *The Leader's Companion: Insights on Leadership Through the Ages*, New York: Free Press.

Wren, J.T. (2006) 'A quest for a grand theory of leadership', in G. Goethals and G.L.J. Sorenson (eds), *A Quest for a General Theory of Leadership*, Cheltenham: Edward Elgar, pp. 1–38.

Wren, J.T. (2007) *Inventing Leadership: The Challenge of Democracy*, Cheltenham: Edward Elgar.

Yetiv, S. (2003) 'Groupthink and the Gulf crisis', *British Journal of Political Science*, 33(3): 419–42.

Young, O.R. (1991) 'Political leadership and regime formation', *International Organization*, 45(2): 281–308.

Yukl, G. (1999) 'An evaluation of conceptual weaknesses in transformational and charismatic leadership theories', *Leadership Quarterly*, 10(2): 285–305.

Zaleznik, A. (1977/2004) 'Managers and leaders: Are they different?', *Harvard Business Review*, 82(1), 74–81 (orig. publ. 1977).

Zelikow, P (with Rice, C.) (1995) *Germany Unified and Europe Transformed: A Study in Statecraft*, Cambridge, MA: Harvard University Press.

Zimbardo, P. (2007) *The Lucifer Effect*, New York: Random House.

Index